DYING UNNEEDED

Dying Unneeded

The Cultural Context of the Russian Mortality Crisis

Michelle A. Parsons

Vanderbilt University Press
NASHVILLE

This book is the recipient of the Norman L. and Roselea J. Goldberg prize from Vanderbilt University Press for the best project in the area of medicine.

This book is printed on acid-free paper.
Manufactured in the United States of America

Library of Congress Cataloging-in-Publication Data on file
LC control number 2013035413
LC classification number HN530.2.A8P34 2013
Dewey class number 304.6'40947—dc23

ISBN 978-0-8265-1972-6 (cloth)
ISBN 978-0-8265-1973-3 (paperback)
ISBN 978-0-8265-1974-0 (ebook)

For James

Contents

Illustrations

FIGURES

TABLES

Acknowledgments

This account would not be possible without the many eloquent Russians who took time to talk with me, sharing their stories. In some cases I was little more than a stranger. They welcomed me into their homes, answered my questions with patience, served me food and tea, and shared their thoughts and experiences. If this telling conveys a sense of how older Muscovites experienced the early 1990s, it is because of the openness and kindness of those same Russians.

Daria Andreevna Khaltourina, a research fellow at the Russian Academy of Sciences Center for Civilizational and Regional Studies, was a source of constant help in many large and small ways from writing letters of support and introduction, introducing me to a research assistant, giving advice, facilitating interviews, and being a friend. Svetlana Victorovna Kobzeva and Irina Alexandrovna Kodjichkena were excellent research assistants, conducting and transcribing interviews. Sveta worked closely with me throughout my stay and conducted as many interviews as I did. Her efforts represent an important contribution to this work. I am thankful for fellowship and companionship with these friends and others during my time in Moscow.

At Emory University, I am especially grateful to Peter J. Brown, a true mentor and wise counselor, and to Chikako Ozawa-de Silva and Carol Worthman for their encouragement and advice. I am very thankful to two reviewers who provided many thoughtful suggestions on how to make this book better. Michael Ames at Vanderbilt University Press was very supportive and easy to work with.

My thanks to Fulbright-Hays for their support of my research abroad and to the National Science Foundation under DDIG No. BCS-0550376. Any opinions, findings, and conclusions or recommendations expressed in this material are my own and do not necessarily reflect the views of the National Science Foundation. Emory University generously supported my graduate studies and funded a summer of preliminary research.

I am thankful to parents who have always supported me in my travels and studies, and have always welcomed me back. My biggest thanks go to my husband, James. James flew to Moscow numerous times during the year I was away. He has made it possible for me to write with two active young boys and a baby girl. James, more than any formal training, has taught me about curiosity, empathy, and open mindedness. If being needed is about giving, James is a needed person.

Introduction

first went to Russia in 1993 and 1994. It was a time largely regarded as lawless and chaotic, *bezporiadok*,[1] or without order in Russian. In St. Petersburg I lived in a sleeper district in a Brezhnev-era apartment building at the then northernmost station of the blue metro line. Outside the Prospekt Prosveshcheniia (Enlightenment Avenue) metro station elderly Russian women stood in lines selling a dried fish, a collection of homemade canned goods, or dried mushrooms on a string. They laid their meager wares on overturned wooden crates or a piece of canvas on the ground.

At this same metro station I watched men with cropped hair wearing leather jackets drive up in BMWs to the collection of kiosks. They offered protection to kiosk owners in exchange for cash. One morning the charred portion of a kiosk frame stood still smoldering in the cold, likely the cost of not buying enough protection from the mafia. On my way to Russian classes one morning I saw a man lying face down in the snow in a concrete planting bed, used for pansies in the spring. People streamed past him through the heavy swinging doors and into the warm blow of metro air. He was dead, a casualty of alcohol and winter temperatures.

During the summer of 1994, which I spent in Yekaterinburg in the Urals living with my friend Nadya[2] and her teenage son, we went to the country cottage, or *dacha*. The *dacha* was located in a small village of *dachas*, surrounded by overgrown gardens. It was an idyllic setting. A small river meandered through the village. Grandfathers fished with their grandchildren. We collected wild mushrooms and harvested vegetables from the garden. I had one of the most amazing meals of my life in that unfinished, wooden hut—a garden vegetable and wild mushroom ragout cooked on a portable gas stove. After a winter of cabbage, onions, and carrots, the ragout tasted incredibly flavorful. That night Nadya and I lay on the bed and talked until late. I often wish I could reproduce that evening—at the *dacha* talking about life with Nadya, after a cold, gray winter.

1

Although I was not aware of it at the time, during the winter of 1993–1994 Russia reached the apex of the most extreme spike in mortality in modern history—"an unprecedented pace of deterioration in a country not at war" (Leon and Shkolnikov 1998, 790). There is only one other instance of comparable demographic decline in the modern era and that is the HIV/AIDS epidemic in sub-Saharan Africa. During a five-year period from 1990 through 1994, total life expectancy in Russia fell more than five years. Male life expectancy dropped more than six years to fifty-eight years; female life expectancy dropped more than three years to seventy-one years (Notzon et al. 1998). The sharpest declines occurred in 1992 and 1993, the first years of neoliberal economic shock therapy. In 2011 male life expectancy in Russia, at sixty-three years, still had the dubious distinction of being among the lowest for its income level (World Bank 2013). The sex difference in Russian (and Belarussian) life expectancies is the largest of any country in the world. In 2011 women lived, on average, twelve years longer than men, or seventy-five years (World Bank 2013).

The summer Nadya and I spent together, the increase in mortality was on the brink of abating, but the crisis was entrenched. Before I left Russia through Kazakhstan, Nadya's son attempted suicide in the apartment bathroom.

MORTALITY

The questions I initially set out to answer were about death. What made the early 1990s so life threatening? Why did so many Russians die? But I found that in answering these questions, death was less important than life. Patterns of death are deeply embedded in culture and have more to do with the question "How do we live?" than with the question "How do we die?" The mortality crisis opens a window on Russian life and vitality, and the spontaneity of social connections that make life worth living. Nevertheless, my initial research question was along the lines of "Why did more Russians die in the early 1990s?"

In his May 2005 "State of the Country" speech, Putin identified the demographic crisis (*demograficheskii krizis*) as one of the most important problems facing Russian society. The demographic crisis revolves around both increasing mortality and decreasing fertility. Fertility fell from an average of 2 children per woman in 1989 to 1.4 in 1994 and 1.2 in 1997. By 2011 the rate had rebounded a little to 1.5 (World Bank 2013).

The population of the Russian Federation, estimated at 148.7 million in 1992, declined by almost 7 million until 2009 when it began to grow again (World Bank 2013). And while a declining population is not unique in the world—Russia joins other European and East Asian countries with extremely low fertility rates—a rising mortality rate in an industrialized country is unique.

Troubling demographic trends go back to at least the 1960s when the Soviet Union became the first industrialized country to sustain a mortality reversal. In 1965 Russian men's life expectancy began to decline and women's life expectancy began to plateau. This is in contrast to substantial improvements in life expectancy during the past half century in most areas of the world. Since the 1960s there have been periods of improvement in Russia, but in 2011 Russian men's life expectancy, at sixty-three years, was no better than it was a half century earlier.

The historical divergence in life expectancies between Eastern and Western Europe is dubbed the East-West divide (Vàgerö and Illsley 1992). Sociologist Watson (1995) pinned the mortality divide from the mid-1960s to 1990 on perceived relative deprivation compared to the West and social exclusion, especially among unmarried men. Family life benefited women more than men. "Despite the physical demands it makes, a woman's family role under state socialism (given that she was also employed) was also a resource and a way of creating meaning; it was *the* way of coping" (Watson 1995, 932). Watson's analysis is insightful for mortality in the early 1990s too.

From 1992 through 1994 mortality registered a dramatic increase in Russia. The increase in mortality was so striking that initially there was some concern as to whether it was an artifact of better death recording. It is now well established by epidemiologists that the data represent a real phenomenon (Leon et al. 1997; Notzon et al. 2003; Notzon et al. 1998). While increases were also striking in the Baltic states (Estonia, Latvia, and Lithuania), Belarus, and the Ukraine, the most severe increases were seen in Russia. Both men's and women's mortality were affected, but men's declined more markedly, widening the already-pronounced sex difference. In 1992 the sex difference in life expectancy at birth was ten years; by 1994 it was over fourteen years (World Bank 2013). Shkolnikov, Field, and Andreev, citing Watson's work above, surmise that the sex difference is due to the fact that men and women "cope with stress in different ways: Compared with women, men are more likely to abuse alcohol, engage in violent or suicidal behavior, smoke more, and eat less healthily" (2001, 153).

Surprisingly, excess mortality in the early 1990s was concentrated in the wealthier and more developed regions of Russia. In the western metropolises of Moscow and St. Petersburg, male life expectancy decreased by 7.7 and 7.1 years, respectively, from 1990 to 1994 (Leon and Shkolnikov 1998). This compares to the national average of 6.1 years (Notzon et al. 1998). Those born between the years 1936 and 1954 have been identified as the generation suffering the greatest proportion of excess deaths in the early 1990s when they were between forty and fifty-five years old (Leon et al. 1997; Notzon et al. 1998; Walberg et al. 1998). Working-class men with less education were particularly at risk (Chenet, Leon et al. 1998; Malyutina et al. 2004; Plavinski, Plavinskaya, and Klimov 2003; Shkolnikov, Leon et al. 1998).

The post-Soviet mortality crisis in Russia has been the subject of epidemiological and social science literatures since the mid-1990s. The principal causes of excess mortality are cardiovascular, injuries (suicide, homicide, and other injury), and alcohol-related deaths, including alcohol dependence syndrome, alcohol poisoning, and chronic liver disease and cirrhosis. Alcohol-related deaths have received the most attention (Leon, Shkolnikov, and McKee 2009), with recent studies claiming that a quarter to half of total mortality among working-age men is attributable to hazardous drinking (Leon et al. 2007; Tomkins et al. 2012; Zaridze, Brennan et al. 2009). The literature on the crisis mostly interprets alcohol consumption in the early 1990s as an escape from stress—maladaptive coping. The other theme in the literature on the Russian mortality crisis is the lack of social capital, which is sometimes seen as a holdover of Soviet society (Kennedy, Kawachi, and Brainerd 1998; Rose 1999, 1995) and sometimes a result of neoliberal economic reform (Field, Kotz, and Bukhman 2000; Field and Twigg 2000; Stuckler and Basu 2013; Twigg and Schecter 2003). Along these lines, Field has likened the early 1990s in Russia to a postwar zone (Field 1995, 2000).

Epidemiologist Richard Wilkinson's theory, elaborated in numerous books and articles (Wilkinson 1996, 2005; Wilkinson and Pickett 2009), is that income inequality drives mortality patterns in the industrialized world. It does so primarily through its deleterious effect on social connections. Russia is an example of how social connections are steeped in culture—to the extent that it is possible to misrecognize them from an outside perspective. For some scholars, Russian forms of social connection, especially but not exclusively during the Soviet era, are discredited as evidence of corruption and lack of trust. Therefore, Russian social connections themselves are seen as pathogenic. This is in contrast to Russian accounts of the crisis in the early 1990s that point to how political and economic dissolution undoes social connections.

I decided to focus my research in the city of Moscow where excess mortality was among the most severe in the early 1990s. In Moscow, I conducted interviews among the ages most at risk of dying then—that is, men and women between fifty-five and seventy years old in 2006 and 2007. My research, to a degree I did not initially recognize, is about a certain *generation* of Muscovites—their life histories and the intersection of these with the history of the Soviet Union and the world in the twentieth century.

With support from my anthropology department at Emory, I traveled to Moscow during the summer of 2004 to make contacts, gauge the feasibility of my research, pilot test interview guides, and brush up on my Russian, which I had not spoken for ten years. Encouraged, and funded, I returned to Moscow in July 2006 for eleven more months of fieldwork. I planned to do sixty in-depth interviews and a representative survey of a neighborhood in a northern sleeper district, along with participant observation in the daily lives of a subset of my interviewees. I managed forty in-depth interviews with the help of a research assistant and dropped the survey entirely. I added two sites of participant observation at a seminar on post-Soviet mortality in Kiev, Ukraine, in October 2006 and a seminar on alcohol policy in Moscow in March 2007. These seminars brought together social scientists who study the mortality crisis.

My ethnographic research primarily took place in 2006 and 2007, although I also draw upon my experience living in Russia in 1993 and 1994, during the apex of the mortality crisis. I intended to focus on the early 1990s, and did so in the interviews. I also came to understand that my informants often spoke broadly about post-Soviet times and did not always make distinctions between the early 1990s and later 1990s, or even the 2000s. I spoke with those who survived, although many had friends and family who died. These would be major methodological problems in an epidemiological study. My objective, however, was not to establish causal associations but rather to understand the perceptions and experiences of middle-aged Muscovites in the early post-Soviet period. Memories do tend to hold the meaning and emotion of past experiences (Schacter 1996). They also combine the past and the present, as new information merges with old. In that way, memories mimic postsocialist culture.

The evolution of my project, from a general question about why Russians died to an account of what made life worth living for a certain generation of

Muscovites, owes much to the method of ethnography—living in Moscow for more than a year, observing, listening, and participating in people's lives.

ETHNOGRAPHY

Ethnography is the cornerstone method of anthropology, although it may also refer to a book that describes in detail the way of life of a specific group of people—the Nuer of Southern Sudan, East Harlem crack dealers, migrant workers in Israel, or "mail-order" marriages. Ethnographic research entails participating in the lives of people through a period of extended fieldwork. As a method, ethnography purports to open a view on these people and their lives from the inside—the emic perspective. Ethnographers attempt to explain how these people see the world around them and to throw light not only on what they think, say, and do but also on how and why they think, say, and do those things. It is a lofty goal that assumes ethnographers will be able, at least in part, to put aside their own cultural viewpoints and judgments to open their minds and immerse themselves in another worldview and way of being. In my case, the point is not to simply write about Russia's most recent transformation and its mortal consequences but rather to represent ordinary Russian points of view on the subject. Of course, there are many points of view even among elderly Muscovites, but the idea is to seek cultural ideas and logics that undergird these points of view.

In this way, there is some pressure for an ethnographer to make sense of things in order to write about them coherently, although there are some ethnographers who consciously resist this. This pressure to understand and make sense of Moscow very nearly led to my undoing as an anthropologist. I thought I had made a mistake about my project, and possibly about my career. I had gone into anthropology because I loved living in different countries, learning new languages, and talking with people who lived different lives. But the pressure to make sense of things took the joy out of the experience. I would come home at night thinking, "This is impossible. This place makes no sense. I can't make any sense of things." I was struggling to craft a coherent story about Moscow, Russia, mortality, and culture.

One day walking home, discouraged, I had a small epiphany. One of the defining characteristics of the city, and perhaps the country as a whole, is a "sense" of incoherence, absurdity, and unpredictability. Of course, I knew this from living in St. Petersburg, Yekaterinburg, and Moscow in 1993, 1994, and 2004. I knew this from Russians who told me that their life was incomprehensible and absurd. I knew this from reading other ethnographies about Russia where informants warn their anthropologists: "It is impossible for you Westerners to understand our lives . . . trying to understand us rationally. Russian reality is based on absurdisms—economic, social, even scientific. All our life is based on absurdity, impossibility. Russian daily life is simply absurd and preposterous" (Ries 1997, 94). I knew this from my own feelings about living in Russia: the exhilaration and the frustration.

Russian émigrée Boym writes of estrangement and longing as part and parcel of what she calls ironic nostalgia—"a good balance between homesickness and the sickness of being home that is necessary for a cultural mythologist" (Boym 1994, 290). Even for her people, Russia refuses to submit. This is how she charms and this is how she frustrates. She is never completely known and always retains her ability to surprise, in both pleasant and unpleasant ways. Russian poet Fyodor Tyutchev's observation is widely quoted:

> You cannot understand Russia by your mind,
> Cannot measure her with a common yardstick:
> She has a special character
> You can only believe in Russia.

Under the pressure to be a social scientist, to make sense of things, and ultimately to write something with a point I had become blind to the obvious. Once I accepted that things did not have to make sense, indeed that my point could be that things did not make sense, I relaxed. I listened. I stopped trying to test everything I heard against some hypothesis I was working on in my head. I began to enjoy Moscow, myself, and my work. This, I believe, was when I started to do ethnography. As an observer of culture, I started to wonder about things that, at first, had no apparent relation to mortality.

But why should ethnography have anything to say about mortality—ostensibly the ultimate biological outcome? After all, epidemiology has identified a population at risk—middle-aged, working-class male Muscovites—and the primary causes of the mortality crisis—cardiovascular deaths, alcohol-related deaths, and injuries. Epidemiologists have also proposed drivers of these particular causes of death: a lack of social capital, harmful drinking behaviors, and the stresses of neoliberal reform. In that sense it is possible to argue that the answer to the question "Why did Russians die?" has already been answered. Russians, without a sense of community or safety net, responded to stress by drinking themselves to death. Simplifying it like this is not meant to diminish epidemiology, but ethnography accomplishes something different.

At a minimum, ethnography aids in the interpretation of epidemiological findings—the statistics that indicate associations between variables. In the case of Russian mortality, this ethnography helps explain puzzles in the epidemiological literature. Why are certain social connections associated with poorer health, while others are associated with better health? Why is alcohol drinking often associated with better health? Why do the effects of drinking vary among men?

Epidemiologists attempting to explain these findings have offered interpretations, but they are often prefaced with an admission that the findings are "difficult to explain" or "difficult to interpret" (Bobak et al. 1998). Some interpretations are little more than conjecture about life in the Soviet Union and Russia. Others are more cautious. Malyutina et al. admit, "we need to clarify the reasons for excess mortality in non-drinkers" (2002, 1453). Some aspects of the mortality crisis remain poorly understood despite an impressive amount of epidemiological research.

Beyond interpretation, ethnography provides answers of a different order to the question "Why did more Russians die?" Ethnographers attempt to understand how individual health and behavior is tied up with larger social processes. By highlighting how political and economic structures make some choices more possible than others, ethnography is an antidote to a perspective which assumes that individuals make lifestyle choices that determine their health. In the case of Russian mortality, it is necessary to explore not only lifestyle variables such as diet, drink, and exercise but also the meanings of these, in addition to family roles, gender, work, morality, exchange, economy, and history. Political economy and culture give rise to lifestyles and give meaning to life. Some epidemiologists openly acknowledge that broader questions remain unanswered. In a recent article Leon, Shkolnikov, and McKee write, "We are still lacking an adequate account of what underlying mechanisms may have transmitted the shocks of the collapse of communism . . . to the behaviours of individuals" (2009, 1634). I consider this a call for ethnography, which elucidates that middle ground between political economy and individuals.

Ethnography offers a broad, holistic approach that deals in culture, a contentious concept even among anthropologists. Some anthropologists see a danger of essentialism and naïveté in cultural analyses, especially in an era of global capitalism. Others stake a claim for culture—the logics and meanings undergirding social practices. I find myself among those in the latter camp, but these logics and meanings are clearly part and parcel of political economy too. Especially among the generation of older Muscovites, who spent most of their lives in a society marked by more homogeneity in housing, education, work, and leisure pursuits, culture is apropos. Today's Russia is different—younger generations of Muscovites respond to a more diverse set of cultural logics and meanings. They may not respond to the same cultural logics and meanings as older Muscovites, or they may respond to them differently. When writing about culture, there is always the danger of stereotyping Russians, but I believe in a concept of culture as shared and tacit understandings that make it possible to think, act, and live among others—part common sense, part disposition, part discipline.

While epidemiologists strive for standardized surveys of representative samples, ethnographers pursue more circuitous and amorphous paths in collecting their data through conversations, unstructured interviews, or merely spending time with people in different settings. The insider, or emic, view is held paramount. Concepts and categories used in analysis should be meaningful to members of that culture. In some cases, that means letting go of ideas and assumptions that lead ethnographers to the field.

Ethnography may even change the very questions that send researchers into the field by continually presenting a stream of cultural data, stubbornly resistant to certain questions and unexpectedly yielding to others. My interviewees knew about the demographic crisis and mortality. But raising the subject in interviews only seemed to derail the flow. Asking about interviewees' own health did not work either. The people we talked with were eloquent storytellers when asked about their lives and how things had changed in the early 1990s. They were intent on answering the question "What makes life worth living?" And what made life worth living was a sense of being needed. Ethnography went far beyond placing behavioral risk factors in cultural context. Older Muscovites' perspectives on life brought into relief other perspectives on life—including those held by Western scholars. As a result, this account does not merely "add culture" through stories and anecdotes. Rather, it draws attention to cultural logics and meanings underpinning emic concepts such as being needed and etic concepts such as social capital.

Being needed is the central concept around which this ethnography spins. The early 1990s eroded this generation's sense of being needed. In the end, I argue that being *unneeded* is related to mortality. In this way, I traveled full circle from my initial questions on mortality back to mortality, but only after ethnography forced me to loosen my preconceptions and listen to what people wanted to tell me. The result is a thoroughly cultural account of the experience of a generation of Muscovites. Mortality is but one aspect of this generation's experience, and one that they themselves do not necessarily privilege. But retaining a focus on mortality illustrates how culture—even at its most sublime—gets under the skin and inhabits the physical body. Being needed serves as a bridge between political economy and mortality, or between historical events and individual lives—and deaths.

Older Muscovites would find accusations of a lack of social connection in Soviet society as responsible for excess mortality highly ironic. According to many of them, social connections suffered as a consequence of the fall of the Soviet Union and the introduction of capitalism.

BEING NEEDED

In hindsight, the importance of being needed made itself plain very early in my fieldwork when I was meeting with contacts and explaining my project. In a cow-themed Moo-Moo cafeteria, a Russian cardiologist listened politely to my idea of interviewing people between the ages of fifty-five and seventy. "Ah, yes, nobody needs them [*nikomu ne nuzhny*]," he said, as if it were a well-known fact. His words struck me as cruel, but he clearly did not mean them that way. I remember the remark because it confused me. His demeanor was so straightforward. Did he really believe that nobody needed them? At the time, I felt that I did not fully understand his meaning, but I did not dwell on it. As I interviewed and later read over interview transcripts, the expression was repeated again and again in reference to post-Soviet life. "I became unnecessary to the state," said one man. "They said you aren't needed anywhere," another explained in reference to losing work. "Who needs us? Who is needed now?" said a woman about the death of a friend.

Over time it became clear that being needed was about having something to offer others. For most of their lives, having something to offer others (something in short supply, a favor, a contact) translated into social status. In everyday life, an economy of shortages promoted an "economy of favors" (Ledeneva 1998). Ledeneva writes about needed people (she translates it as "useful people") "who were in demand when something was needed" (115). Older Muscovites spoke about suddenly feeling unneeded in the early 1990s—both unneeded by the state and by others around them.

Referring to their many years of work experience, one former defense factory worker lamented, "What rich experience—it just seemed that we would still be needed." They found a sense of neededness where they could. Teachers were thankful they were still needed by their students, if not the state. A man, unneeded, was needed again when he took care of his granddaughter. Mothers were needed by their children and grandchildren.

Being needed was gendered. "A lot of [men] felt unneeded, useless, defective." But "a woman tries to be needed in whatever situation—to find herself somewhere where she is really needed." And: "[A woman] is always needed because she is in the family." Men's sense of neededness centered on being able to adequately provide—a possibility that narrowed substantially in the early 1990s. Women's sense of neededness was more diffuse and included, importantly, being able to hold their families together in times of hardship. In this sense, the early 1990s meant that women were sometimes quite desperately needed. They were undoubtedly burdened by this responsibility, but they may have also been preserved by it.

As much as this book is about a particular generation, it is also about a particular experience—becoming unneeded. As will become clear, being unneeded is a distal driver of the mortality crisis. Being unneeded translates social collapse to bodily death from cardiovascular and alcohol-related causes. Being needed is related to the death of the body, but it is also related to the life of the soul. This is a story about mortality, but in order to understand it in cultural context, the story must start with vitality. What makes life worth living?

VITALITY

In Russia, a soulful person is a person who gives—a needed person. A soulless person holds back. Soulfulness is related to generosity and communion. A generous person is "wide-souled" (Pesmen 2000, 151). In Margaret Paxson's beautiful ethnography of a Russian village, a soulful person is open and expansive, generous and hospitable, while a soulless one is controlled and disciplined (Paxson 2005, 79). The soul (*dusha*) emanates from an individual but is not the property of an individual. Dale Pesmen, who has written a deep ethnography of the Russian soul, quotes a friend who explains, "Dusha isn't in individuals but in their union" (Pesmen 1995, 71). The Russian soul has a directionality—outward—and a sociality. Soulful social connections "are vectors, dynamic in nature, that move out from the individual and into the world" (Paxson 2005, 100). Wierzbicka writes, "The Russian 'duša' is not simply an individual human soul but a 'soul' that comes into being, and that lives, in the 'obščenie' (communing talk) with other people" (2003, 427).

The soul extends outward, offering individuals more space (*prostor*). A social soul enlarges the experience of the self. In certain social interactions "the self is unlocked," writes Paxson (2005, 100). But space can also threaten the self with its unknown and unbound qualities. There is the possibility of losing oneself in all that space. To keep space safe, it must be bounded. In social communion, "The self is unlocked, and there is some boundedness around the group" (100). Social connections grant individuals more space, but they also keep individuals bound. And in keeping them bound, they keep them safe.

In Soviet times, social connections served to enlarge space and possibilities for people and to help them get around the System (*Sistema*). So they had a transgressive quality, an alternative morality, whereby rules could be broken. Limits could be pushed back, constraints eased. Where the System closed off possibilities, social connections might open them up again. And in this way, social connections also imparted a sense of freedom from larger, more powerful forces in Soviet society—the political economy of Soviet socialism. Through social connections individuals might attain, however fleeting, a feeling of collective freedom from Soviet order, even as social connections also depended on the this same social order.

Older Muscovites were often nostalgic for Soviet order (*poriadok*) because it ordered social connections. People's positions vis-à-vis the Soviet state influenced what people could give to other people—the ways they could be soulful and needed. Work was the principal means by which Soviet citizens were ordered by the state. At work, Russians had personal connections and access to resources and services. Someone in the Soviet bureaucracy could arrange permission to build a *dacha*. A friendly butcher could set aside a good cut of meat. A test proctor could help a student pass an entrance examination. Collectively, people often circumvented the state, but they depended on the state to do that. Order here refers to both the order of the state and the order of social relations because they are mutually constitutive.

The paradox of space (*prostor*) and order (*poriadok*)—the unbound and bound quality of social relations in Soviet society—resolves into the even higher-order concept of freedom. For these elderly Muscovites, freedom was not always compromised by the Soviet state. In some cases, the constraint of the Soviet state heightened a sense of freedom. As people, using their connections, collectively pushed against the limits of the state, and as those limits bent back or gave way, they experienced a sense of freedom. This was a freedom that hinged on constraint. From a Western perspective it might seem an impoverished freedom, and oftentimes, it must be said, Russians were not successful in pushing back the System. The System refused to bend or it pushed back, sometimes quite violently, especially under Stalin. But the System loosened over time. And when people did manage to get around the rules, to circumvent the System or to collectively redistribute goods and services, this was a triumph of people against the state. When people were successful in asserting themselves against the Soviet state, they had a sense of freedom from determination by the state—its politics, its economy. This freedom felt imminently human, almost spiritual, because people attained it through human relationships bent on overcoming everyday trials. Freedom was space (*prostor*), but it was a space contingent on the order (*poriadok*) of social relations and the state.

The abstract concepts of space, order, and freedom speak to the vitality of Soviet life. The spontaneity and serendipity of social connections asserted themselves against the System even as they were rooted in the System. But how do such cultural abstractions speak to the mortality crisis? When the state fell, a framework of social connections also fell. Elderly Muscovites spoke about not knowing people or not being able to place people in the new Russia. This severely compromised their ability to act together. Furthermore, what they had collectively asserted themselves through and against had fallen apart. There was a sense of chaos and disorder (*bezporiadok*) against which people could not act. This translated into a profound sense of social isolation and powerlessness, which are related to alcohol-related mortality, homicides, and suicides. Recent epidemiology shows that these feelings are also related to cardiovascular mortality through physiologic processes that are still being elucidated. While social epidemiology has shown that social isolation and perceived control have serious emotional and physical health consequences, it has failed to explore how the logic of isolation and powerlessness may be culturally and temporally specific.

Elderly Muscovites spoke about being unneeded. Fundamentally, being unneeded is about the loss of ability to give to others and thus to intervene in social life. Being needed is also tied up with abstract ideas of space, order, and freedom. On one side, being needed opens into an account of Russian vitality, spirituality, and life; on the other side, being unneeded narrows into an account of Russian mortality, disorder, and death. Deep, even philosophical cultural currents drive patterns of health and death in Russia as elsewhere. In the language of Durkheim (1979), who wrote about national rates of suicide in the 1800s, population statistics are subject to social currents.

RUSSIA

This book is not intended as a history of twentieth-century Russia, but some basic background is necessary, especially in the areas of Soviet history, its economy, and the so-called transition to capitalism.

The Russian Revolution in 1917, inspired by the political philosophy of Karl Marx (1818–1883), ushered in seventy years of socialism, originally envisioned as the historical stage after capitalism and before communism. In Marx's political philosophy the means of production are socialized during a dictatorship of the proletariat, while communism is a stateless, classless society, following socialism. In 1961 Nikita Khrushchev, head of the Communist Party from 1953 to 1964, proclaimed that the Soviet Union would be communist by 1980. In the 1970s, Leonid Brezhnev, his successor, clarified that the Soviet Union was in a long historical stage of "mature" socialism. Communism was never attained.

Vladimir Ilyich Lenin led the Russian socialist state through its tortuous first years until his death in 1924, by which time it had become the Union of Soviet Socialist Republics (USSR). Under Joseph Stalin's rule from 1928 to 1953, the Soviet Union underwent a period of extremely rapid industrialization, urbanization, and collectivization, accompanied by ruthless repressions and famine in the 1930s. The 1940s were marked by World War II and more famine. The late 1940s and early 1950s, before Stalin's death in 1953, were the height of the Soviet state, marked by economic growth and developments in science and technology. Signs of the economy slowing were first apparent in the 1960s, although most Russians may not have recognized this until the mid-1970s and Brezhnev's period of "stagnation." The generation of older Muscovites in this book came of age during the height of the Soviet state.

The Soviet state was paternalistic, providing full employment, housing, health care, and retirement pensions to its citizenry. It also aimed to create a New Soviet Person instilled with socialist values such as collectivism. "The New Soviet Person was to be not only clean, sober, and efficient but also prepared to sacrifice his or her individual interests for the good of the collective, in sharp contrast to the ideal of liberal individualism" (Hoffmann 2003, 10). Soviet ideology promoted the collectivist ethic at work and at home.

The economy of the Soviet Union was a planned economy, based on a series of five-year plans. It was weighted toward heavy industry, not consumer goods. Centralized planning was hampered by misinformation and hoarding of supplies (Verdery 1996). Due to these and other factors, there were chronic shortages of consumer goods. People often waited in long lines to buy food and other necessities. They made due without items such as deodorant or washing machines. There was an element of unpredictability and happenstance in consumerism. While this often led to frustration, it also created moments of serendipity. Informal economies of barter between firms and exchange between individuals served to redistribute goods and services in the shortage economy (Kornai 1980; Verdery 1996). Procuring goods had little to do with money and everything to do with personal relationships and connections. While Western observers may view this as corruption, older Muscovites often remember it as more humanistic.

By the time Mikhail Gorbachev came to power in 1985 it was clear that the System was in dire need of reform. Gorbachev instituted a period of glasnost and perestroika, or openness and restructuring. Initially, this may have inspired hope for a better future, but the machinations of reform soon grew unwieldy. The Baltic states (Estonia, Latvia, and Lithuania) seized the opportunity and began clamoring for independence from the Soviet Union, emboldening other nationalist movements. Amid a failed hardliner coup in August 1991, Boris Yeltsin, then president of the Russian republic of the Soviet Union, rose in popularity and power. In December of that same year, Yeltsin met with the presidents of Belarus and the Ukraine and dissolved the Union of Soviet Socialist Republics, thus eliminating Gorbachev's position. The Soviet Union, an empire of fifteen republics, no longer existed.

The years immediately following the dissolution of the Soviet Union were chaotic in Russia, as it embarked on a "big bang" or "shock therapy" approach to transitioning from a socialist planned economy to a capitalist free market. This approach had its roots in economist Milton Friedman's ideas and was inspired by neoliberalism in the West, heralded by Ronald Reagan in the United States and Margaret Thatcher in the United Kingdom. Solidified into the Washington Consensus in 1989, neoliberal reforms were supposed to result in a liberalized, stabilized, and privatized economy. In

Russia, privatization occurred very rapidly, and many of the state's biggest assets were divvied up among Yeltsin's "family" (*semya*), or cronies. This process was accompanied by hyperinflation, high levels of unemployment, and widespread poverty.

During Yeltsin's years, the Russian mafia also rose up to fill a power vacuum. By the time of his resignation in 1999, Yeltsin was very unpopular, regarded by many as a corrupt alcoholic. In comparison, his successor Vladimir Putin was thought to have restored order (*poriadok*). Putin, either as president or prime minister, has held political power in Russia since the year 2000. He has deep connections with Russian law enforcement, business, and the mafia. Many Russians admire his ability to command order and stand up to the West. But there is growing unrest, in the West and in Russia itself, with his authoritarianism and the silencing of opposition.

POST-SOVIET ETHNOGRAPHY

Post-Soviet ethnographers regard a "transition to capitalism" as a misnomer. Transition implies a move from one known state to another. The early post-Soviet era is better regarded as transformation, rather than transition, where the future was continually being created with unpredictable results (Berdahl 2000; Buyandelgeriyn 2008; Gal and Kligman 2000; Hann, Humphrey, and Verdery 2002; Hemment 2004a; Shevchenko 2001). Verdery (1996) shook up some of the assumptions behind the idea of transition with her question, "A transition from socialism to feudalism?" She advocated that ethnographers attend "to what is happening rather than . . . what ought to happen" (228). "Transition" erases the variability of whatever came before and the variability of capitalism. It pulls attention to the before and after with labels such as communism, socialism, and capitalism rather than to that which resists labels. Anthropology can be an antidote to narrow conceptualizations. It is possible to speak of "national capitalisms" (Kennedy 2001) or, for example, "Wild East" capitalism (Lindquist 2001c) in Russia during the early 1990s. More recently, Collier (2011) has staged another anthropological intervention in the use of the concept "neoliberal" to understand Russian economic reform in the 1990s. He argues that too much is left obscure about neoliberalism. Neoliberal economic reforms are not "a rigid ideological project" (2). They are also cultural constructions involving compromises with Soviet social welfare. The post-Soviet cultural landscape is one marked by change, continuity, and emergent hybrid forms. The past is crucial in understanding the present. That being said, there is also debate about the usefulness of the concepts "postsocialism" or "post-Soviet" (Humphrey 2002a). Sampson, who works in the Balkans, has declared postsocialism over: "the shock has worn off" and the new order is "embedded in people's consciousness" (2002, 298). While this is certainly happening, post-Soviet is still a trenchant concept for the older Muscovites of this study. "I prefer everything *sovkovoe,*"[3] or Soviet-style, one said. "I have not yet restructured myself."

There is no escaping memory and nostalgia in post-Soviet ethnography (Todorova and Gille 2010). In her book on nostalgia, Svetlana Boym defines it as "a longing for a home that no longer exists or has never existed" (2001, xiii). In Russia there is nostalgia for both the past and "for the unrealized dreams of the past and visions of the future that became obsolete" (xvi). Post-Soviet nostalgia is not merely the longing for Soviet society but for the future that never was. This was not necessarily the utopian "radiant future" of communism promised by Soviet ideology, but certainly an expected, taken-for-granted future. For middle-aged Muscovites nearing retirement when the Soviet Union fell, their future of a well-deserved retirement with an adequate pension was irretrievably lost. Particularly for this generation, memories comment on the present and future of a new Russia. Along with other postsocialist ethnographers (Dunn 2004; Kideckel 2008; Paxson 2005; Stillo 2013; Uehling 2004), I consider memories not only as an imperfect record of the past, but also primarily as commentary on the present. The romanticized past is a constant specter in the narratives older Muscovites tell. The radiant future becomes the "radiant past" (Burawoy and Lukács 1994). In this, older Muscovites revealed their perspectives on the present.

The radiance of the past emanates from social connections in the Soviet era. In her ethnography of a Russian village, Paxson (2005) argues that nostalgia about the past is fundamentally about the quality of social relations. In the East German discourse of nostalgia "metaphors of community and kinship have become increasingly prevalent. 'We used to live like one big family here . . . now no one has time for anyone else'" (Berdahl 1999, 219). Elderly benefactors of a Moscow soup kitchen mourn "the loss of interpersonal relations and a move toward individualization" (Caldwell 2004, 201). Their ways of "making do" are still intimately tied to sociality (Caldwell 2004). Ledeneva's seminal work on *blat*—"the use of personal networks and informal contacts to obtain goods and services in short supply" (Ledeneva 1998, 1)—illustrates how social connections in Soviet times were put to good use. Material pursuits in Soviet times were tied up with social ones.

Social connections in Russia remain a way of living a moral life amid circumstances widely regarded as immoral. Oushakine (2009) argues that Russians foster social connection around loss or tragedy. Pesmen (2000) writes about soulful communion, often when drinking alcohol together, that contests the new Russian order. In Zigon's work on morality, "working on the self" (2010, 245–46) is done through communion (*obshchenie*) with others. Drawing on Wierzbicka (2003), Zigon argues that *obshchenie* "allows individuals to mutually develop each other and themselves . . . creating new moral persons" (2010, 97). Russian social connections allow individuals to access a moral space beyond the self and beyond the mundane. When middle-aged Muscovites lament a loss of sociality, they are commenting on a perceived loss of morality. In this, their voices join with other moral critiques of free market capitalism by individuals and institutions in society, the Russian government and Russian Orthodox Church among them. Nevertheless, morality and sociality are changing in tandem (Zigon 2011; Bazylevych 2010).

When I first began to think about this project, there were very few references to the Russian demographic crisis in the anthropological literature (Rivkin-Fish 2001, 2003). Rivkin-Fish refers to the discourse of Russia's "dying out" (2001, 29). She writes, "Physical crisis is mirrored in moral fragmentation; biological degeneration represents the nation's social and ethical demise" (29). She points out that nationalists and advocates of Westernization alike think recovery "involve[s] changing the nature of social interactions, reconfiguring human relations, and healing the social bonds of daily life" (29) rather than merely changing politics. Recently, Rivkin-Fish's work on fertility (2006, 2007, 2010) has considerably expanded the anthropological literature on that aspect of the demographic crisis. Leykin's work on the politics of population in Russia (2011a, 2011b) also focuses primarily on fertility and pronatalism. She discusses the mortality crisis as part of the larger demographic crisis, even if Russian population prescriptions do not. Post-Soviet health in Russia is broached more broadly in Rivkin-Fish's work on reproductive health (1999, 2000), Raikhel's work on addiction and treatment (2010; Raikhel and Garriott 2013), and Lindquist's work on alternative healing and magic (2001a, 2001b, 2001c, 2006). The mortality crisis is sometimes noted as background (Pesmen 2000), as part of a larger discourse of decline (Oushakine 2009), or as related to stress and disempowerment among the working class (Kideckel 2008), but it has not been ethnographically examined in its own right. Ethnographers see alcohol consumption in the region as creating social identity (Kideckel 1984) and social communion (Pesmen 1995, 2000), even as they acknowledge its destructive effects on men and women (Metzo 2009). Drinking alcohol is bound up with masculinity, and when other avenues for expressing masculinity recede it may become problematic (Zdravomyslova and Chikadze 2000; Creed 2011). Drinking together is status leveling and offers alternative moralities (Koester 2003; Sokolov 2006).

Gender is extensively treated in the anthropology and sociology of Soviet and post-Soviet society, although literature on masculinity is more recent (Kay 2006, 2007; Kukhterin 2000; Meshcherkina 2000; Utrata 2008, 2013; Utrata, Ispa, and Ispa-Landa 2012). According to many scholars the transition to capitalism made women more vulnerable in Russian society as they were disproportionately unemployed and social services such as child care were withdrawn (Attwood 1996; Gal and Kligman 2000; Hemment 2004a; Kuehnast and Nechemias 2004; LaFont 2001; Watson 1993). Bridger, Kay, and Pinnick claim, "It is . . . undeniable that women have borne a disproportionate share of the economic fallout of transition" (1996, 193). Hemment writes that "structural adjustment policies led to the dismantling of the social security system and sharp cutbacks in the health care system, affecting women disproportionately" (2004a, 817). There is some dissent on this point (Ashwin 2000; Kiblitskaya 2000). "There has been a tendency to consider the collapse of communism in terms of a balance sheet of losses and gains for women. . . . This approach . . . ignores the fact that men as well as women are challenged by the end of the Soviet era" (Ashwin 2000, 19). A crisis of masculinity, reflected in mortality and self-destructive behavior among the generation of men born around the Great Patriotic War, was openly acknowledged in Soviet society starting in the 1970s. Zdravomyslova and Temkina claim that many practices of masculinity were countercultural, including "friendship among men, drinking in groups, sports, getaways, and sexual philandering" (2012, 28). The late Soviet man "has created for himself a space relatively independent of the state where he can actualize the practices of true masculinity" (28–29). Others agree that masculinity is constructed through transgressive or oppositional practices. "A certain kind of modestly destructive mischief has been a key emblem of Russian masculinity" (Zdravomyslova and Chikadze 2000, 48; Ries 1997). Social scientists also locate the crisis of masculinity in the post-Soviet weakening of men's ability to provide for their families (Kiblitskaya 2000; Zdravomyslova and Chikadze 2000). Creed (2011) proposes that cultural dispossession and unemployment among post-Soviet Bulgarian men shifts the performance of masculinity to other spaces, in this case a ritual of folk masquerade, often accompanied by drinking and lewd or violent behavior.

There is no doubt that men were more likely to die in Russia in the early 1990s. While men are more likely to die than women in most places, the difference between men's and women's mortality in Russia is currently the largest in the world and widened appreciably in the early 1990s. An interpretation of historic differences in mortality of Russian men and women requires an understanding of men's and women's position under the Soviet state, social practices, and, most importantly, what makes life worth living for men and women in Russia. There is consensus among older Muscovites that men more easily became unneeded in the post-Soviet context.

ORGANIZATION

The organization of the book reflects my own discovery—that mortality, while the focus, is not the point of departure. Therefore, I save most of my discussion of mortality until Chapters 6 and 7. Instead, after a chapter on methods and Moscow, I explore the Russian cultural paradox of space and order. Space opens up through relationships of neededness, but these relationships also order space. People help each other, giving things that are needed and becoming needed people. The paradox of space and order is the cultural frame of this ethnography. The book then progressively narrows its focus, going from paradox to being needed to mortality. The narrative flows from life to death. The last chapter before the conclusion broadens out again to complete the frame—showing how the paradox explored earlier relates to the experience of freedom.

The first chapter of the book describes the Moscow cityscape—its monumental avenues and quiet courtyards. The focus of the chapter is a recorded conversation between two old friends reminiscing about one of Moscow's radial streets in Soviet times. In their telling, space (*prostor*) references social relations and freedom, physically and metaphorically framed by the Soviet state. In the early 1990s the collapse of the state created chaos and disorder (*bezporiadok*), indeterminacy rendered dangerous without the limits of order—both state order and the order of social relations organized through the state. This chapter also provides more details on my ethnographic methods and the particular challenges of doing ethnography in Moscow.

Chapter 2 further explores the cultural paradox of space and order. Paradox is uniquely able to hold contradictions without sacrificing the concept of culture. Older Muscovites' concern with unbound space (*prostor*) and the constraint of order (*poriadok*) is reflected in an appetite for the spontaneous and transgressive and nostalgia for the Soviet past. Soviet order created the very possibility for social relations that served to circumvent and oppose Soviet order. A Russian sense of space and freedom, which is connected to space, depends on thwarting order through social connections. The space-order paradox sheds light on another, theoretical paradox in social theory—that of structure and agency. Western social theorists often assume structure binds agency, while the Russian point of view is diametrically opposed: structure creates agency.

The next two chapters on war and work provide a background on this generation's lives and illustrate how the paradox of space and order manifests in Soviet history, work, social exchange, and gender. This generation of Muscovites was born between 1936 and 1951—around the time of the Great Patriotic War, as World War II is called in Russia. The early hardships of war were given meaning through cultural tropes of sacrifice and collectivity. For this generation, poverty in the early 1990s recalled the war and postwar period, more than forty years earlier. The progressive trajectory of their lives swung back on itself. Moreover, their sacrifices were in vain and they themselves were rendered unneeded—without anything useful to offer the state or others around them. This generation had been needed by the state, first for postwar reconstruction and then to labor for the radiant future. They had also been needed by others, to survive the war and postwar hardships, and later to secure the goods and services the state did not provide them.

Chapter 4 establishes Soviet work as the principal nexus of space and order. Work was how Soviet citizens were integrated into the state but also how they collectively crafted their own space apart from, and sometimes opposed to, the state. This was a space for spontaneous action. Work also defined how and why people were needed by the state and by each other. At work people had access to connections, services, and goods that they used in practices such as *blat*—the use of personal networks to redistribute goods and services (Ledeneva 1998). People were needed because they could offer things to others; what they could offer was largely defined by where they worked and what they did there. The loss of work meant the loss of a social status based on the ability to give.

Chapter 5 describes how the destructive logic of shock therapy violently collided with the progressive logic of the Soviet state. The stories of Ivan and Lidia show how gender influenced the experience of shock therapy. While women were overburdened at home, to some extent these domestic responsibilities protected them from being unneeded. Men, whose domestic role had been narrowly defined as breadwinner, were much more vulnerable to being unneeded with the loss of work, salary arrears, or a diminished ability to provide, especially when set against ostentatious social inequality. Being unneeded set men on a desperate search for egalitarian social communion. A masculine predilection to push against order proved deadly when that order gave way in the early 1990s.

Chapter 6 outlines the contours of Russian mortality, drawing on the epidemiology of the crisis. The early 1990s marked a dramatic rise in mortality unprecedented in modern history. Working-class, middle-aged men living in the more developed regions of Russia, chief among these Moscow, were most at risk of dying from cardiovascular problems, injuries, and alcohol-related causes. In the epidemiological literature, which primarily focuses on alcohol, mortality is related to the Russian predilection for drink and a lack of social capital, often seen as a legacy of Soviet times.

Chapter 7 begins with an exchange on the Russian soul. The Russian soul is social and bears marks of both space and order. It offers individuals an existence beyond the confines of the self—a social expansiveness. With this come dangers that are held in check by the limits of order, in its interpersonal and institutional forms. Harm to the social soul renders the physical body vulnerable. This chapter links cardiovascular and alcohol-related deaths to being unneeded and to ruptures of the soul. I contrast this with Western epidemiologists' emphasis on a lack of social capital in Soviet/Russian society and the use of alcohol as an escape. An anthropological reading of epidemiological studies makes sense of some puzzling epidemiological findings, such as the association between better reported health and alcohol use, an association between mortality and nondrinking, and an association between poorer reported health and reliance on civic associations.

Finally, I return to the theoretical frame to argue that Russian freedom, *svoboda,* is held in social relations that grant the individual both a sense of transcendence and autonomy from determination by larger forces, be they historical, political, economic, or cultural. Middle-aged Muscovites experienced a sense of freedom in a sociality that was intent on separation from and opposition to the state. The early 1990s in Russia made *svoboda* less tenable precisely because individuals no longer had a clear view of space and order.

DYING UNNEEDED

When I tell people about the Russian mortality crisis after the fall of the Soviet Union, they often ask me to repeat myself. More people died? They assume that Russians, at long last, had freedom. Why would they die? One answer to this question, and one I commonly give, is the increase in cardiovascular and alcohol-related deaths, which together constitute the bulk of excess mortality. People are often content with that answer. They understand that this time may have been stressful as people lost their jobs and savings. What happened in Russia, however, was more than an economic depression and the dissolution of the state. In their own words, middle-aged Muscovites felt *ne nuzhny* (unneeded). Social isolation and powerlessness have consequences for health, but their logics vary by place and time. Another answer to the question "Why would they die?" is more provocative: Russians died precisely because they were free—free of the order that had provided them with the means to interact with those around them. The idea that Russians died because they were free is polemical. It is a way of challenging the popular, if tarnished, Western account that the early 1990s brought freedom to Russia. It also hints at an emic perspective that resists Western ideas of freedom, especially when they are bound up with processes of social disintegration and inequality.

Not all Russians died, of course. Mortality was most pronounced among the middle-aged in the capital city. These were the "generation of victors" born around the years of the Great Patriotic War. They came of age at the height of the Soviet state. Just as Russia was embarking on a scientific and technological revolution that propelled the Soviet Union's economy during the 1950s and 1960s, this generation entered the workforce. After the suffering and sacrifices exacted during the war and reconstruction, the 1950s and 1960s were heady times. Later as the economy slowed and reform became inevitable, a radiant future—if not the radiant future—was still possible. When the Soviet state collapsed at the end of 1991, hope in a Soviet future was lost. In 1992 economic reforms meant that industry contracted severely, inflation skyrocketed, social services receded, and chaos reigned. For many ordinary Russians, hope in any future was threatened during this time.

This generation not only lost their work and savings—they lost their lives. Socially isolated and disempowered, many men died alcohol-related deaths as they tried to repair a sense of neededness by drinking. Women were protected from alcohol-related and cardiovascular deaths due to their central role in the family—they were still needed. The order this generation had used to navigate in society, to know others around them, and to interact socially was of little use in the chaos of that time. They died unconnected, unbound, unmoored.

World political economy had fatal consequences in Russia in the early 1990s. The rise of global neoliberalism, the fall of the Soviet state, and the introduction of economic reforms reverberated through Russian society, affecting social connections and the everyday possibilities of action that hinged on them.

CHAPTER 1

Moscow

M oscow is a city of extreme contrasts. Initially I found it a very difficult place to do ethnography, but we made our peace. In this chapter I use a conversation about a Moscow city street to highlight the experience of space in Soviet Moscow and its transformation. Space, or *prostor,* is a highly significant concept in Russian. In the Soviet organization of the capital city, Muscovites found the space to spontaneously make things happen. The confluence of state and space helps explain why mortality in the early 1990s was especially severe in the capital city. When the state collapsed, so did bounded spaces of personal and collective expression.

MOSCOW TRANSFORMED

One evening while having tea with Tatiyana and Lidia, Margarita recounted a trip to Novyi Arbat street with Tatiyana. Both Tatiyana and Margarita worked on Novyi Arbat at the State Committee on Material and Technical Procurement (Gossnab) from 1965 through 1974. Novyi Arbat is a portion of one of the main radial streets that extends from the Kremlin westward toward the White House, former home of the Russian parliament and now a Russian government building. Originally named Kalinin Prospekt, Novyi Arbat is a broad street with a series of identical high-rise buildings shaped like open books lining both sides. Since Soviet times, it has changed dramatically, with casinos, department stores, shops, restaurants, cafés, and parking lots.[1] The neon lights rival those of Las Vegas. Because of the parking lots, the street has narrowed somewhat. The broad sidewalks are also effectively narrowed by café seating.

In 2006 Margarita had not seen Novyi Arbat street for more than fifteen years and she was flustered. *Krutitsia* she said over and over, a word that literally means rotating or spinning. She was referring to the neon lights and electronic signs, which do indeed spin. *Krutitsia,* however, also refers to business activity, as noted by Pesmen, *"Krutit'sia* had long meant to engage in business . . . from petty speculation to buying and selling large lots of goods and 'something serious in the shadow economy'"; it "is running around in control, hustling, or out of control, 'like a squirrel in a wheel' or 'like in a meat grinder'" (2000, 192–93). The bright blinking lights, the advertisements, the concentration of selling and buying struck Margarita as wild and frantic. To her it was disordered. "A horrible thing is happening," she said over and over. Lidia sympathized: "Nothing of Russia is left."

When I audio-recorded a later interview with Margarita (her friend Tatiyana and Tatiyana's daughter were also present), I asked her to tell me again about going back to Novyi Arbat. The excerpt below is lengthy, but it gives a sense of how this generation interprets change in Moscow and introduces the concept of space (*prostor*).

> Margarita: Oh, that was terrible. I told you, Michelle, first of all, we worked there at Prospect Kalinin,[2] right? I said, "Tan, let's drop by . . . Novyi Arbat," I say. Oh, when I saw. . . . We worked there. Oh, horror, everything lit up, illumination, oh horror! All of it, oh horror! That was before the New Year, wasn't it Tanya? I don't remember.
> Tatiyana: It is always like that there.
> Margarita: Oh what a nightmare! I say, "Tan, I haven't been here for many, many years." We worked there at one time. Oh, no, but before it was good. And now I don't like it, absolutely, some kind of wildness. . . .
> Tatiyana: But there, there really, now there all those casinos, all those. . . .
> Margarita: A nightmare, a nightmare, some kind of horror.
> Tatiyana: Yes and there are cafés, everything like that.
> Margarita: A horror, horror![3]

At this point, Tatiyana's daughter interrupted to ask, "And what was there before?"

Tatiyana: Understand what it was like there, I. There was space [*prostor*]. There each one of those books [a reference to the high-rise apartment buildings, shaped like open books, which line the street] definitely had its own café. It did, sure. But it had them so that the ministry workers could eat there.

Margarita: Yes, we went to the cafeteria Angara.

Tatiyana: Yes, there was Angara, and Moskvichka. And above them a café. They were spacious [*prostorniye*], all of it. And between them there were railway and airline booking offices. And that was it. All the rest was simply space [*prostor*]. There was a store and above it two ministries on the right and left and a café. Another book, and likewise another, different ministry to the left. There was a café there too and there was vast space [*prostor*]. Well how to explain?

Margarita: There was a Synthetika store . . . gifts. . . .

Tatiyana: Well, yes, yes, that is, all [the shops] were lower-end. A store or a café or a grocery or such a store. . . . I mean people walked by. . . .

Margarita: A delicatessen.

Tatiyana: Yes people walked by and, if they were going on or to work, they stopped in and bought everything they needed. And clothing. And it was affordable to each person, that is each one of those people, whether they worked there or. . . .

Margarita: That's right.

Tatiyana: Or they had simply arrived from Georgia, from Armenia or from wherever, or they simply passed by and it was generally such a quiet atmosphere. Now, when you come out there on Prospekt Kalinin it is, of course, just, I don't know, terrible for those who worked there and saw something different.

Margarita: I was just in shock. Literally.

Tatiyana: Yes, in shock. Why? Because there are those spinning casino advertising signs, the touts. And what is more there is no more of that space [*prostor*]. Each door there, some shop appears. Some new doors which were not even there before. And all of those touts calling for you to come in. Of course it makes such an impression that you already understand that it is for a certain . . . not for everyone but for a certain type of people. That's it. It wasn't like that before. Before everything was very simple and very easy. That is how we saw it.

SPACE ON THE STREET

Tatiyana's and Margarita's comments reveal how central city space in Moscow has been reordered. They concentrate on two aspects of the old Novyi Arbat—buildings that were sites of state functions such as ministries and ticketing offices and the space of the street, which includes the cafeterias, cafés, and stores. In one reading, space is simply physical space that has now been taken up with new commercial establishments, outdoor café seating, and parking lots. Another reading considers space as a metaphor for the quality of social relations in Soviet society. The buildings housing state ministries and ticketing offices framed the space of the street. Again:

> [The cafeterias and café] were spacious [*prostorniye*], all of it. And between
> them there were railway and airline booking offices. And that was it. All
> the rest was simply space [*prostor*]. There was a store and above it two
> ministries on the right and left and a café. Another book, and likewise
> another, different ministry to the left. There was a café there too and there
> was vast space [*prostor*]. There was a store and above it two ministries on the
> right and left.

In this sense, the space is created and framed by the state, but it is set apart from the state. Tatiyana and Margarita mourn the loss of undetermined space.

Tatiyana and Margarita struggled to explain the quality of the space. "Well, how to explain it?" The space was "vast," "quiet," "simple," and "easy." Everyone walked in that space, no matter where they worked, where they lived, or where they came from. The space was a site of personal and collective expression and action, framed by the structures and functions of the state. This is in contrast to the transformed street, which is "not for everyone but for a certain type of people." The space that once existed for ordinary people—ministry workers, tourists, others—is now space for a certain class of people with money to spend. Space in the city is no longer a preserve from politics and economics but is invaded by capitalist logic. Instead of a space of spontaneity and indeterminacy, where social relations were merely framed by the state, now social relations are intimately colored by the currency of capitalism that orders, indeed quantifies, both places and people in units of rubles or dollars.

The fact that Tatiyana and Margarita also characterized Soviet-era cafés, shops, and grocery stores as spacious suggests that state enterprises could also be domains of social expression and autonomy. Although there were surly clerks and empty shelves, these were sites where individuals asserted themselves as individuals, and not merely state citizens, through moderate consumption. The limits on consumption were frustrating, but not any less rewarding. In fact, finding something special at a good price was a minor triumph in an economic system plagued by shortages and low-quality goods. In 2004, my Russian tutor told me that finding one pair of stylish Italian leather shoes was exciting in Soviet times. "Now everything is available, but there is no money to buy it." No more sense of surprise and serendipity in consumerism.

Another interviewee also told me that Moscow is now a different city. Around the year 2000 she returned to an area of the city where she had once lived for eight years, walking from the Byelorussian train station to Pushkin Square along a northwestern portion of Tverskaia Ulitsa, which radiates from the Kremlin and Red Square.

> Those were my own places, and I didn't recognize my own street. It was all banks. I came to Pushkin Square, got on the metro and returned home. I even cried because that is not my city. That is for sure, for sure. I will not drop into a store where I could before because it is entirely boutiques there. [. . .] I have nothing to do there. They won't even let me in there. They will say, "Grandma, where do you think you are going?" For sure. Banks, boutiques, restaurants, where they will say, "Not dressed like that." [. . .] So that street is perfectly strange, it isn't mine.

Here too the street and city are no longer her own—"because that is not my city." She said, "I have nothing to do there. They won't even let me in there [. . .] it isn't mine." It is as if actual, physical urban spaces have shrunk for a certain generation. They no longer feel as though those spaces are theirs to inhabit.

Caldwell recounts an episode where an elderly friend refused to drink coffee at a coffeehouse on Tverskaia Ulitsa. She told Caldwell that she found the space uncomfortable. "The café was not an appropriate space for people like her" (Caldwell 2009, 102). Instead, she and Caldwell sat on an outside bench with bottled juice and water. Caldwell ties this to a discussion of the morality of space. She suggests that the coffeehouse confused "the anonymity of a public space with the intimacy of a private space" (124). My friends also thought this type of space was not simple, but this was due to a sense of exclusion. Instead of a space where people's interactions were framed by the political economy of socialism, this space was subsumed by the political economy of capitalism. In this way social inequality was written into the space in a way that clearly read social exclusion to older Muscovites, many of whom had never seen such lavish cafés with their trendy clientele and expensive coffee during most of their lifetimes. These spaces were no longer "for everyone but for a certain type of people." Even when a friend is buying coffee or the touts are inviting them inside, older Muscovites know these spaces are not for them. Spaces of capitalism effectively communicate social inequality in Russia, as in the West. Westerners, too, are highly attuned to these messages, and they determine where people go and where they do not. Older Muscovites felt this restriction of space acutely. Space in Moscow is now highly stratified.

Tverskaia Ulitsa (formerly Ulitsa Gorkovo) has always been a highly symbolic space in Moscow. Rüthers, drawing on Thorez, describes the street in the postwar years, contrasting the grand architectural facades with the courtyards behind them. "In the everyday life, two seemingly contradictory spaces existed: the anonymous and monumental in the front, and the retreat into the back as a space of self determination" (2006, 255). Writing about St. Petersburg, Nielsen draws a similar distinction between Nevskyi Prospekt and the courtyards (*dvori*). The *prospekt* is civilization; the *dvor* "a closely guarded bit of untamed nature" (Nielsen 2006, under "A. *Prospekt* and *Dvor*"). The contrast between state architecture and personal space marked Moscow and St. Petersburg in Soviet times. In Moscow, in particular, the facades of the street were originally a testament to Soviet power; the courtyards a testament to its malleability. The street represented state order while the courtyards represented the idiosyncratic and spontaneous social life that asserted itself in the interstices of state order—a bit of contained disorder. One made the effluence of the other possible. But, as Rüthers herself illustrates, the street itself evolved into a site for the expression of individuality.[4]

> Citizens came to Gorky Street in their best clothes to spend their time at
> leisure. They went window-shopping and strolled up and down Gorky Street
> between Okhotnyi Riad and Pushkin Square, all the while showing off to

themselves and to the world the achievements of socialism. They thereby took possession of the public space as one of leisure, consumption and fashion, a space of urban lifestyle offering identity. (2006, 261)

The public space was appropriated and used in ways that Soviet planners could not have envisioned. It is worth noting that the city of Moscow itself has a facade and courtyard—the center, radiating from the Kremlin, and a vast periphery of apartment blocks, or sleeper districts. The layout of the city reflects both the state and the society that flourished in counterpoint—a "reconciliation between authority and the people," as Boym describes Moscow (2001, 115).

Certain post-Soviet spaces painfully testify to what has been lost for this generation. It is not just the loss of the state and a stable order but the space to circumvent and be free from that order.

Prostor

In one Russian-English dictionary the first definition of *prostor* is "space; expanse." The second is "range; scope; freedom" (Katzner 1994, s.v. "prostor"). *Prostor* is emblematic of Russia as a whole, both geographically and spiritually. When Valentina told Sveta and me, during our first interview on a bench by a pond, that Russia was a wild country, I asked her to clarify. She mentioned the thousands of kilometers, the forests, the rivers, Siberia, and Lake Baikal. She spoke of the distances and proportions. It is nature—untamed—and it is expansive—unbound. According to Caroline Humphrey, "freedom has always been a highly spatial idea in Russia, and is associated with sheer openness, endless space (*prostor*)" (2007, 7). A friend at the English club told James that Siberia was the only place in Russia where one could be free. In this sense, space (*prostor*) is possibility.

Space is also uncertainty, even angst. Living with possibility, where limits are constantly renegotiated, is tiring. In Pesmen's ethnography of Omsk in the early 1990s a friend says, "That spaciousness (*prostor*) tires me out. Spaciousness. With a sort of indeterminacy. It's hard for me to incorporate, to learn to live with that space" (2000, 283). A widely repeated refrain is, "It isn't allowed, unless you really want to." One day when I could not talk my way past the guard at the academy, I felt that I had failed. Living in a place of unpredictable possibilities makes it hard to know what exactly is possible and what to expect.

Space is also an analogue for the expansiveness of the Russian spirit. On the bench by the pond, Valentina spoke of Russians' wide nature and emotional richness by which Russians accomplish great things but also "get carried away." She described Europeans as "somehow narrow, [going] from this to that." Valentina continued, "On the other hand, a sense of form, discipline—that is what is difficult for a Russian person. That's why it has always been necessary [. . .] to force, pressure." The Russian spirit is essentially untamed, in need of boundaries.

Over a century ago, in an essay on "bourgeois democracy" in Russia, Max Weber (1995) lamented the importation of capitalism into Russia. His point was that Western capitalism did not have "any elective affinity with 'democracy' let alone with 'liberty'" (109). But he also insinuated that democracy and liberty would come to Russia only when "they are backed up by the determined *will* of a nation not to be ruled like a flock of sheep" (109). Weber may have been right about capitalism, but his reference to sheep is misleading. It is precisely because Russians are determined "not to be ruled like a flock of sheep," precisely because Russians are not sheep, that they have been ruled by an iron fist. And this is also the reason many Russians have preserved *prostor*—spiritual freedom—in times of oppression.

MOSCOW

I vividly remember landing at Sheremetevo airport just north of Moscow in March 1993, more than a decade before ethnographic fieldwork. I would spend more than a year living in St. Petersburg, studying the Russian language and teaching English. My first memories of Russia, though, are of Moscow. At Sheremetevo, the airport immigration official signaled for me to step forward. A tall blond man dressed in drab green, he looked the part. He didn't smile, but he did ask me if I spoke any Russian. Nervous, I forgot to conjugate the verb. "I to speak a little," I offered. He nodded me on and I felt some relief that he had not found a problem with my visa.

Outside, snow was on the bare, brown ground in patches. We took an older gray bus and then the metro to a friend's apartment in the north of Moscow. The metro was awe inspiring, but outside the spring thaw meant that we walked through dirty, wet slush. The first vibrant green of a Moscow spring was still to come—tender leaf buds that are so anticipated after the winter. And the city itself was desperately in need of repair and maintenance.

With so much concrete the color was overwhelmingly gray. Soviet socialism had fallen and the gaudy colors of Western capitalism—signs, advertisements, storefront displays, neon lights—were still absent.

Despite this, and the smallness of the two-room apartment, my first impression was that the Soviet state had adequately provided for the city's population. It was not a luxurious life, but the public transportation system was enviable and the centralized heating definitely worked. After dinner we had a rectangle of vanilla ice cream wrapped in silver paper. It was so rich it evoked cheese—in the best possible way. That evening I soaked in a hot if slightly rust-colored bath and sank into a lumpy bed, which converted into a sofa. A red Persian carpet adorned one wall. With a large square down pillow and a red plaid wool blanket covered by a white duvet I felt very cozy.

Russia was actually in chaos. People had been thrust into poverty with the reforms of 1992. The industrial sector was fairly grinding to a halt and along with it the livelihoods of millions of individuals. People who were working were not being paid. Each day the price of food rose while the value of the ruble declined. There were shortages of milk, bread, meat, and oil. Organized crime was filling the power void. The summer of 1993 would represent a brief reprieve before the darkest winter of this period, during which almost one million Russians lost their lives prematurely. Although I remained unaware of the magnitude of the mortality crisis until years later, I saw and heard enough during the winter of 1993–1994 to know that something had gone seriously awry with Russia's "transition to capitalism."

CONTRASTS

When I returned to Moscow in June 2004 to do some preliminary research, the city was changed. I flew into the new Domodedovo airport south of the city and took an express train to the metro. I had arranged to rent an apartment near the Sportivnaia metro station, located across the river from Sparrow Hills and Moscow State University. On the outskirts of St. Petersburg in 1993 we paid $200 per month for a renovated three-room apartment. In 2004 I paid $500 per month for the two-room apartment near Sportivnaia. Two years later I paid $700 for the same Moscow apartment, and that was a bargain. Apartments in the center of Moscow were renting for thousands of dollars per month. The southwest area of the city is known as relatively green and ecologically clean. In the fifteen years of increasing geographic stratification, the southwest was also relatively more affluent. In contrast, the southeast was known as working class and poor. As a general rule, Moscow's wealth is concentrated in the center while the periphery is poorer, and this pattern is increasing with time. In June 2004 Tverskaia Ulitsa, the main boulevard that radiates from the Kremlin and Red Square northwestward, was awash in shops and designer boutiques. As I walked down the street, I felt awkward in practical shoes and a black travel skirt. Although I knew the city had changed, I had packed with 1994 in the back of my mind—no heels, no whites, and no dry cleaning. I felt short and frumpy, out of place. I must admit that on Tverskaia a part of me mourned the Russia I knew before.

Moscow is a city I both love and hate. My husband, James, after his first trip there in the summer of 2004, described it as "New York on steroids." On the streets it is an aggressive city, especially in the center. Russians will tell you that Moscow is a business city, as opposed to the more cultural city of St. Petersburg. I took a friend and Atlanta-based flight attendant on the metro, where she was shocked that someone exiting rudely pushed her. What to say? I myself learned to push on the metro. At first I thought racing toward an empty seat on the metro was beneath me, but I had my days. I was disgusted when I saw young men and women absorbed in music or reading while their elders stood, holding onto the overhead handles or vertical posts. But there were times when I too avoided looking around and held onto my seat. Once, in line for transportation to Sheremetevo airport, the people in front of us ran over to the still-approaching minibus and began to climb inside the open door of the moving vehicle. The people behind us peeled away from the line, also hurrying toward the minibus. I told James to do the same for fear he would miss his flight. I then watched him struggle to lift a large suitcase through the door and up the steps of a moving vehicle before it came to a complete stop at the place of the original line. Something about that saddened me. James almost always holds back in such situations. At my urging, he was learning to fight. The feeling of being forced to participate in demeaning behavior was not restricted to foreigners. On my way to a honey festival, after being roughly crammed into the corner of a complimentary shuttle bus, I heard a Russian middle-aged woman tell her son, loudly and angrily, "This is so barbaric."

I frequently tell people that Russians may appear rude or unhappy in public but in their homes they are hospitable and open. In general, this is true. But it is also true that even in Moscow kindness happens on city streets. And given the harshness and anonymity of the city, this kindness seems all the more sincere and sweet. On more than one occasion, it made my day. Once when I was five months pregnant a cashier at the Pushkin Museum of Fine Arts waved for me to enter. "But I haven't paid," I dumbly insisted. "Aren't you 'in the condition'?" she asked. Well, yes, I was. She waved me through again. I am sure she thought I was a bit thick, and not only around the middle.

Moscow is a seductive city, both racy and charming. There are four concentric circular main roads that overlie Moscow, forming a giant dart board around the Kremlin center: the Boulevard Ring, the Garden Ring, the Third Transport Ring, and the Moscow Automobile Ring Road, or the MKAD, which is the city bypass. During the summer of 2004 I made a point of walking above ground as much as I could. I used a black marker to trace my routes on a map of the city. Once I arrived at Leningrad train station from St. Petersburg at four thirty in the morning before the metro opened. Overnight I had ridden in a poorly ventilated yet remarkably well-heated third-class sleeper car (*platzkartnyi vagon*). Each open *platzkart* wagon has fifty-four sleeping berths arranged down one side of the car and on either side of partitions on the other side of a narrow aisleway. Instead of lining up and pushing with the throng through the metro doors at five, I walked in the cool morning air around the Garden Ring Road to the north and then the west. It was twilight and the streets were practically deserted. Occasionally a car would speed by in one of fourteen available lanes. A bright sun rose at five. I cut in toward the center at Petrovka Street, which meets the inner ring road at the Bolshoi Theatre in just more than a mile. The words "road" and "street" seem inadequate to describe these broad avenues lined with imposing Stalinist architecture.

When I miss Moscow, though, caught unawares by a sudden memory followed by a faint longing in my throat, I am almost never thinking of the center streets. I am thinking of quiet courtyards with tired, crooked benches. The paint on the wooden planks of the seat and back—red and blue or yellow and green—is peeling. An older woman (always called a grandmother in Russian) might be sitting quietly, reading or keeping watch, bundled in an old sweater even in summertime. Younger women gather together, animatedly gossiping about neighbors, dropping their voices and looking at strangers who walk by. A child climbs or spins on the old painted iron play equipment. Men of any age might be sitting on another bench at the opposite end of the yard, often drinking together, talking loudly if they have been at it awhile and sleeping against each other if they have been at it even longer.

When I remember these courtyards, in my mind it is summertime. It is warm with a soft breeze—weather for a light sweater. A shaded path might be lined with rustling birch trees. In June in Moscow the poplar trees shed their cotton-ball fluff—summer snowflakes floating in the air. In places it is hard to avoid inhaling the fluff before it descends to the ground and clusters together. At some point a Soviet-era leader, Khrushchev according to legend, ordered thousands of poplars planted throughout the city. I have always found the two or three weeks of poplar fluff magical, although it is a practical nuisance.

Courtyards of the city periphery are often nestled between the prefabricated five-story apartment buildings, which are now slated for replacement. Khrushchev had them built quickly during the 1960s in order to remedy the housing shortage. In his memoirs Khrushchev writes, "In my day the goal that was set above all was to build as much housing as possible with the least expenditure of monetary and material resources" (Khrushchev 2006, 291). Ostensibly, he thought that there would be less destruction to five-story buildings in the event of war. There was also no need to provide elevators. Russians generally regard Khrushchev's apartment buildings as poorly constructed and bug infested. They are known as *khrushchoby,* a play on the words Khrushchev and *trushchoby,* or slum.

Moscow is full of extreme contrasts. Boym (2001) writes about Moscow as the "big village" and the "Third Rome," a site of history and prophecy— traditional, cosmopolitan, or apocalyptic in its myths. Soviet Moscow was at once both an "intimate city" and a "megalomaniac capital" (97). It still holds these contrasts. In the small Orthodox churches, dark and hazy, the walls are lined with icons surrounded by thin pale candles, dripping wax. Here a priest in a long black robe swings a smoking incense censer attached to a chain, and a hidden choir chants a haunting refrain. A middle-aged woman may sit in the pews, her head covered and bowed under some silent burden of grief. At the boisterous outdoor Luzhniky market traders hawk their imitation Gucci bags and Prada shoes loudly every morning before packing them back into the ubiquitous plastic plaid-patterned rectangular bags. There are new sushi restaurants, myriad *kofe haus* and *shokoladnitsa,* and the utterly delicious fall salads made in tiny apartment kitchens from the last misshapen *dacha* tomatoes, cucumbers, apples, and tiny red onions on the windowsill, all chopped and heavily doused in oil. There are walks through vast and plentiful parks, heartfelt chats over tea in the kitchen, the raucous singing and yelling of a group of teenage boys in the courtyard after a Spartak soccer game, the numerous toasts at a smoky business dinner in an expensive Azerbaijani restaurant. Some things are as they always were, some are lost along with Soviet Russia, and still others are strictly the new Russia, in existence only since the mid-1990s.

Any Russian will say that Moscow is not Russia. A Russian friend studying in the capital told me that when he visits his hometown he asks his friends and relatives, "How are things in Russia?" It is a joke, but there is something to it. Another woman cautioned me, "Don't ever draw conclusions about what happens in the country by what happens in Moscow." Moscow is not Russia. And yet, when I repeated this refrain to another Russian acquaintance, she responded, "It is and it isn't." Two centuries ago Russian historian Karamzin wrote, "whoever has been in Moscow knows Russia." Despite the differences with other cities in Russia, Moscow remains Russian.

Moscow, however, is busier, wealthier, more diverse, more stratified, and more cosmopolitan than even St. Petersburg, the other big city in western Russia. One academic told me St. Petersburg was a dead city, "uninhabited, hardly breathing." "Understand, there is no money, so no impulse like in Moscow. Moscow! I love Moscow, with her furiousness, her dynamic, her fever, with everything, everything, everything. . . . There is life in her." It is true that most of Russia's wealth is concentrated in Moscow. The head of the Russian Academy of Sciences institute I was affiliated with told me, "Moscow is a special city. She very much differs from all other cities in Russia. Very much another character, other moods, other prospects, other opportunities, another pace of life." The contrasts and complexities of Moscow made fieldwork challenging.

METHODS

In the early months of fieldwork in 2006, I felt pressure to interview people, even in everyday conversations. I thought I should ask questions and push people further. In some sense it made my interactions with people unnatural and unsatisfying. I had planned to do sixty in-depth, audio-recorded interviews that included questions on childhood, schooling and education, work, family, recent changes in Russia, and health. I knew that this meant I had to do about an interview per week. This doesn't seem like much, but it is a good-sized sample for in-depth interviews of an ethnographic study, especially interviews that include some life history. I had some friends and acquaintances I could ask for interviews, but I wanted time before asking permission to audio-record them. I contracted a research assistant, Sveta, who was a graduate student interested in politics and society at the Russian Academy of Sciences institute where I was affiliated. She and I made a few false starts together.

INTERVIEWS

In August, Sveta and I decided to glue announcements around my neighborhood, inviting citizens fifty-five to seventy years old living in Moscow for at least fifteen years to participate in a survey sponsored by the institute, with compensation. A couple of young men in their early twenties, who were talking in the courtyard, taunted us as we glued announcements on the boards next to the building doors. "Are you from the apartment management?" Sveta responded with a laugh. "Uncultured," she muttered under her breath. The very next day I checked on the announcements to find that many had been torn away. I was not surprised when no one called.

The following week we decided to approach middle-aged and older people in courtyards and parks. On one afternoon we talked to six women and one couple. Two grandmothers sitting in the courtyard said that they would answer questions. One was obviously much older than seventy and seemed to be in the early stages of dementia. Looking beyond us she mechanically asked, "Could I perhaps have some clothes, a new skirt, a warm sweater . . ." before her voice trailed off. A young man sitting idle in the courtyard, perhaps feeling protective, pointedly asked us what we intended to do with the grandmothers. After a few minutes it was clear that he was not going to leave. We said we would come back another day to talk. I left feeling as if I were preying on the elderly. One woman walking home with groceries in a business suit didn't hesitate to tell us no. Another woman, walking toward the Novodevichyi Convent, also said no, twice. A couple chasing their grandchild around the pond outside the convent walls explained they were just visiting Moscow. A woman feeding ducks said, "My life has already passed. I like to feed the ducks. I have nothing interesting to say and I don't need money. I get five and a half a month [5,500 rubles]." Sveta and I sat down on one of the benches by the lake for a while and talked. I was honest about my distaste for this type of recruitment.

As we got up to leave we passed an older woman, but not too old—I'll call her Valentina—reading a book on another bench. Sveta looked at me. I looked at Sveta. I didn't have the stomach for another rejection that day. But Valentina saw us hesitate. "Girls?" We introduced ourselves and Sveta asked if she would be interested in doing an interview. She was keen. In retrospect, we should have done it immediately. But I felt drained and something in me did not want to pull out a notebook and turn on an audio recorder. Instead, as storm clouds gathered in the sky, we chatted about her book on Mozart. "Russians are not Germans," she said. "We're craftier." She spoke of Soviet Russia. "We had no illusions. But the human aspect of that time. . . . Everything is sold now. Before we would have been ashamed." She was a music teacher at a college and invited us to attend one of the recitals. We wrote down her phone number and promised to call in order to set up a time to meet again. As the wind swept up, we walked toward the apartment blocks. She was not specific about which direction she was heading. I made a point to tell her where I lived and then said goodbye.

For a few days, Sveta tried to get in contact with her by telephone and was only able to speak to her husband. Valentina wasn't home; perhaps she would be home later that day. When Sveta and I met for coffee we tried once more. By some stroke of luck Valentina answered the phone and Sveta set up a meeting time on the same bench by the pond. This was the only interview Sveta and I did together. We were relieved that it went well, but after Sveta had transcribed our hour-and-a-half conversation, she was frustrated. "She says a lot, but I don't always know what she thinks. She doesn't say much that is definite." Valentina spoke too carefully. There are times in the interview when she clearly comes close to saying something and then backs away from it, her voice trailing off. This may be due to the fact we were audio recording; it may simply be the way Valentina expresses herself. Or, most likely, it is due to the fact that Valentina did not know Sveta and me from anywhere—we did not have an introduction. Oddly enough, in a city so large, I saw Valentina twice more that year by chance. In another city park we exchanged a few words. On the metro we acknowledged each other. She looked slightly uncomfortable and I was concerned she thought I was following her.

Sveta and I never again recruited on the streets. Instead, we primarily relied on friends and family for introductions to people who expressed an interest in talking about their lives. Sometimes these people were also strangers. Darsha, a friend and scholar at the institute who also happens to have a knack for getting people to agree to things, arranged interviews with her mother, her mother's friend, a neighbor, a taxi driver, and a pensioner she met on the electric train. While interviews with recommended friends were usually less stressful, the interviews with the taxi driver and pensioner may have been freer. The taxi driver could speak about infidelities and the failure of his marriage and the pensioner could tell me about his father-in-law's role in Stalin-era repression without fear that it would find its way back to anyone in their social circles. I promised confidentiality, but social recruitment of this type necessarily compromises that promise, as it is difficult to provide rich ethnographic detail about people's lives and disguise their identities at the same time. Except for Valentina and perhaps the pensioner mentioned above, everyone I interviewed was connected to someone else I knew. Many of these people will appear in the following pages. To the extent possible, I have tried to disguise people's identity without losing depth or authenticity of detail.

INTERVIEWERS

This type of social recruitment was slower, so we decided that Sveta would also conduct interviews. In January I also hired Ira, the daughter of a middle-aged friend, to help with transcription. She also ended up doing some interviews on her own. Sveta and Ira used the interview guide I had developed. Below is a list of selected questions from the guide. I encouraged Sveta and Ira to approach each interview as a conversation, allowing it to flow naturally. They were familiar with my flexible style of questioning from their transcription work. Not every question was asked in every interview and often we asked new questions. Each of us had a unique interview style. I would not have asked some of the questions the way Sveta and Ira did, and I am sure they cringed at the all-too-frequent moments in my interviews when it is clear that I have not understood something or am having trouble phrasing a question. In Sveta's and Ira's interviews the Russian language is not an issue. Interviewees use idioms and cultural references freely. The exchanges reveal common assumptions that Russians, even of different generations, have about life. I was more apt to interrogate these: "What do you mean by 'simple people'?" Sveta's interest and knowledge in the area of politics is evident, although it is not always shared by her interviewees. My own questions about health fall painfully flat most of the time. I gave up asking them after a while. Ira, by contrast, is not a trained social scientist and her questions are more tentative and halting but also less encumbered. Her interviewees tell stories without worrying about how to describe their lives to a social scientist. She interviewed a close relative, a friend of her mother, and two neighbors.

Sociodemographics
How old are you?
Where do you live now?

Childhood
Can you tell me a little about your family?
What are your earliest childhood memories?

Schooling
Can you tell me some of your memories about going to school?
How did you spend your free time?
What hopes did you have for your life? Did you think of certain things in life that you wanted for yourself? What were those things?

Family formation
How did you meet your spouse?
How many children do you have?

Work
What work do/did you do?
Have you ever been without work?
Do/did you enjoy your work?

Social change
How do you describe what happened in Russia during the early 1990s?
For whom were the changes easier/harder?
Did men and women experience the transition differently?
What are some positive and negative points of the Russian transition?
In your opinion, what is freedom?
How do you feel about the future for your children and grandchildren?
What do you think will happen to Russia in the future?

Present

When you think back on your life, what do you think is most important?

If you were to give advice to young people about life, what would you
tell them?

PLACE

Interviews ranged in length from a half hour to two-and-a-half hours. Most
interviews were conducted in the homes of interviewees and almost always
over tea or even a meal. In one case, I was sent home with a jar of homemade
applesauce and a sweater to keep me warm. Academics were interviewed in
shared offices, often over tea. A male member of a Russian sobriety society
met me at the spa where he gives massages. After the interview he offered to
give me a shoulder massage. I held three interviews in parks or courtyards. One
of these was with Darsha's taxi driver. We met at a northern metro station. I
had told him I would wear my long hair up and that I was pregnant. "But will
I be able to tell?" He met me with a branch of fragrant lilac and we headed to
the nearest courtyard to find a bench. It was a beautiful spring day in mid-May,
though, and they were all occupied. I indicated another courtyard around the
corner of a five-story apartment building. He was the only interviewee who
hesitated about the audio recorder, indicating that he would tell me more if
I did not use it. We compromised by starting with the recorder on, agreeing
that he could fill in other details when I turned the recorder off. As we chatted,
an older woman approached us. In very general terms he introduced me and
then she began updating him on news of friends and neighbors. I turned off
the recorder. Her son drove up along the courtyard in an older Lada and made
small talk about the materials he was transporting for his apartment renovation.
It turned out that I had led him back to the courtyard outside his own apartment
building. As soon as the older woman went back inside with her son he admitted as much. We laughed and moved to yet another courtyard where we talked
with the recorder on for about an hour. At that point I turned it off. We continued for perhaps another half hour or so and then talked about summer plans—
the *dacha,* his lady friend, fishing.

The one interview I conducted in my apartment was hijacked. Over tea
and pastries Maria told me how she became involved in the sobriety movement, diagrammed her theories on God, Jews, aural colors, cosmic energy,
and the coming "golden age" when Russia will be the savior of a lost world.

Eventually I was the one being interviewed. And yet her thoughts during the interview and at the alcohol policy seminar where I met her touch on a number of central themes of this work.

INTERVIEWEES

Our interviewees belong to different social circles, which I should briefly identify. Sveta and I both interviewed academics (eight total), primarily affiliated with two Moscow academies. Sveta interviewed engineers and workers of factories located in Klimovsk, a formerly closed city of Moscow Oblast' (the densely populated federal jurisdiction surrounding Moscow city), which is also Sveta's hometown. Ira and I interviewed three individuals who lived just outside of Zelenograd, another formerly closed city, administratively part of Moscow city although it lies within Moscow Oblast.' Zelenograd was an electronics city in the Soviet era and is now sometimes touted as Russia's Silicon Valley. It is home to a number of national and multinational electronic and computer companies. I interviewed three members of a Russian sobriety society, whom I met at a seminar on alcohol policy, which is further discussed below. I also interviewed two men from a weekly English club that I attended.

In total we did thirty-eight audio-recorded interviews. Sveta and I each did seventeen; Ira completed four. We were not strict about the age limits, and thus our interviewees' ages ranged from fifty through eighty, although most of them were indeed between the ages of fifty-five and seventy. There were twenty-three women and fifteen men. They were also not strictly from Moscow city, but also from the surrounding area, Moscow Oblast.' Nor is our sample representative, in any sense, of the population of Moscow city and Moscow Oblast.'

I continually asked Sveta and Ira to prioritize individuals with lower levels of education, preferably men. At one point, Sveta told me that it was not possible to find such men around Moscow. It was clear that she meant it was not desirable. In a later email she wrote, "But, honestly, in general I have very few acquaintances without education, practically none. In Russia it is in general very rare. And besides this, people without education don't like to speak into a recorder—they don't understand why that is necessary. But I will try." When she did manage to conduct an interview with a less-educated woman she emailed this: "True, it is short, but with a perfectly uneducated person (joke!)."

UNSTRUCTURED INTERVIEWS

In addition to the semistructured interviews, I conducted what are referred to as unstructured interviews, or simply asking questions and having conversations. I took notes when I felt it would not disrupt the interaction. Otherwise I waited until I was free to write down as much of the interaction as memory permitted. These interactions included ongoing conversations with friends and acquaintances or something interesting I overheard, sometimes only peripherally related to my research questions. When individuals knew what I was doing in Russia and were forthcoming about their opinions on the subject, some of these conversations approximated the social change portion of the semistructured interviews. One summer afternoon when I was reading in a courtyard outside my apartment building, a neighbor initiated a conversation. His views were unabashedly nationalistic and anti-Semitic. I suspect these would have been muted in an audio-recorded interview. In early September 2006 Sveta invited me to her family's *dacha* where her parents were spending the weekend. "You can interview them," she laughed, a little ambiguously. Their grandson by Sveta's sister ran around excitedly and took my hand to show me a small fir tree and the last cucumbers and tomatoes in the garden. Sveta's parents and I spoke at some length about my research and their experiences but I didn't audio-record anything. It is possible I was too cautious in this regard. On the other hand, potential friendships were more valuable to me than even the most faithfully rendered textual data.

PARTICIPANT OBSERVATION

My colleague and friend at the Russian Academy of Sciences institute, Daria Andreevna Khaltourina, has written about alcohol's role in the mortality crisis (Khaltourina and Korotayev 2006, 2008). At her urging, I attended a seminar on post-Soviet mortality in Kiev, Ukraine, on October 12–14, 2006 ("International Seminar on Mortality in Countries of the Former USSR. Fifteen Years after Break-Up: Change or Continuity?").[5] In December 2006 she and I began to email funding agencies about supporting an international seminar on alcohol policy in Moscow. In part due to the prominence of this theme in the public health literature and its perceived public policy importance, funding was quickly secured from the Wellcome Trust and the Nordic Center for Alcohol and Drug Research. The seminar, entitled "Developing Effective Alcohol Policy for Russia: World Experience and Russian

Realities," was held March 1–2, 2007, at the Russian Academy for Civil Service of the President of the Russian Federation.[6] I assisted Darsha with writing letters and proposals for funding and accompanied her as she took care of logistics.

Seminar presenters included prominent scholars on the mortality crisis, alcohol use, and alcohol policy from the Russian Academy of Sciences, the London School of Hygiene and Tropical Medicine, and the Max Planck Institute for Demographic Research, among others. The press and a few members of Russian sobriety societies also attended. Panels addressed Russian alcohol consumption, alcohol mortality, and alcohol policy experiences in Russia and abroad. This seminar and the Kiev seminar were important sites of participant observation among social scientists who have written extensively on the mortality crisis.

I also took part in day-to-day activities of Muscovites of all ages who were my friends. We shopped, drank tea, prepared meals, rode the electric train, went to the *dacha,* barbequed, planted potatoes, visited monuments and museums, went cross-country skiing, and took trips together. Later in my fieldwork I asked some of my closer, older friends if they would do a formal interview with me. They were happy to help. And what I learned is this: even my most enlightening interviews were but the thinnest slivers of people's lives. Margarita did not talk about selling her childhood home; Tatiyana did not mention her son's death.

My deeper understanding about how older Russians have experienced the transformation of their world did not come from conducting interviews; it came from participating in people's lives. I heard Margarita's agitation while she told her friends about her first visit back to Novyi Arbat street in fifteen years. I slept over at Margarita's place where the neighbor across the stairwell has publicly accused Margarita of being a witch and scratched the peephole in Margarita's door beyond the point of usefulness. I saw Margarita burst into Tatiyana's apartment in a fit of nerves over the sale of the country home her father built before he was sent to the front in 1942 and never came back. And then Margarita and I took an early morning trip by bus, electric train, metro, another electric train, and by foot to this country home, which abuts a new development of villas, surrounded by a high cement block fence. I took pictures of her and the house that day and was embarrassed, later, when she cried with gratitude over the prints.

Shared experiences are the lifeblood of ethnography. And yet they are the ones that have been the most difficult for me to capture and write down.

Frankly, sharing these experiences feels like somewhat of a betrayal. I profit through others' trust. Besides this, these experiences are emotional. When I returned from the field I taught a medical anthropology course. One class session I lectured about my dissertation research in Russia. I projected a few pictures of Margarita's country home, including the one with Margarita's backlit silhouette in front of a semicircular window and inset door dressed with fine lace curtains. With that picture on the screen behind me, I had to stop briefly to collect myself. Anthropologists talk about shared experiences as participant observation, taking part in social life in an observant and reflexive manner. It is the cornerstone of ethnographic research. I appreciate this now more than I did even during my fieldwork. Yet I am not quite satisfied with labeling friendships as participant observation.

Moscow is undoubtedly one of the hardest places to do ethnography, at least the ethnography I envisioned. Moscow and her inhabitants fiercely resisted simplifications and generalizations. I began to sympathize with students of anthropologist Ruth Benedict, who thought that Russian emotional bipolarity was related to the practice of swaddling babies (Gorer and Rickman 1962). It did seem that life in Moscow was swayed by currents of mania and melancholy. Telling a coherent story necessitates simplification and generalization. There is no way around it. But I also hope to preserve some of the messiness inherent in Moscow life by allowing contrasts and contradictions to surface throughout the story. One way to do this is to explore paradox.

MORTALITY IN MOSCOW

Tatiyana and Margarita's dialogue on the transformation of Novyi Arbat is helpful to open a window on the experiences of this generation. However, the points of reference are right before the fall of the Soviet Union and fifteen years after the fall. The mortality crisis, as we have seen, peaks in the early 1990s. At that time Novyi Arbat had not yet been transformed. The quality of the space, however, had been compromised by the collapse of order—the order of the Soviet state and the order of social relations that hinged on the state. The frame around the space had ruptured and changed the quality of the space from "simple" and "easy," bounded, to unknown and dangerous. This time is commonly described as chaotic and *bezporiadok* (without order). If we think of Novyi Arbat, the physical space was still there in the early 1990s, but the framing was uncertain. This changed the quality of the space from a bounded one in which people experienced spontaneity and indeterminacy in contradistinction to the state. Instead the space became unbound and, consequently, more unpredictable. There was less a sense of autonomy and play and more a sense of dissolution and danger. People did their own thing. Unbound by the logic of Soviet society and not yet bound by another logic, people drifted away from each other. Urban areas, especially Moscow, were more affected by the crisis because that is where the presence of the state was most felt. In the metropolis people's sense of space and the social relations within space were defined most fully by the state.

Male life expectancy in Moscow decreased by 7.7 years from 1990 to 1994, compared to the national average of 6.1 years (Leon and Shkolnikov 1998; Notzon et al. 1998). Epidemiologists Leon and Shkolnikov consider these "surprising geographic differences":

> The abrupt economic and social changes that occurred tended to be most significant in those regions that, by virtue of their relative affluence and good communications, were most susceptible and open to change. For example, the abolition of price controls and removal of restrictions on private commercial activities in 1992 led to rapid changes in the nature of life in Moscow. In contrast, the economies of more isolated, remote, and less developed areas have changed at a slower pace. (1998, 790)

A more complicated story about the "changes in the nature of life in Moscow" describes how the Soviet city, Soviet work, and gender created space for efficacious social interaction.

It is clear that the state organized urban space in Moscow. As the state receded in the early 1990s, the space expanded outward and the rules and resources that constituted social interaction were in flux. Muscovites describe this as disorder (*bezporiadok*). Space, in order to be safe, needs order.

CHAPTER 2

Paradox

A few months into fieldwork some fellow Fulbright scholars told me the story of another anthropologist, who, on his last day in the city of St. Petersburg, "lost it" on a bus. They couldn't remember why. Perhaps he was pushed or berated for not having the correct change. In any case, he let out a loud string of expletives in English. When he met up with them afterward he was still shaken. They told me it was completely unlike him to react that way. I sympathized with the anthropologist, but the story was funny because of its implied irony. Anthropologists are supposed to fit in and understand local practices. In many ways, it seemed like a story about anthropological failure.

Months later, toward the end of my own fieldwork, I stood in a long line at Kievskyi Station to buy train tickets. When my turn came at the window, the woman sitting behind the glass told me that foreigners had to purchase tickets in a special office. This was true when I lived in Russia in 1994 (although even then I often managed to purchase tickets as a Russian), but the dual pricing system for train tickets—one price for Russians, another for foreigners—had long been defunct. I told her as much, but she was immovable. I raised my voice, asked for her name. I told her that she was wrong, did not know her job, and that times had long changed. I ranted about not having a Western salary. Her face remained stony. By that time there was not one person in the hall who did not know that I was a foreigner, that I wanted train tickets, and that the cashier wasn't going to sell them to me. I moved to where my husband James, in Russian fashion, was holding a spot in another line. He raised his eyebrows ever so slightly but didn't say a word. The young woman behind us caught my eye, smiled, and, shrugging her shoulders, said, "Russia—the land of miracles." "Exactly," I responded. I bought the tickets without any problem at the neighboring window.

"Land of miracles" refers to strangeness, otherworldliness, and unpredictability. What happens is beyond explanation. It means something along the lines of "only in Russia"—an ironic statement about confounding circumstances. As the "land of miracles," Russia is unique and other, even to its inhabitants. Anything can and will happen. When I tried to ask interviewees about their future or the future of Russia, the most common response was "Who knows?" This openness and indeterminacy, as we shall see, is an integral part of Russian character and society. It opens up a space of spontaneity and possibility that is sometimes hard to bear unless it is, in some measure, bound.

I began to think about these episodes—the anthropologist on the bus and the anthropologist in the train station—differently. They did not seem so much anthropological failings as Russian triumphs. Russia had done her work; she'd gotten under the skin. My reaction was more authentic than any anthropological coolness I might have mustered. I drew unnecessary attention to myself, but the Russians who witnessed the outburst were not perturbed. Such an occurrence is normal, even expected, in the land of miracles. It has long been a central part of Russian identity. As Boym writes, "Russian, and later Soviet, cultural identity depended on heroic opposition to everyday life" (1994, 3). I am a product of a middle-class American upbringing, a particular family, and my own temperament. In public I am often reserved and temperate. In losing it, I may have become more Russian—more direct, open, and emotional. Russia drew me out. The moment was liberating. These moments, however much they frustrate, make one feel alive. The individual revolts against authority and is rewarded with a feeling of autonomy. Significantly, this moment had another reward in the Russian context. A stranger and I experienced a fleeting bond related to a struggle against imposed authority. For a moment, we stood united in our recognition of an absurdity we had no control over.

The relationship between order and a sense of autonomy or freedom is central to the story I tell. In the West the Soviet state is commonly regarded as a totalitarian state, where power was centralized and absolute. Citizens of a totalitarian state are not free; their lives are controlled by political authority. Many post-Soviet scholars would agree that this is a far cry from what the Soviet state was able to achieve. Katherine Verdery is succinct: "contrary to the original 'totalitarian' image, socialist states were weak" (1991, 426). More recently Alexei Yurchak's notion of deterritorialized milieus is instructive. Deterritorialized milieus are "tightly knit networks of friends and strangers who shared some interest, occupation, or discourse" (2006, 131). These networks "drew on the system's possibilities" (132). Yurchak also writes of "being *vnye*"—living "simultaneously inside and outside the system" (128). Sitting around the kitchen table, among an intimate circle of friends and relatives, Soviet citizens inhabited space that was set apart from the state. That space, however, was not immune from the influence of the state. In fact, the state specified the form and quality of the space. What made the space exceptional was precisely its relationship to the state—just as a deterritorialized area is defined by its relationship to a territory. The Soviet state was central to the logic and significance of social relationships and the experience of freedom in Soviet times.

When the state collapsed, social order was compromised—the order of the state and the interpersonal order. The space where Russians sensed autonomy, indeed freedom, expanded infinitely outward, no longer held in check by the interpersonal order nor by the limits imposed by the state. Space became boundless, dangerous, unbearable, even deadly. "Everyone went their own way" more than one middle-aged Muscovite told me, as if society were spun by a centrifugal force outward.[1] Individuals, spun far apart, ended up alone and isolated. "Each his own way, someone to robbery [*razboi*], someone else to binge drinking [*zapoi*]." The Russian "craving for *freedom*, to lay all caution and pretense aside, no matter the risk" (Nielsen 2006, under "Interlude: Vitya") was set loose. In a greater tragedy, Russians' attempts to reestablish social connections with others, to regain a sense of order, sometimes placed them at risk of dying.

For a long time I did not understand this. Instead I saw a paradox I could not resolve—a nostalgia for order alongside a thirst for thwarting it.

SPACE AND ORDER

However much they complain about the vicissitudes of the System, Russians feed off of spontaneity and unpredictability, the unexpected. Social connections frequently render the official rules of the System inapplicable. "No" does not necessarily mean no. When I talked about this with my landlord over tea, he said that it might be easier to live somewhere where rules were clearer, but he also noted that when his mother lived in a small village in

French-speaking Switzerland she found it unbearably boring. Misha told me, "Those people would stop for a red light in the middle of the night." Having lived two years in French-speaking Switzerland, I had to agree that many of them probably would. Then again, so might I.

Toward the end of my fieldwork, Ira's husband drove Ira, Ira's mother, and me to a friend's house. On the highway, he commented, "In America the cars probably stay within the lanes." I replied, "And Russians would probably find that boring." They all laughed. Ira's mother said, "Well you've learned something about Russians." Rules are not always fixed; this grants individuals space to maneuver. It opens up the door to spontaneity and the unexpected.

In the summer of 2004, my friend Lena and I attended a Fourth of July celebration sponsored by the American Chamber of Commerce. When we arrived, the guards at the gate were not letting any more people into the Kuskovo estate where the festivities were being held. Lena tried to talk her way past to no avail. She then rolled up a bill into a tiny cylinder, gave it to one of the guards, and, grabbing my hand, marched us through the gate without waiting for any indication of permission, verbal or otherwise. The guards—there must have been at least five of them at the one gate—had machine guns slung over their shoulders. Once inside Lena laughed at my obvious discomfort. "What do you think they're going to do?" That evening we watched fireworks over the lake. Every few yards along the lake shore there were fierce-looking German shepherd police dogs with their handlers. Lena did not seem to notice. Later Lena and I were stuck in traffic as we tried to leave. It looked like it would be impossible to make a left turn. There was a young policeman standing nearby. Lena leaned out the window and sweetly asked, "Are you in charge here?" He said he was. Lena then asked, "How do we get out of here?" He promptly stopped traffic and we were able to turn left. I asked Lena why she went through this exchange, instead of simply asking him to help us turn left. She said, "You have to make them think they are very important and then they will do something for you." As much as Russians bemoan these situations, they are highly skilled at circumventing rules through social connections, whether long-standing relationships or fleeting instances when an agent of the System is rendered human. Misha, my landlord, spoke of the accomplishment of making a human connection with a policeman—by offering him a cigarette or telling a joke and making him smile. It does not always work, but when it does it is rewarding. Authority becomes human and malleable.

Anthropologist Finn Sivert Nielsen, who did ethnography in St. Petersburg in the early 1980s, once tried to get a drink with his friend Vitya. It proved difficult. They ended up in a hallway behind a door marked "No admittance for unauthorized persons" drinking to the health of an obliging, drunk waiter of an establishment where no wine was being served. Nielsen reports the words of Vitya. "Do you see why I'm happy to live here, and would never consider emigrating to the West?" (2006, under "Interlude: Vitya"). This sense of satisfaction depends on thwarting rules through social connections.

An appetite for the unpredictable and contingent coexists with a yearning for order. This was one of those contrasts I had so much trouble trying to reconcile during the first period of my fieldwork in Moscow, before I realized that reconciliation runs the risk of distorting the very culture I wanted to understand. In *Culture: A Problem that Cannot Be Solved,* Charles Nuckolls advocates an anthropological theory of paradox. "A paradox is an idea involving two opposing thoughts or propositions that, however contradictory, are equally necessary to convey a more imposing, illuminating, life-related, or provocative insight into truth than either factor can muster on its own right" (1998, 273). Paradox lends culture dynamic and generative possibilities. It is culture's vitality. To resolve paradox is to fatally distort culture.

Paradox has a special affinity for Russia, where Russians themselves consider their country a place of paradox, contradiction, and absurdity. In fact, an exclamation of "Russia!" might mean just that—difficult to understand, impossible to resolve. Pesmen recounts a Russian who spelled it out for some American visitors. He uttered "Russia!" and then clarified "by adding the usually implicit word 'paradox'" (2000, 289).

Muscovites thrived at beating the System, and yet many of them, at least among the middle aged, were nostalgic for the old System and the order it imposed. The nostalgia for Soviet order reflects a yearning for the social connections of the past, which were structured and granted potency by the Soviet order. In addition, it reflects a yearning for a particular sense of space or freedom crafted through these connections that is only possible when the official System is routinely circumvented and contested. In Soviet society people were granted a sense of collectivity if only because they were all subject to the state and its version of history. Their lives were to variable degrees organized by the state, especially through their work. This type of collectivity could be construed as Soviet or, alternatively, as anti-Soviet. In another sense, individuals were integrated through social connections that served to compensate for weaknesses in the System or to right perceived injustices in the System. This sense of collectivity was more intimate and idiosyncratic, even as it bore the mark of the state. Social identity and action depended on the existence of the state, even when they undermined the authority of the state. Social connections, notwithstanding whether they were more superficial, deep, fleeting, or long-standing, were compromised with the dismantling of the Soviet system, the core around which they were organized and put to use. Although the Soviet system imposed rules and limits, these were hardly static. By the time of Brezhnev, who was the head of the Soviet state from 1964 through 1982, the System was widely considered unsystematic and incomprehensible. Soviet order created space for spontaneous social action and, in fact, enabled that action. Over time, these possibilities for autonomous social action grew as the authority of the Soviet state waned.

When middle-aged Muscovites mourn the loss of the Soviet system, they are principally mourning their ability to think and act in a coordinated way with other individuals around them in a way that is creative and not fully determined by the political economy. In many ways Soviet society permitted the thoughts and actions that sustained it, but also those that eventually loosened it.

STRUCTURE AND AGENCY

Central to this work is another, theoretical paradox that represents one of the abiding concerns of social theorists, particularly anthropologists. Anthropologists often speak and write of structure and agency. Indeed, the central preoccupation of anthropologists is showing that who we are and what we do is bound up with the structures of our society. There is a troubling paradox in this, and perhaps most troubling in the West, where we have an idea of the autonomous self, free to act, and a more muted idea of structure that determines self and action. How can the self and the self's actions be autonomous and yet determined by structure? The short answer to that question is that structure opens up possibilities for agency, even as it closes others off.

Post-Soviet ethnographers also grapple with the relationship between agency and structure. Burawoy and Verdery (1999) draw on the theory of Jürgen Habermas (1989) to suggest that the collapse of state and economy granted more importance to everyday practices.

> Our view of the relation between macro structures and everyday practices
> is that the collapse of party states and administered economies broke down
> macro structures, thereby creating space for micro worlds to produce
> autonomous effects that may have unexpected influence over the structures
> that have been emerging. In the language of Jürgen Habermas . . . the
> disintegration of the system world has given freer rein for lifeworlds to stamp
> themselves on the emerging economic and political order. (Burawoy and
> Verdery 1999, 2)

Burawoy and Verdery posit that the disintegration of the system allows the lifeworld—"a reservoir of taken-for-granteds, of unshaken convictions that participants in communication draw upon in cooperative processes of inter-pretation" (Habermas 1989, 124)—to flourish. This elides the crisis of the 1990s, which was a crisis not only of the system but more importantly of the norms and values of the lifeworld. "Taken-for-granteds" and "unshaken convictions" were in short supply. Habermas's theory posits that the central problem of modernity is the colonization of the lifeworld by the system. The system gives shape to the lifeworld and makes communicative action pos-sible. The system's demise in Russia, at least initially, also harmed the life-world. Structure begets agency.

That said, societies continually create structure, and moments of chaos transform into moments of greater stability. Agency opens up again in new ways. Russia is an especially stark example of this process. Of course, indi-viduals have different access to the rules and resources of structure, and thus agency is channeled differently. So while many in post-Soviet Russia are wielding new rules and resources, some are not, and channels of agency are restricted. Kideckel argues that, among industrial workers in postsocialist Romania, "worker collective agency and resistance has largely evaporated" (2008, 12). Structure limits agency.

Dunn's ethnography of workers in a baby-food factory in Poland sug-gests that socialism and capitalism hold different forms of power or differ-ent "emancipatory potential" (2004, 173) for workers. Capitalism atomizes workers who find themselves "individually as well as collectively disem-powered" (173). But capitalism, like socialism, offers power through its own logic. In capitalism power is channeled in practices of consumerism; under socialism power was channeled in practices of redistribution. There is a further difference. Under socialism power or agency was often informal or oppositional. Under capitalism it is more fully subsumed by structure. "The construction of the self-managing, choosing individual . . . is an integral means of regulating social actors so that the capitalist-democratic political economy runs smoothly" (166). Dunn's argument suggests that the relationship between agency and structure itself may be reconfigured by particular forms of modernity. Agency reflects structure.

Most middle-aged Muscovites did not celebrate the early 1990s as a moment of independence from the incursions of state and economy into their social worlds. Rather, they experienced these years as chaotic and disordered. Agency was momentarily hindered by the collapse of state and economy because agency had co-opted the mechanisms of state and economy for its own ends.

GIDDENS ON STRUCTURE

Giddens's (1984) theory of structuration is an attempt to resolve the paradox in a way that treats structure and agency as mutually constitutive in social practice. Giddens describes the structure-agency paradox as a tension between the "active, reflexive character of human conduct" and "human behaviour as the result of forces that actors neither control nor comprehend" (xvi). "The basic domain of study of the social sciences," according to Giddens, "is neither the experience of the individual actor, nor the existence of any form of societal totality, but social practices ordered across space and time" (2). An agent only comes into being through social practices, and these social practices, repeatedly expressed, express structure. Taking Giddens seriously means a focus on Russian culture must fall above the level of the individual and below the level of the state. Structure and agency are both found in this interstitial space that is constituted through social practices.

In Giddens's theory, structure refers to the rules informing social practices and the resources drawn on in social practices. Giddens takes particular pains to clarify that rules are primarily held in individuals' "practical consciousness" by which he means that most rules are unspoken and unwritten, and are not consciously known by individuals. Structure is manifest in individuals' knowledge of what to do next or how to "go on" (1984, 23). Structure is submerged under the visible in society, orchestrating the social practices through which it is made manifest. In the Russian case, structure is not the state but the rules and resources of social practices, some of which derived from the organization of the state.

In Giddens's theory, structure has no concrete existence apart from social practices, although structure is not social practices per se. Structure refers to the rules and resources drawn on in social practices. Giddens writes, "Structure is not to be equated with constraint but is always both constraining and enabling" (1986, 25). As structure closes off certain possibilities of action, it opens others. To clarify this he turns to language:

> This is easily demonstrated in the instance of learning a first language. No one "chooses" his or her native language, although learning to speak it involves definite elements of compliance. Since any language constrains thought (and action) in the sense that it presumes a range of framed, rule-governed properties, the process of language learning sets certain limits to cognition and activity. But by the very same token the learning of a language greatly expands the cognitive and practical capacities of the individual. (1984, 170)

Giddens writes that structure is not the same as constraint and is "always both constraining and enabling" (1986, 25), but I contend that structure both enables and disables through constraint. This is readily apparent using the example of language. It is only through rules and limits that individuals are able to express themselves in language. Language is not static, though, and individuals' use of language may bear against these same constraints, applying pressure. It is true that structure constrains and enables, but it does both through constraint. Constraint is central to the concept of structure.

Another analogy may further help to explain what I mean by constraint. Streams and rivers carve out their paths in a landscape. Once established, these channels are exploited and become more permanent aspects of the landscape. Yet, in time, erosion may result in new waterways. Waterways are constraining, but that is how they produce current and erosion. The constraint of the waterway leads to force and change. Without constraint the force of water is dissipated across the landscape and rendered less powerful to change the landscape. In society, structure enables action and change precisely because it constrains. In constraint lies possibility.

I use the notion of constraint to flesh out one of the central points of this work—constraint is integral to the Russian sense of freedom.

AGENCY

In Giddens's theory the agent retains some separation from social practices. Agents only exist through social practices, but they are able to "reflexively monitor" social action. Although most of the agent's "knowledge" is located in practical consciousness, the actor wields the rules and resources of structure and thus must be, in some mindful sense, separate from structure. An agent separate from structure, though, must be primarily involved in repetitive day-to-day routine that contributes to the continuity of both the agent and social life. "Routine is integral both to the continuity of the personality of the agent, as he or she moves along the paths of daily activities, and to the institutions of society, which are such only through their continued reproduction" (1984, 60). Giddens's agent is theoretically able to "act otherwise" (1984, 14), but must, for the most part, act predictably in order to perpetuate a consonant self and society. Agency is mainly channeled in the service of reproducing selves and institutions.

Pierre Bourdieu has had more influence than Giddens in anthropology, and his practice theory also reserves an agent separate from structure and therefore bound to act in ways that reproduce structure. Bourdieu's (2004) agent internalizes structure, and this internalized structure, or habitus, is a system of dispositions that are both structured and structuring. That is, dispositions are the embodiment of external structures and also the reproduction of external structure. If Giddens's agent is located in the mind, Bourdieu's agent is located in the body, as habitus. Bourdieu's agent is in danger of being entirely swallowed up by habitus and able to act only through the generative properties of the habitus itself—structure writ small. This agent is not able to "act otherwise" because such action always lies outside the realm of the possible or thinkable. Action can never transgress habitus. Bourdieu, however, contends that action is not purely rote because habitus is itself generative.

> As an acquired system of generative schemes objectively adjusted to the particular conditions in which it is constituted, the habitus engenders all the thoughts, all the perceptions, and all the actions consistent with those conditions, and no others. This paradoxical product is difficult to conceive, even inconceivable, only so long as one remains locked in the dilemma of determinism and freedom. . . . Because the habitus is an endless capacity to engender products—thoughts, perceptions, expressions, actions—whose limits are set by the historically and socially situated conditions of its production, the conditioned and conditional freedom it secures is as remote from a creation of unpredictable novelty as it is from a simple mechanical reproduction of the initial conditionings. (1977, 95)

But Bourdieu concedes that the habitus leads to practices that tend "to reproduce the objective structures of which they are the product" (2004, 72). Despite "an endless capacity to engender products," habitus results in a social theory taken up with routine and habit, as in Giddens.

There are limitations in these two theoretical accounts of agency. One is that the agent remains separate from social structure to a certain degree, ensconced in either the mind (as in Giddens) or body (as in Bourdieu). The other is that there is less importance granted to spontaneity and indeterminacy than to repetition and reproduction. In some sense these theories are too intent at showing how structures determine the possibilities of individuals' action and thought.

Perhaps most relevant to anthropology is the way that neither of these social theories entertains the possibility that the contours of agency may be a product of culture and political economy. If both structure and agency are located in the interstitial space of society, and if societies are distinct, then the relationship between structure and agency must be, to some extent, variable.

The Russian paradox of space and order grants more room for spontaneity, indeterminacy, and contradiction. Space grants agency, but agency needs order to play off. Without order, space is too wide open and agency is diffused. The space-order paradox also suggests that the friction between space and order imparts a particular sense of freedom from order. Thus constraint and boundedness is integral to the Russian sense of freedom. Without constraint, freedom is frightening, pointless, and potentially mortal.

SOUL

Agency is located not in the individual, but between individuals. This necessitates freeing the individual from the mind and body to bleed out into the space between individuals in society. This will become clearer through reflection on the social character of the Russian soul, *dusha,* elaborated in a later chapter. For now, it is enough to visualize the individual as a space around the body where the soul resides and interacts with other souls. If an individual is located in society, then an individual can come to emotional and physical harm through the weakening of social practices because these *are* the individual. When social structure is in crisis, so are individuals.

Individuals must share rules and resources in order to communicate and collaborate. But individuals are positioned differently in relation to those rules and resources. This indeterminacy in social practice grants a feeling of unpredictability and spontaneity that is an essential part of life. Perhaps counterintuitively, the spontaneity and indeterminacy of social life grant a sense of control because unpredictability is evidence that the reign of routine and habit may be interrupted. In these reprieves, individuals have a sense of freedom from determination. There is more to this story, but it is better told through an ethnography of Russian space, order, and freedom.

Clearly, structure makes agency possible. Individual agency is a misnomer. Agency is always social. Thoughts, actions, and words require constraint in order to make them meaningful and potent. Thoughts take form only within a mental framework. Actions must act upon something. Words only make sense as part of language. Individuals are differently constituted and positioned in a matrix of social practices. Together, individuals hold and use social structures, often conflicting ones, to create new avenues for thought, speech, and action. Agency challenges the very structures that make it possible by pushing up against them, exerting pressure, and causing change.

Nonetheless, the availability of more-or-less stable social forms enables us to conceive of others, imagine their motivations, and know them. Because we have a framework through which to see and interpret the complex social world around us, we can think and we can act. In essence, we can be social beings.

CHAPTER 3

War

That felling, I lived through that felling—our patriotic war. That was a nightmarish time. I need to tell you that the sun was always crimson, the whole time, [...] as if it were washed in blood.

—interviewee

For this generation, war was the dark beginning against which their radiant future shone. The early 1990s reminded middle-aged Muscovites of the war. History was no longer progressive; their sacrifices were in vain. They remembered those sacrifices and also a lost sense of collectivity that made sacrifices worthwhile. The seeds of neededness, order, space, and the mortality crisis of the early 1990s are all found in the war.

WAR AS BACKDROP

On June 22, 1941, the Germans mounted the largest ever wartime land invasion, Operation Barbarossa. The aim of this three-pronged attack was to take over the portion of Russia lying west of the Ural Mountains, including most of Russian industry and the cities of Moscow and St. Petersburg. The front was eighteen hundred miles long; it comprised more than four million soldiers. They marched through the Baltics to Leningrad, through Belarus toward Moscow, taking Smolensk, and through the Ukraine to the Volga, taking Kiev. The Red Army was unprepared; in a little more than five months it lost seven million soldiers. In total, twenty-seven million Soviets perished in the war from 1941 to 1945; nineteen million of those were civilians. Almost 15 percent of the entire Soviet population died during a four-year period. Absolutely and relatively, the war cost Russia more in lives than any other country. In comparison, Germany counted seven to nine million war dead, representing 8 to 10 percent of the population.[1] Compared to the early 1990s, when excess deaths represented perhaps 1 percent of the population in a four-year period, the war was a demographic disaster of another order.

Eventually the Red Army was able to repel the Germans, and Russia played an important part in ending World War II. The significance of the war in Russian history, in present-day culture, and in Russian collective memory is crucial to any understanding of the country. Although Tumarkin (1994) has written about the fall of "the cult of World War II," under President Vladimir Putin the cult enjoyed a rebirth. Victory Day, May 9, is a national holiday complete with military parade on Red Square, fireworks throughout the city, and old war movies on television.[2] The holiday is perhaps second only to New Year's Day in its cultural importance to Muscovites (Forest and Johnson 2002), although this will undeniably change with more time. Most of the men and women who served are now over eighty-five years old, but the generations after them have not forgotten the cost their parents and grandparents paid, often with their own lives.

The generation we interviewed was too young to have served in World War II, or the Great Patriotic War as it is called in Russia, but the war and its aftermath are this generation's earliest memories. The oldest men and women interviewed remembered their fathers' departures to the front and their returns, if they did return. Sometimes they remembered their mother's departures to the front. Many remembered their mothers' hard work, at home or digging trenches. The war served as the backdrop to their lives. It was their starting point—the ashes from which they arose. Their earliest memories are punctuated by war; their biographies begin with war: "And my father was missing in action in the Great Patriotic War. They called him up on the twenty-second of June, when I was still in my mother's womb. The only thing he said—if a boy is born call him Tolik, which she [my mother] did. That is all, and I was born the second of October, 1941." A woman went to collect her seventh-grade diploma around June 25, 1941: "We were all young, and we, we didn't know what a war was. You think, we're graduating—a noise, a yell, and they took them to the front. They killed, by the way, our teacher, God bless him." One explained, "We had just begun school and the war started," while another said, "I finished one school year before the war." One of the women we interviewed was born in June 1942 in the town where her family had been evacuated. Another began his life a few months after Germany surrendered. "I was born the fifteenth of July 1945 at nine in the morning. . . . The war had ended. The year 1945 the war ended."

After the war things did not immediately improve. A drought led to the famine of 1946–1947. Interviewees reported eating weeds, acorns, and the bran of grain. One man, who would have been five at the time, remembered the day his mother brought home a bag of dried fish. "Eat as much as you want," she told him. One woman remembered waiting all night with her grandmother for bread with their ration coupon. She spoke of the crush of desperate bodies and stolen coupons. In December 1947 the ruble was devalued and inflation took off. Poverty was widespread; finding work was difficult.

In part because of the destruction of the war, there was a shortage of adequate housing. Living space per resident declined throughout the 1940s. Most urban housing was in the form of communal apartments, where families lived together and shared the kitchen and bathroom. In Moscow in 1947 a significant proportion of the population lived without running water, plumbing, or central heating. Outside of Moscow the situation was more dire (Filtzer 2006; Manley 2006). In the countryside, many people had lost their homes in the war. They dug out shelter in the ground or in a hillside and lived in these "dugouts."

The war interrupted education. The eldest of this generation started school and then stopped for the duration of the war. Others started late. Schools were overcrowded and undersupplied. One man restarted school in the second grade in October 1945 at thirteen years old, although "there was nothing to write with—no blackboard, nothing." He said, "We would gather and tell each other stories. There was nothing else to do." Another wrote in the margins and spaces of newspapers with a sunflower stalk. "There wasn't anything—whatever the teacher said, that is what we memorized." An entire class shared one primer; students sat four to a desk. Elementary education was four class years. "Incomplete secondary education" was seven years, and that only became compulsory in the late 1950s.[3] After seven years, students might continue their studies at a vocational technical school or *tekhnikum,* a trajectory encouraged after Stalin under Khrushchev (1953–1964). Higher education was available to those with "complete secondary education," or ten class years. However, many of this generation went to work in factories after only four or seven years of schooling. They sacrificed their education first to fight fascism and then to build socialism.

The stories of Lyudmila and Viktor illustrate well how these early memories influenced the experiences of this generation during the early 1990s.

Lyudmila

Lyudmila's father died before the war in 1938, when she was two years old. They lived in Kaluga Oblast,' to the southwest of Moscow. "We were six children and mama raised us alone. She worked in the technical school and as a person of the steppe." By this Lyudmila meant that in addition to working for a wage, her mother worked the land, growing food and raising animals. They were forced to evacuate fifty kilometers southeast as the Germans advanced in the fall of 1941, losing their cow in the process. Lyudmila would have been five years old then, and she remembered waiting in a ditch for older evacuees to bring back food as German shells exploded, raining debris on them. Separated from their mother, Lyudmila and her siblings temporarily resettled in a village that was shelled: "Oh, there we stayed in some sort of house going to pieces. Oh, glass flew and everything there. Somewhere a shell would explode [. . .]. The glass flew and everything on the face of the earth. . . ."

As the Germans retreated, they burnt villages. There were no houses standing when Lyudmila and her family returned to their home village. They dug out the *samovar* (a "self-boiler," or a giant tea kettle of sorts with a spigot) that Lyudmila's mother had buried and built a clay-walled dugout to live in. They were poor and hungry. After school, Lyudmila worked on the collective farm where she turned hay and transported it by horse and cart. She hauled water and firewood for her mother. Lyudmila and her sister went to festivals in other villages to beg and gather the frozen potatoes that had been left in the fields during the winter. Her mother made potato cakes from them. They collected horse sorrel, an edible weed related to buckwheat. "We walked through the field collecting sorrel. We collected sorrel, we picked it. Oh! We ate grass." They used sorrel to make cakes but Lyudmila remembered, "They are dry, you can't swallow them." There were no winter coats and no shoes. "We were destitute, destitute. Lord, we walked around in winter, walked, skinny, and we had no shoes to walk in! And we wore foot wrappings and those foot wrappings came out through holes when we walked."

After Lyudmila finished seventh grade at eighteen years of age she moved near her sister in Moscow Oblast' where she worked in construction, living in a workers' dormitory. She dug trenches, hauled mortar, and unloaded sand and stone chippings by the truckful at night. In winter they had to break up frozen sand first in order to unload it. After a year she transferred to a mechanics factory in a nearby city. She was married and had a daughter, who was raised by Lyudmila's mother until she was seven years old. Then Lyudmila struggled to work two shifts and care for her daughter while her "hooligan" husband drank. She thought her personal life had not gone well, but she spoke fondly of her work: "I was among the best workers, I was on the [. . .] factory honor role. [. . .] With work, with work I did very well." She remembered the time her pension was to be 132 rubles. Under the Soviet system, she would have retired at fifty-five years of age in 1991.

> We figured out everything about the pension. It was enough for us. And when we would go on the pension. We will work, [then] we'll retire. It was enough for us. All of us saved for our funeral. And it was adequate, enough. A 132-ruble pension and here [then] sausage was two rubles [per kilogram] and meat two rubles. But then suddenly it was all over. And it turned out there was no manner of pension.

In 2007, at seventy years of age, Lyudmila was still working in the factory. In the early 1990s her retirement pension and savings, which represented approximately three years' pension at the time, both evaporated. She was still waiting for her savings to be reimbursed. "I had five thousand in savings. So far nobody has returned it to me." Lyudmila's daughter, who was present during the interview, asked her mother, "What will they return to you? Are you still. . . ." Lyudmila interrupted,

> No, now they are paying in full. I was talking with [a friend]. She said her aunt signed up for three thousand in old money. Then when they paid it out, then it came to sixteen. Instead of three it came to sixteen. At first they gave by one thousand. Then they decided to return all of it. But how they returned it all, with a percentage [interest] or how, I don't know. So I have five

thousand somewhere, and I don't know how much they will return to me. Will they return five thousand or even more?

She will likely never receive her five thousand rubles, which in 2007 was only worth about two months' pension. When Sveta asked her what the most important thing in her life was, Lyudmila said, "Oh, to rest [. . .] To rest a little." Sveta asked her where, but Lyudmila wasn't referring to a vacation. "Well, to stop working. Yes, if only to stop working. If only. But by the look of it, it won't happen for me. Probably while my legs still go, as long as I don't crumple, then probably, that's it." Rest was the expected reward for her years of labor, but for Lyudmila there is no rest.

When Sveta asked Lyudmila about the early 1990s, Lyudmila spoke again of the poverty of her youth. Sveta tried to clarify, "But that was before, right? Not after perestroika." Lyudmila said, "Well, but afterwards too. How we didn't have anything. People were also frayed [in reference to clothing]." She continued by telling a story about needing a winter coat in the late 1940s. To Lyudmila, economic shock therapy looked a lot like war-ravaged Russia. In a terrible sense it was as if the poverty of her youth and the poverty of the early 1990s had merged together. Thirty-five years of her life, from age nineteen when she started work in the mechanics factory to age fifty-five when the Soviet Union fell, fell out of view. Her marriage had not gone well, but she had been proud of her work in the factory. Yet she would end life where she began it—in poverty and need. Many in this generation were forced to reevaluate their past during the early 1990s. Their lives circled around to the poverty of their youth, which they believed they had overcome.

Viktor

Both of Viktor's parents went to the front in 1941 when he was still an infant. His mother left immediately on June 22 as she was with the People's Commissariat for Internal Affairs (the NKVD, precursor to the Committee for State Security, or KGB) and ran eleven reconnaissance missions in the enemy's rear. His father left in August. He and his grandmother returned to her village in southeastern Ukraine. He vaguely remembers his grandmother pulling him, along with a rooster, in a wagon across a small bridge. This was about the time the Germans were advancing on Kharkov in northeast Ukraine, the largest Soviet city the Germans took during the war. A German shell hit the bridge and the wagon overturned. He and the rooster ended up in the water below, and his grandmother jumped in after them. Later she would tease him about jumping in to save the rooster. At six years old, Viktor began work on the collective farm as a cowherd grazing calves. Those were the years of famine; the collective farm was how Viktor and his grandmother survived. "I remember my first workdays. They didn't give us wheat. A little corn, seeds, four oil cakes or mill cakes, as we called them then, two cans of milk. I was a shepherd, a little shepherd. [. . .] Those were my workday payments." At six years of age these workday payments made an impression on Viktor and he was thankful for the collective farm.

His mother returned from the war, demobilized in 1948, but his father, who survived, did not return to the family. He remembers childhood fights where he threatened other children, "I'll tell my papa," and the other children replied, "You don't have a papa." When his mother remarried, he went out into the street and told his playmates, "Well, now I have a real papa." In 1952 the family moved to Sevastopol where eleven people lived in a three-room communal apartment. Viktor finished seventh grade and began work in a factory. He continued his schooling at night and became a secondary school history teacher.

This is how Viktor described his generation:

> In history our generation is called the generation of the victors, because
> our fathers were victorious and we are the generation of victors, that is the
> generation [born] at the end of the thirties, forties, and even fifties—a few
> before the war, during the war and after the war. Our parents came back then,
> those whose parents did come back. I remember in our class there were forty
> students in the first grade, and in response to the question of our teacher,
> "Whoever has fathers, raise your hand," only six or seven students raised
> their hands, no more. Even though there were children of different ages in
> the class, from seven through thirteen years of age. [. . .] I remember, when
> we went to first grade, my [step]father took me by the hand and led me to
> school. That was one of my memorable days. I stood with pride and looked
> at everyone and thought, "You don't have fathers, but I have one." Of course,
> that was all childish. But I was proud to have a father, because there were
> not many fathers, there were not. And that was the tragedy of my generation.
> And such a tragedy that revealed itself afterwards. Unfortunately, many men
> of my generation drank themselves to death. [. . .] That was the echo of
> war, so to speak, the echo of growing up without fathers, growing up without
> mothers.

Viktor summarized the early 1990s thus:

> I became unnecessary [*ne vostrebuemym*] to the state. History is not needed.
> [. . .] We ourselves walked through that history. We didn't need to go
> through the war. We didn't need to go through collective farms. We didn't
> need to go through it—how we labored in the factories. Almost all of my
> generation after seventh grade left for the factories, and some even earlier
> after fourth grade. We went through that, and in 1954, 1956 we went to
> Virgin Lands,[4] to all those projects. We are history. We apprehended this
> history not only in school, but we believed it. Yes, we really believed in that
> radiant future. We believed, we believed.

Viktor thought even history was no longer needed—the war, collectivization, factory work, and labor projects. Like Lyudmila, Viktor thought his life
efforts were in vain. Moreover, the sacrifices of an entire generation were
unnecessary.

In 2007, Viktor and his wife Vera consoled themselves that their students
still came to see them, to ask advice, and to borrow books. "It means a lot,"
Vera said. Multiple times during the interview with Sveta, a former student,
Vera said that she and Viktor were thankful their students remembered them.
"Thank you students, for not forgetting." It was not simply about remember-
ing, though. It was also about the fact that the students came for advice and
borrowed books. "Books are our riches," Vera said. They might not be able
to offer much, but tea and books were within their means. Vera told Sveta,
"We are still sought-after [*vostrebovany*] by our students." Both Viktor and
Vera used forms of the word *vostrebovannyi,* which has the sense of being in
demand, sought after, necessary, or useful. Those that are not *vostrebovany*
are dispensable, expendable, and unneeded.

BEING UNNEEDED

There was another expression with a similar meaning that was much more
common: needed by nobody (*nikomu ne nuzhny*). It is clumsy to translate,
but it is central to the story of the demographic crisis in the early 1990s.
The phrase has been included in other ethnographies of Russia. Rethmann
notes how the Koriaks of northern Kamchatka Peninsula use it daily to
mean "nobody needs us, we are worthless" (Rethmann 1999, 205). She
writes, "Koriaks' convictions that they do not matter lead to self-neglect and

outbursts of pain, soothed only by radical bouts of drinking" (205). *Needed by Nobody* is the title of Höjdestrand's ethnography of the homeless in St. Petersburg.

> Once I began my fieldwork in St. Petersburg in 1999, I heard the phrase "needed by nobody," *nikomu ne nuzhen* . . . more or less every day. "Needed by nobody" is a set expression that conveys the worthlessness or rejection of something or someone. It can be used disparagingly to belittle others or . . . to convey subjective feelings of loneliness and vulnerability. As the logic goes, those who are not needed are, in Douglas's terms, matter out of place, dirt embodied, for real human beings are by definition immersed in social webs of mutual responsibility and protection. (Höjdestrand 2009, 2)

Here being unneeded expresses social exclusion. In her conclusion, Höjdestrand acknowledges "most Russians in the 1990s were in a manner of speaking, homeless" (195).

For my informants, many of whom still had some close social relationships, being unneeded expressed a particular logic of social exclusion, based on no longer having anything to offer others. This was a terrible position for a generation who had been brought up in hardship with an ethic of mutual sacrifice during and after the war. Officially this mutual sacrifice was for the greater good of the state. Unofficially mutual help was practiced in networks of social connections which often served to circumvent the state. In the late 1980s these social networks would have been broadest for the generation of victors after two or three decades working. They were on the cusp of retirement. They were in the position to make things happen—for themselves, yes, but more importantly, for others around them, including their children who were establishing themselves. Then, suddenly, their work and retirement were no longer certain. Their social connections were insecure. They could hardly help their own children. "Nobody needs us," they said again and again. What they meant was, "We have nothing to offer."

ECHOES OF WAR

The Great Patriotic War may seem peripheral to an account of the more recent Russian mortality crisis. However, those at greatest risk of dying were born in the years 1936 through 1951. They were the generation of victors Viktor describes above. The war exacted a tremendous Russian sacrifice, a sacrifice that was officially interpreted as necessary for a Russian victory over fascism and as necessary for the future of socialism and communism. Viktor's wife Vera asked, "How is it possible to forget the Great Patriotic War? When we won, and we are a victorious people? Is it even possible? All should bow before our mother Russia." In this view Russia paid the price for an Allied victory and changed the course of history, as only Russia could. Vera added, "And only we could have withstood such a war. Only we [could have], only we, the Russian people." The sacrifices and deprivations of the 1940s were not in vain, at least not until the Soviet project failed. Then the future that the war was supposed to have secured disappeared.

Professor Vladislav, who headed the institute where I was affiliated during my stay in Moscow, told me:

> I myself remember [. . .] the wartime generation of Russians, who lived
> through the war—men and women. They had, naturally, different fates.
> They came through that war in different ways. But those people, you know,
> they had a beautiful identity, a social identity. They understood what it was
> to be Russians. They understood what the government was, what they were
> responsible for. They answered not only for their family. They were ready to
> answer, especially men, for the situation around them.

Professor Vladislav was perhaps speaking of his parents' generation here, but it is likely some of that social identity, based on an idea of what had been fought for and what was being built, was imparted to the next generation. The Great Patriotic War became a central aspect of Soviet identity for certain generations. "For the majority of post-war citizens, being Soviet was easy. . . . 'Sovietness' was a natural attribute of all those who had fought in the war, either actually at the front or metaphorically on the 'home front,' and survived" (Fitzpatrick 2006, 272).

When the Soviet Union fell and much of the Russian population was thrust into poverty, this generation would recall the Great Patriotic War and its aftermath. Everywhere this generation was confronted by scenes they could only comprehend as analogous to the postwar years. During her interview, Lyudmila conflated conditions in the late 1940s with those in the early 1990s. Another man described his impressions upon seeing street children in the early 1990s. "At the train stations, in every underground space, it was as if, the impression was that suddenly a war had ended, just like when our war ended or even before the war ended." At least twice in 2007, walking through informal markets outside metro and train stations, where individuals sold various odds and ends laid out on tarps or overturned crates, Margarita told me with some disgust, "It is just like after the war." And then she would add—half angry, half baffled—"But there was no war." And certainly there was no victory. The fifty-seven-year-old taxi driver I interviewed said, of those older than himself, "They will never understand what happened. No war, nothing. And everything fell apart."

The chaos and poverty, panic, and despair of the early 1990s had only one historical parallel for this generation. But this analogy with postwar Russia brought with it a terrible reckoning—it was as if all of their life efforts from the war onward had been futile.

SACRIFICE FOR A RADIANT FUTURE

This generation's lives were measured against the war and its aftermath. Compared to the deprivations of the war and postwar period, life had steadily improved in the 1950s and 1960s. During the 1970s and 1980s stagnation set in, but it remains true that most of this generation had never seen their circumstances dramatically worsen. They had only ever seen them improve.

The worst of Stalin's repressions, in the late 1930s, occurred before they were born. For most, the promises of Soviet socialism rang true during their formative years and through the 1960s. A radiant future was possible, based on the incredible rate of progress in rebuilding western Russia after the war. "Well, we lived in hard times, all the population lived in hard times, but somehow we lived, found work and all the time thought that it will be better, that there will be improvement. [. . .] We lived with such instilled hopes." And another woman remembered, "We thought that now there is poverty, now we will endure, but afterwards we will live. [. . .] It seems to me that everyone thought it would be better." In addition to the fact that lives did improve in the 1950s, hopes and expectations for further improvement were high.

Sacrifice, long an important motif in Russian culture and orthodoxy, was also central to Soviet citizenship. The Soviet state made constant use of the notion of sacrifice to goad the population to rebuild the country and ensure the radiant future of communism. When that future was lost, it was as if the war and the sacrifices to build socialism were in vain. Even in 2006 and 2007 middle-aged Muscovites said, "What did the people fight for? But now look at what is being done!" The sacrifices they had made—in lives, housing, education, and labor—counted for little.

According to many informants, there is no more radiant future. Where society is going is unclear to them. In an interview a female defense worker lamented:

> And what we have now, I don't even know. There is no ideology now,
> nothing to aim for. Before we had that we were aiming for communism. How
> was it? Well we had some sort of dream that there would be communism,
> meaning that it will be better and better. Although it seemed as if the
> lines were getting longer, but all the same we thought that all of that was
> temporary. Afterwards it will be better. Work! We are going towards a radiant
> future. But now it is unclear where we are going.

A male engineer concurred: "When we started to build socialism and then communism people at least knew what they were building. Now nobody knows what they are building in Russia, and there is not one slogan—'Let's build capitalism.' Nobody says that we are building capitalism even though we have the most bandit capitalism that ever was in eighteenth-century Europe."

COLLECTIVITY

While this generation recalled the war during the early 1990s, for them the late 1940s were essentially different from the early 1990s, however much the hardship and poverty seemed comparable. Vera described herself and her husband, Viktor, as "children of the war." She lost her father during the war, yet she said, "I remember those years like a wonderful, beautiful dream. No, no, no, I don't want to say that, but somehow. . . . We lived friendly [*druzhno*]." One woman, who lived in Kazakhstan during and after the war, said, "And you know, despite these hardships, we lived, we lived somehow very friendly [*druzhno*], very friendly, and we tried to help one another." She spoke of Kazakh and Russian children sharing an apple or dried mare's milk cheese. "We didn't disdain each other." This time was special, "even a happy time for mama and all those relatives [who had fled eastward from the front]."

During interviews individuals struggled to describe the society in which they came of age, one that no longer exists. Soviet society was a "tight society"; "we all lived alike." Vera said, "We lived friendly. [. . .] Now, of course, we are upset. [. . .] We are very upset that we are strangers in one country—strangers." She referred to the political party of Putin and Medvedev, United Russia, with irony: "What sort of United Russia? It is funny to even say it, and I don't want to say it." Vera thought Russia needed another 1941. "Truly we need another war in order to unite us, so that we are together. But now, what disorder [*bezporiadok*]! Neighbor doesn't know neighbor. That's just, that's just . . . That's a catastrophe. It's really scary! How can it be so? Sorrow unified people, they were together, holidays together. And now we don't know each other. Is that really good? A person dies—we don't know about it." According to Vera, war and sorrow are the only ways to bring Russians together. "We're that type of people," she said. People not knowing other people—"neighbor doesn't know neighbor," "now we don't know each other"—is a mark of disorder.

A male engineer spoke of the collective that was knit together during Soviet times. This generation is no longer unified by participating in a big social project. "But now they have torn everyone apart. Everyone has disbanded. Everyone has once again begun to work to survive. Each one for himself and the culture of consumption." People are much more concerned with securing their own lives. Another man similarly told me that everyone wants "to live their own private lives."

These memories made claims about the true Russian character—"that type of people." Viktor said, "We love to be a collective. And we tear ourselves apart. You should never break tradition, do you understand? Yes, individuality is also necessary to nurture, but we are Orthodox and that is solidarity, solidarity [*sobornost'*]." Viktor used a Russian word that comes from the root *sobor,* meaning both cathedral and assembly, or gathering. Boym notes that the word is an "untranslatable antipode to the Western concept of the individual and identity" (1994, 87). Viktor considers solidarity an essential Russian quality, deep and spiritual in nature. His meaning is clear. What is happening now is not Russian. He derides the new Day of Unity on November 4, a holiday plagued by nationalist demonstrations. "Unity between whom?" Viktor asks. "Unity-holiday, and the whole month they tootled to us about the Bolsheviks, how bad Stalin was. They showed films and on the fourth of November again films about the bad Bolsheviks. [. . .] That was on the day of Unity. Do you understand? As a historian I was ashamed. Do you understand? Ashamed, ashamed. *Then* there was unity."

Memories are socially constructed. The Soviet state legitimated and crafted memories of the war and the postwar period. Moreover, accounts of middle-aged Muscovites are laced with nostalgia. Connerton notes that "images of the past commonly legitimate a present social order" (1989, 3). However, in the case of older Muscovites, memories often serve to comment critically on the present. As seen above, one way they do this is to emphasize collectivity, solidarity, or unity in the past, focusing on the war and the radiant future. They exclude sentiments of individuality, inequality, or conflict, which are reserved for characterizing the present. Beyond the question of whether these memories objectively reflect the past, they surely reflect something about the post-Soviet experience for this generation. That experience is marked by a feeling of social isolation, in contrast to the collectivity and unity of Soviet times.

A sense of collectivity is undoubtedly part of their early experiences, forged through the war and the difficult years after the war. People shared struggles to feed themselves, house themselves, educate themselves, and secure a better standard of living. The state provided a master narrative of progress: the radiant future of Soviet communism came only after sacrifice and hardship. Indeed, sacrifice and hardship resonated with people's experiences. The destruction of the war and the destitution of postwar Russia meant that hardship and sacrifice were a daily reality. Whether or not hardship and sacrifice were interpreted as furthering socialism was another matter. But as people's lives improved, a more radiant future with better housing and more consumer goods would have been believable—the master narrative reflected experience. As anywhere, people internalize messages that resonate with their experience.

POSTWAR DEMOGRAPHICS AND GENDER

Many in this generation lost one or both parents in the war. In the years after the war Russia had almost seven hundred thousand orphans who were raised in children's homes. Viktor's childhood coup, when he told his playmates that he had a "real papa," reflects the demographic consequences of the war. An estimated twenty-seven million people had died, three fourths of whom were men (Zubkova 1998, 20). The state reacted to this demographic catastrophe by introducing the 1944 Family Law, which made divorce more difficult and granted state aid to single mothers and mothers of three or more children. Any mother could place her children in a children's home and retrieve them at a later date (Bucher 2006, 14). In the same law, single mothers could no longer sue the father of their children for support (Bucher 2006, 15), given that the state was prepared to assume responsibility. Fathers were no longer legally required to take responsibility for offspring outside of marriage.

The state was intent on increasing the birth rate and replacing the lost population. As a side effect, fathers were divested of legal responsibility in the domestic sphere. Men retained the breadwinner role and were expected to bring home a paycheck. Their social identity centered around work. As Viktor notes, the consequences of a fatherless generation were only fully revealed later and perhaps most fully in the early 1990s when men were unemployed, unpaid, or unable to adequately support their families. During those years, the breadwinner role itself was at stake.

Many women, even before the war, managed their households and worked as wage laborers without much help from men. Under Lenin's and then Stalin's push to industrialize Russia women entered the workforce en masse during the 1920s. In 1939 women represented 39 percent of the workforce; at the end of the war they were 56 percent of the workforce, although this declined a little in the postwar years (Clements 1991, 271). Women's salaries, however, were less than men's throughout the Soviet years. Men were always regarded as the primary breadwinners; women's wages were supplementary. Nonetheless, women fulfilled both productive and reproductive roles in society.

Professor Vladislav spoke of the faded image of men as saviors, an image promoted by Soviet war propaganda. The image retains little cultural currency. "The war, yes, yes, yes. The man was the savior, you know there is the image of the Russian men-saviors, saviors. [. . .] The woman was the guardian, the guardian of the family, children, homes." According to Clements,

> In the iconography of the war, and undoubtedly in the minds of many Soviet soldiers, women came to stand for endurance, rebirth, and the tenderer emotions rare in the world of combat. Women as well must have drawn sustenance from this vision of themselves, for it honored their contribution to the war, justified their suffering, and legitimated their own deep feelings about their succoring role within the family and the community. (Clements 1991, 272)

At some point soon after the war, the image of men-saviors who sacrifice for the future of Soviet communism lost relevance in greater society. The ethic of sacrifice was preserved, but it was most relevant in the domestic sphere. "The practice of self-sacrifice in favour of future generations became reoriented towards one's own children" (Ledeneva 1998, 102). While the image of men-saviors eroded, the image of women guardians expanded into domestic martyrs after the war.[5] Sacrifice became the purview of women. Professor Vladislav told me that men were no longer the saviors, that now "the woman must comfort, support, and sometimes save the man." He, along with others, told me that the best men had died in the wars of the twentieth century. Women became the saviors of those who were left.

ORDER

Particularly during the late 1940s the Soviet state was reasserting itself. Stalin used the war to galvanize his vision of the Soviet project. Central ideology, organization, and control were tightened, along with renewed persecution of Jews, intellectuals, and students. This period of time was the height of the Soviet state, but it also contained the seeds of collectivity and individuality apart from the state. It is tempting to equate order with the Soviet state, but order, in the memories of older Muscovites, is fundamentally knowing other people—an interpersonal order. This order is akin to Giddens's structure: invisible rules that facilitate social practices. Many of these rules would have depended on the existence of the state, but they were not determined by the state.

Children of the war were inculcated in the morality of sacrifice but also independence and spontaneity, as the state struggled with "reconciling order and heroism" (Livschiz 2006, 204). In her seminal literary analysis, Dunham (1976) wrote about early yearnings for freedom after the eye-opening experiences of the war. The desire for more freedom was contained by the state through a "Big Deal" permitting moderate middle-class materialism in exchange for continued support of the regime. More recently historians have argued that the general population was much too destitute to yearn for anything other than to rebuild their individual lives (Zubkova 1998; Filtzer 2002). But as they rebuilt their lives, aspirations surfaced. The radiant future began to apply to individual lives as well as the communist project, and the state tolerated this development. Fürst (2006a) recognizes this time as the maturation of the Soviet state and claims that the reassertion of state control coincided with growing individuality. "Thus, precisely in the regime's highly developed sense of control rests the very possibility to avoid, undermine and reinterpret" (12). Postwar Soviet order inadvertently created space to circumvent and contest that same order.

At least retrospectively, the informants of this study found the roots of their social identity in the war and postwar years, notwithstanding that they themselves were too young to serve. After the war people's growing aspirations for their own radiant future eventually exceeded the state's ability to deliver. In order to deal with this problem, people cooperated to push against the limitations of the state and form alternative channels of redistribution.

The two dimensions of order and space in the Soviet era had their roots in the war but were later epitomized in the workplace. According to Livschiz, the solution to reconciling order and heroism (individuality) was found in the promotion of "love for labour and work that emerged as a key theme and ultimate demonstrator of patriotism and peacetime heroism" (2006, 204). At work, individuals were integrated into the state's industry and bureaucracy. Work also helped organize social connections that circumvented and co-opted state control and structure. In the next chapter we will turn to work to understand the intertwined relationship between order and space during this generation's working years.

THE ECHO OF WAR IN MORTALITY

Some scholars interpret the age distribution of excess deaths during the mortality crisis as the impact of early childhood experience on mortality. Demographers Anderson and Silver (1989) find elevated cohort mortality for Russian men and women born during the war, especially those in western Russia. There is literature suggesting that risk of cardiovascular disease is, in part, determined by early experience, even as early as fetal and infant growth (Barker 2001). For the most part, this cohort would have been in utero during years of hardship and stress. They often had restricted diets when they were young and poor diets thereafter. Many men smoked and drank heavily throughout their lives. Perhaps very early, biological vulnerabilities to cardiovascular disease may have developed, compounded and mitigated over individuals' life courses. It is also true that biological vulnerabilities and their life-course histories are the bodily imprints of larger political-economic processes. Moreover, the meanings given to vulnerabilities such as a wartime childhood may also attenuate or heighten their biological impact. This generation grew up as the generation of victors. In the early 1990s they became the generation of losers. Such a radical retelling of their lives' worth affected their health.

At the alcohol policy seminar in the spring of 2007, two women of the sobriety society Sober Russia were in attendance. As the seminar drew to a close, Maria stood up in the back of the amphitheater and proclaimed loudly that Russians needed to learn from their own history. She continued emotionally, "You are not looking at reasons, but consequences. Russians can't live for themselves, for their pockets. There is no more 'radiant future.' We need to talk about our own people, the war, our 'radiant past.' You need to talk about that and if you don't talk about that you aren't talking about Russia." It is not possible to understand the mortality crisis without some understanding of Russian history and this generation's place in it. I scribbled frantically in my notebook as Maria made an anthropologist's appeal to look at mortality in context. Although the seminar's scholars recognized that rising rates of alcohol consumption and alcohol-related deaths coincided with the demise of the USSR, they were focused on risk reduction strategies through government regulation to limit access and control quality. In Maria's opinion, though, high levels of alcohol consumption were a consequence of a new Russian society where the logics of individualism and monetary accumulation reign. In Soviet times a radiant future was the glorious future of a truly communist Russia. While Maria does not see any radiant future for Russia, she refers to the past, Russian history, as radiant. The war in particular symbolizes a moment of Russian history where Russians were brought together by collective sacrifice at the same time that the Soviet state was in ascendance. The state asserted itself, on the one hand, and, on the other, individuals did what was necessary to survive, often relying on each other. "Russians can't live for themselves," Maria said. In Soviet times Russians lived depending on each other to address the difficulties and absurdities of daily life in the Soviet Union. When the Soviet Union was dissolved in December 1991, so were the social logics by which people were connected.

Above all, this generation mourned the loss of being needed. Both the ideology of the Soviet state and the logic of social relations emphasized that people were worthy and had status based on their ability to offer something. They gave their labor to the state. They offered favors and goods to others around them. In Russian ethnography being unneeded means "hurt and pain" (Rethmann 1999, 205) and "loneliness and vulnerability" (Höjdestrand 2009, 2). These come from the loss of ability to give to others. Fundamentally, being unneeded is about the loss of ability to give to others and thus to intervene in social life. Social epidemiology has shown that social isolation has serious emotional and physical health consequences. Ethnography shows how the logic of social isolation is culturally and temporally specific. Being unneeded is how many middle-aged Russians experienced the early 1990s. Being unneeded is also why some of them did not survive those years.

This chapter has touched on early hardships suffered by the generation of victors and the meaning given to these hardships in terms of sacrifice and collectivity. These meanings were promoted by the state, but they were powerful precisely because they resonated with everyday experience. These meanings, however, evolved through this generation's lives. Collective sacrifice for the radiant future of Soviet communism, emblematized in men's wartime service, was displaced by collective sacrifice among family and friends, emblematized by women's daily struggles. Older Muscovites, identified as victorious in Soviet history, attempt to reassert the meanings of sacrifice and collectivity through their memories of World War II. They do this against a strong tide that sees their sacrifices as a failed project—ultimately unnecessary.

CHAPTER 4

Work

We were sorry to lose everything that we had already acquired. What rich experience—it just seemed that we would still be needed [*nuzhny*].

—interviewee

This chapter explores the role of work in the lives of this generation. New wealth redefines past labor. The chapter begins with the experiences of Galina and Margarita before introducing the idea of "socially useful work." Work was the central way almost all citizens were integrated into the order of the state; yet, work was also how Muscovites acted collectively in space set apart from the state. Work gave people a sense of knowing each other and organized social relations, *blat* among them. The practice of *blat* further reveals what it means to be unneeded in post-Soviet Russia.

THE GOOD YEARS

Most of this generation entered the workforce during the 1950s and 1960s after postwar reconstruction and during the scientific and technological revolution. The standard of living had likely returned to prewar levels by 1950 (Filtzer 2002) and the economy began to expand. Schwartz's classic *The Soviet Economy since Stalin* (1965) calls the late 1950s "the good years." The Soviet Union made remarkable progress in military industry after the war, testing the atomic bomb in 1949 and the hydrogen bomb in 1953.

79

In 1957, Sputnik 1 was launched into orbit; Yuri Gagarin became the first Russian astronaut in 1961. That same year Khrushchev predicted communism by 1980.[1] It was a heady time. Chubarov describes the political promises of that time as "overoptimistic, utopian objectives" (2001, 141).

At the time most people dreamed of better futures. They saw that the standard of living was rising, part of the postwar Big Deal that permitted middle-class materialism in exchange for continued support of the regime (Dunham 1976). In the decade from 1955 to 1965, a third of the population received newly, if poorly, constructed accommodations, many of these private apartments (Filtzer 2006). This alleviated some crowding as people moved out of communal apartments. Even into the early 1970s people's lives were improving, albeit slowly. However, by the late 1970s it was clear the economy had stagnated. Shortages and queues were evidence that the system was not working as it should. People made up for the deficiencies in the system by relying on personal connections to secure consumer services and goods.

The generation of victors grew up during a period of progress. By the late 1980s the youngest among them had worked for at least fifteen years. In the Soviet Union women could retire after twenty years; men could retire after twenty-five. The formal retirement ages were fifty-five and sixty, respectively. Just as they were poised to reap the benefits of the Soviet system, the system unraveled. An employee in the defense industry, born in the early 1950s, explained:

> And remember we always said that, let's say, our generation, generally those
> who were born in the fifties, the famine was over . . . we had passed through
> the war. . . . We lived well on petrol dollars into the seventies. We entered
> work in good enterprises. We earned well, [had] interesting work. That is,
> it appeared as if we would be the first generation, that our life would go by
> without that [war, famine, poverty]. . . . And suddenly, it was such a collapse
> at the peak of everything.

The experiences of Galina and Margarita illustrate two Soviet work histories and how the collapse irrevocably altered an expected future.

Galina

Galina was born in 1942 about three hundred kilometers south of Moscow where her family was evacuated during the war. After her father returned from the front the family lived in barracks where two adults and four children were crowded in one room. "They gave us the worst room in the barracks, the coldest. Our mattresses froze to the beds in the morning. We lived there, oh six, seven years." Two more girls were born and the family moved to a room in a house. The three oldest children moved out before the family received a three-room apartment. Galina finished seven class years and in 1959, at the age of seventeen, began work in a factory painting sewing machines in the paint and varnish section. For her work, which was classified as hard and harmful, she received 120 rubles a month in addition to cooking oil and milk.

In a few years she decided to go to an evening *tekhnikum* for further training in economics. While attending classes she worked in quality control at another factory, which produced gate valves used in chemical processing. Her salary was only 60 rubles, but lunch was provided. After she received her diploma she was lucky to be promoted to an engineer-economist position at the factory. This raised her salary to 126 rubles per month (90 rubles in salary plus 40 percent in bonus). "That was good money; a good thick winter coat cost 120 rubles." To Galina, work at the factory was marked by discipline and precision.

> I assessed the industrial capabilities of the factory, how much of what the factory could [produce], as far as everything was in the hands of economists, you know. They already saw where each configuration would lead, where each piece of equipment purchased [would lead]—in that everything was planned precisely. [. . .] In the factory everything was precisely counted, literally, and the factory was like. . . . My father said it worked like a watch. It worked precisely. Understand me. We delivered equipment precisely; we executed our program precisely; if the program stalled we tried to get back on schedule within three shifts. But now I look. . . . We were very highly disciplined: we came at eight o'clock, lunch at twelve, you didn't go out anywhere, understand? We were precise, nobody went anywhere. We were very disciplined, very disciplined. And now I don't observe that. A complete collapse, a complete collapse.

When perestroika began, Galina was not against reform.

> When perestroika proclaimed a market economy we understood that there would be a market salary. That was the deception of the people—that a salary would be a proper salary. And they bought us on that. They deceived us on that. We thought there would be a big salary and we supported

everything only because of that. Everyone thought the salary would be big. And once there is a big salary that means we will live better. But it turned out the opposite.

In 1992, at fifty years of age, Galina was three years away from retirement. That year the factory was privatized and Galina received shares in the enterprise. She used privatization vouchers to buy more shares for a total of forty-one shares, the maximum permitted. She was told they would be worth four hundred thousand rubles. She was forced into early retirement in 1993, but for the first six months received only unemployment benefits. These payments were erratic and she and her husband, who had also lost his job at the same factory but without a pension, borrowed money from her retired sister in order to make ends meet. Her husband was fortunate enough to find work as a security guard. Technically Galina was not supposed to work as a retiree, but she too was soon working.

> It was only possible to find work as a security guard or a cleaner because the factories everywhere were all in decline. There was a contraction in production. And through a connection I got a job in a college, I was a guard there and I cleaned the floors. That paid four hundred rubles there or four hundred thousand, now I don't know. It was in 1995. I've already forgotten the units [. . .] and my pension was somewhere around three hundred rubles in addition.[2]

Three years after she was forced to retire from the factory, Galina returned in order to do something with her shares in the company.[3] She was shocked to see that the landscaped flower gardens had been overrun by wormwood plants and a birch tree was growing out of the roof over her former department. In better times, the factory director had told his employees that there was not a factory like it in America. "As a result, they plundered that factory, they took it away." With her forty-one shares she received 8,000 rubles. She supplemented that amount and bought an automatic washing machine for 10,500 rubles.

Together Galina and her husband managed during this tumultuous time. Given they don't have any children, they are saving what they can for the day when one or both of them will not be able to work. They read detective books, watch television, and do crossword puzzles in their free time. For most of their lives they worked under the expectation that they would become comfortable retired engineers with the means to enjoy yearly vacations. Under the Soviet system their pensions would have been equivalent to their salaries. "Of course they [retirees in Soviet times] lived much richer than we do. That is, our pension now is four or five times less [than what it would have been] and what's more the cost of living is such." In a matter of a few years Galina and her husband have become guard-janitors, worried about a day when they will no longer be able to work.

Margarita

Margarita was born in 1940 in a village in Moscow Oblast' where her father, who was involved in the 1930s development of Moscow city, built a house on a lot for his family before he died on the front. Margarita's mother rented out the lower level of the house to the Pioneer camp, a vacation camp of the Soviet youth organization, in the summer and the upper level to students the rest of the year. Margarita finished seven years of schooling and then enrolled in a four-year day course at a *tekhnikum*. She graduated as a technician-mechanic for meat-packaging machinery. She was assigned work at a meat-packaging plant in a city about four hundred kilometers northwest of Moscow, but it turned out they had no opening. So she was told that she had "free choice"—she had to find her own position. Wherever she went in Moscow she was turned away. Eventually she met a man in the village who worked as a manager in the preslaughter treatment section of a Moscow meat-packaging plant. Margarita began to work as a storekeeper in the cold room of the plant.

> Well, the meat comes from wagon, in the wagons, and the carcasses were already frozen. The carcasses were laid on trolley carts, there was a type of platform there, in the cold room of course. A track. The loaders were there at the platform. The loaders lifted those carcasses. They were such men, you understand. And there were these floor-mounted scales and you go up to where the plummets are, you set the weight. So as soon as they sent it, we weighed to know how much was in each wagon. And the men, whole brigades, carted [the carcasses] away in cars to the refrigerated rooms.

In time, Margarita and two other women working as storekeepers were sent for further training, given they were not working in their area of specialization. Margarita began working in the design division of the mechanical repair department with a new diploma in the assembly of screw-cutting lathes, but she didn't enjoy it. She considered her spatial perception poor and wanted to be a mechanic.

When she became pregnant in 1965 she went to the Regional Economic Council (Sovnarkhoz) and asked to be reassigned. In that same year the regional system of economic management was disbanded in favor of centralized ministries. She was told she could work at the State Committee on Material and Technical Procurement, but she would need to learn to type. She worked there for nine years, during which time she had her son, divorced her husband, and received a one-room apartment to the north of the city. After her maternity leave of four months she placed her son in a five-day nursery. She picked him up Friday evenings and they spent the weekends together. She left the ministry in 1974 to work closer to home at a research institute for poultry processing.

> The thing is, that when, before retirement it was mandatory to have a certain length of employment, mandatory that there was an uninterrupted period of work. That was what it was all about, do you understand? And I had in general, quite a normal salary. Before people lived. . . . The most I received was 125, 130 at the institute where I worked. I received 130, and the biggest pension was 132. Do you understand 120, 132 and people lived very well you could say. But now. . . . But now, how much? Everything [money] has changed by a thousand times, right? Well then, now my pension should be 13,000. That's what our pension should be. That's it, but we will not receive anything like that, we won't receive it and we aren't receiving it, so that's that. Oh, what a nightmare! But given I didn't have any savings anywhere, I didn't lose anything—"ever spare, ever bare." Ha, ha. I was living on my salary and so it's nothing. Perestroika or no perestroika it's all the same to me.

But it isn't the same. Immediately following this, she gave a nervous laugh as she recalled vouchers (for stocks in companies to be privatized). She continued, "Michelle, how they deceived us, it is some kind of quiet horror! Oh, I can't. I need to throw away those pieces of paper [vouchers]. I still have them. Oh, what a nightmare, oh! Oh, horror, it is just, anyway it all needs to be. . . ." She didn't finish. When I asked how she was deceived, she told me that organizations should have exchanged the vouchers for cash. "And all of it disappeared, all of those organizations." She attempted to cash in her vouchers through the trade union with no luck. "What a joke! I came. . . . Oh, well I don't even want to talk about it. It's horrible how they messed with people's heads. Especially . . . oh it was terrible. Well all of that was just lost and good riddance. There was never any money, and there is none, and let there never be. So there!"

On her retirement pension she continued to work for an additional eight years in the boiler room of her housing complex. Her salary was fifty-five hundred rubles per month when she stopped. In 2007 her pension was twenty-five hundred. She uses her pension primarily to buy food and medicine for high blood pressure. Public transportation is free. Fees on the apartment are discounted 50 percent by virtue of her status as a work veteran (she completed twenty years of uninterrupted service) and are further subsidized so she only pays two hundred rubles a month. The telephone service is more expensive, but is also discounted 50 percent. She comforts herself, "In principle, you understand, in principle there are people who live worse, it isn't worth getting offended. Everything is okay now. In any case it won't get better. I'm old, not as bad off as others."

Like others in the previous chapter, when Margarita thinks of the new Russia she is reminded of her youth, after the war. That is when she lived in the village. She commuted back and forth from Moscow on the electric train. In the following she remembers a frozen body on the tracks below the platform and the odds and ends the poor and invalid sold around the station—"but that was after the war." In 2007 there were once again people selling around the station. "But now there are rich folks and again that garbage at our station."

> When I was seven, eight, nine, up until eleven years it was difficult. I walked to the train station in my wellies. And I remember we had a lot of water there, now everything is asphalt, but before as soon as it began to rain, you couldn't get through it. I walked on kerosene, we had kerosene cookers then, there was no gas there. [. . .] I remember on the train. There weren't the automatic doors before [to enter the platform area] on the electric train, and they [the tracks] were just there, oh, horror! You go up on the platform and there is someone down below [a corpse], if they were frozen on . . . after the war—poverty and everything . . . they would take off the overshoes, the ankle boots. In a sense you could say they were stealing. And also at the station I remember they sold every sort of nonsense, there were a lot of poor, there were invalids, but that was after the war and then more or less. . . . But now there are rich folks and again that garbage at our station. Some kind of horror! It is a silent horror. They sit, they swear, the grannies, the grampies

and various women, and everything. Oh, again we've returned to the same thing, and they sell every sort of nonsense. Every piece of clothing, every old shoe. Oh, what is that?

Like Lyudmila in the previous chapter, Margarita sees poverty and is reminded of the postwar period, but "now there are rich folks" too.

"SOCIALLY USEFUL WORK"

Work was the one way almost all Soviet citizens were incorporated into the order imposed by the state and participated as citizens. Clarke explains that work was much more than a job in Soviet times:

> People's social benefits and entitlements, their rest and holidays, sporting and cultural activities, access to consumer durables, clothing and footwear, housing, health care, education, and even food are all linked to their participation in the enterprise. The enterprise is the basis of the Soviet worker's social existence: most of the things provided through the enterprise cannot be acquired by any other means, so work defines the worker's identity in a much more fundamental way than it does in the capitalist world. (1993, 24)

Work was a right. "In our generation's time, everyone received their passport [work history card] at sixteen years of age. Sometimes even at fifteen they were in the factory. If you weren't studying, you went to the factory." For those that graduated from a vocational technical school or a *tekhnikum,* employment was usually arranged for the graduates. The state provided a place for most members of society, although it was not always the place desired. Due to labor hoarding there was a constant labor shortage and little turnover. Loss of work—loss of a place in the social order—was rarely threatened.

The fact that the government guaranteed work to its citizenry is but one side of Soviet work. Work was also a social duty and responsibility. Through their work, individuals gave something back to the state and greater society, at least in theory. A younger man in his late forties told me that many people were relieved when the state backed off from their lives. "Before they were constantly talking about the debt to the state, namely to the generations. And they [Soviet citizens] never refused; generally it was as if they heeded the debt." But most of those individuals I spoke with were not relieved when the state fell away. One woman spoke of work under the Soviet state thus:

> In a Soviet city, working people could get a job anywhere and God forbid you didn't work for ten days! They would carry you to work with a military escort. They wouldn't let you fall. That was the purchase then, that was what was good then—they wouldn't let you fall. You will work, whether you want that or not. You will feed society. You will feed your children. And not one poor woman, having even three, four children, feared that her children would die of hunger because there was a society that was obliged to answer, not only for yourself, but for others.

Work was framed as a contribution to society.

An emphasis on socially useful work applied to all work under the Soviet state. Socially useful work was part of the state's greater project of building communism. The 1977 Constitution of the USSR, in part 2, chapter 7, article 60, included the directive: "It is the duty of, and matter of honor for, every able-bodied citizen of the USSR to work conscientiously in his chosen, socially useful occupation, and strictly to observe labor discipline. Evasion of socially useful work is incompatible with the principles of socialist society." In the *Encyclopedia of Soviet Life,* Zemtsov describes the official version of "socially useful work":

> Any work in socialist industry or agriculture that is officially presented as serving the common good. The phrase "socially useful labor" is intended to contrast the virtue of labor performed in state-run enterprises (plants, factories, collective farms, or state farms) with the supposed social insignificance of the work carried out outside the system of state regulation and planning, on private agricultural plots, or in home crafts. Socially useful labor is portrayed as the basis of economic progress as well as the most important formative influence shaping the character of Soviet individuals. Labor outside the state sector is often held to be motivated by greed for personal gain even at the expense of the public. (2001, 299)

An interviewee reminisced of her childhood, "In those times there were beautiful people, who took part in social work, socially useful work." She was referring to work under the Soviet system in contrast to work in the capitalist marketplace. Soviet work was framed as collective contribution; capitalist work as personal gain. According to Tatiyana, even if people retained their work in the early 1990s it no longer gave much satisfaction "because it wasn't for anything. [. . .] There wasn't anything to work for." Another interviewee agreed, saying, "We didn't have any goal to aim for." No ideology framed people's work as socially useful. For this generation, working for personal profit does not have the same import.

The fact that work was a social right, indeed, a social obligation, meant that many people felt as if they had a place in society and that it was useful, especially during the 1950s. Even if they did not feel this, most individuals participated in production in some form; therefore they had a role in society, however minimal or senseless. Vera commented, "If we were orderly [*poriadochnye*], there was work." The Russian word *poriadochnyi* denotes a person who is decent, respectable, and clean living—it is derived from the word for order—*poriadok*. When people suddenly lost their work in the early 1990s, they were no longer orderly, part of a larger order. According to Vera, orderly people who had worked their entire lives finished their days living with the homeless or thieves—those who were not part of the legitimate social order, those who cause disorder. Even if they were only threatened with losing their work in the early 1990s, this effectively communicated that their contribution to society was no longer necessary and they were unneeded. Even their past labor was discredited. Orderly people give to others through their work; disorderly people do not.

PAST LABOR

In the early 1990s, a generation's labor was deemed insignificant. Vera and her husband Viktor worked as secondary school teachers and now live on two meager pensions. Vera says that this is all normal and they are not bitter. In the following Vera recounts seeing oligarch Iosif Kobzon claim on television that he is rich because he worked his whole life.[4] Vera thinks through the implications of Kobzon's claim.

> Listen to what Kobzon says on television, "That is why I am so rich, so much money, because I worked my whole life." And I say, didn't we work? [. . .] We worked, and how we worked. We gave ourselves without holding back anything. That means we. . . . It means [what Kobzon said] we didn't work if

we didn't earn for ourselves. Yes, we don't have good apartments, or *dachas,* or cars, but for us that isn't the point. [. . .] And money—we never chased after it, even though we had a wretched salary at school, you know yourself, and we earned a wretched pension. But we didn't even become bitter . . . ha, ha, ha. Nothing, it was normal. We don't curse anyone, no one. I think everything is normal, normal. We have an interesting, good life. And that our students don't forget us—that is like the measure of a teacher, right?

Not much later she comes back to Kobzon's claim that he is rich because he worked his whole life. "That we earned it, that two teachers earned that pension, it is almost funny! It is as if we really didn't work after all. I don't even want to think of it."

Under the new economic logic, if she and Viktor had worked, they would have something to show for it. Given they have very little, it is indeed as if they never worked. She says she does not want to think about it—about their life's labor rendered invisible. But she does continue to think of it. Below is another portion of her interview with Sveta. Here she rejects Kobzon's claim completely. She wants Sveta to know that their work developed the country and yet they have nothing. Instead, the younger generation benefits.

> Vera: Someone, really, forgive me, deals in millions, and someone is in
> poverty. And they say we have poor and rich like we had rich and poor—
> and so they have remained. But what did my husband and I earn? A
> beggarly pension but we both worked at a school. It is good that we can
> still sort of finagle a bit somehow. I will never accept this time, no. . . .
> Sveta: It is interesting. . . .
> Vera: And I am hurt, I am hurt, for children, for grandchildren, for your
> young generation, although you are conforming, conforming. Well and
> how else? Of course. . . .
> Sveta: There isn't an alternative. We don't have an alternative.
> Vera: And so I don't judge you. [. . .] The older generation had already
> gained something for itself. . . .
> Sveta: Of course, of course.
> Vera: But nothing more comes of that for us. Nothing at all. But you [the
> young] are still living on what our generation built.
> Sveta: Well of course, yes.
> Vera: Thus far you haven't really created anything. That is why I'm hurt.
> Didn't we do something?

In Soviet times each new generation was indebted to the proceeding generations' sacrifices and labor. Each new generation repaid this debt through its own sacrifices and labor in the name of a brighter future for the succeeding generations. Now the younger generations are free to do work that is "for personal gain even at the expense of the public" (Zemtsov 2001, 299) using the infrastructure developed by previous generations. Viktor, Vera's husband, was forceful on this point, although he gave credit to the war generation: "I repeat: All of present-day democratic Russia, all of her economy, rests on what that generation built. Do you understand? Your grandmothers, my parents, do you understand?"

The war generation and the "generation of victors" are not given credit for their contribution to the development of Russia. In fact, Viktor and Vera's generation feel accused of leading Russia astray: "And now they say: 'So you were communists. Bad.' So they plant in people's hearts that your past is 'down the drain,' that whatever you labored at didn't make the grade. That you fought for the country. . . . What kind of country did you fight for?"

NEW WEALTH

It is clear to people that wealth in the new Russia is not a result of hard work. Viktor told Sveta: "Here as the result of privatization we have a group [of oligarchs], well we even know [them], Sveta, you and I. We can count that group on one hand, right? For peanuts or for nothing at all, they took colossal natural riches. [. . .] Abramovich, Khodorkovsky, Fridman in some five or six years: about eighteen or fifteen million."[5] Lyudmila, who continues to work past her expected retirement, had this to say about new wealth and work: "Abramovich is thirty years old. He already has millions of dollars, billions. Has he worked for thirty years? I am seventy, I work, I haven't rested a day. I work. I can't save for my funeral. I work every day and I work even until I'm seventy years old. And he's thirty. He already has billions? How can you not notice that?" She thought all of the rich were thieves, "because the capital was stolen from the beginning." The idea that honest, hardworking people are financially rewarded by their length of service is now a transparent fiction. Another man complained, "But people who worked honestly and so on—they suffered the biggest loss, the biggest loss. Now work honestly and they look at you like you're an idiot! [. . .] So work has lost its meaning as work." Work has lost its meaning because the value of work has to a large degree been supplanted by the value of money.

KNOWING PEOPLE

The "complete collapse" Galina referred to above was not merely a collapse of industrial production; it was a collapse of moral order over time, space, and lives—when trees and people had their proper places at the factory. She told Sveta that a man named Jorge is now director of the factory.

> He arrived from Mexico. Here is what I heard about his biography. He's Russian. His father was a diplomat in Chile. He [the father] is Russian. His mom is Russian and his father dies. He [Jorge] was five years old. Mom marries a Chilean and he [the Chilean stepfather] gives him his surname, his first name. He becomes Jorge. And here's what they say about him: that he killed that father [the Chilean stepfather]. His mother dies and he kills that father [. . .] and with that money he arrives in Russia and somehow he is the owner of the factory of our patron.

Galina had already referred to her former boss as "director" in the interview. As in English, the word patron implies a personal relationship of support and encouragement, not merely a professional relationship. Patron is used in contrast to the new director Jorge. Galina says Jorge is Russian, but he has a foreign name, and by using only his first name, Galina emphasizes his foreignness. When she refers to the old director she uses his last name, as is customary. Whoever he is and whatever he did, Jorge symbolizes the immorality of the new order. The story is compelling in post-Soviet Russia. Jorge acquired money to buy the factory through patricide—a highly immoral act. Jorge's patricide also stands in for the casting away of the older generation. Jorge uses his stepfather's money to become owner of the factory. Jorge is Russian, but in many ways he is not. He has a foreign name, lived in a foreign land, and had a foreign stepfather.

Jorge, like all "new Russians," is both Russian and not Russian—a different Russian who appeared in the early 1990s and did not fit into the old order and was therefore, at least initially, marked as immoral. In the early 1990s, Russians began to refer to the "nouveaux riches."[6] There was an implication that this money was acquired through criminal activities, and the term itself sometimes served as a euphemism for the mafia. In the later 1990s "nouveau riche" evolved to "new Russian." The term no longer implies the criminality that "nouveaux riches" did, but it provides a label for those with money and a showy lifestyle. Older Russians still refer to the rich as "new Russians."

Once, driving among *dachas* on the outskirts of Moscow, we asked a Russian working in his garden how to get back to the highway. "Go straight ahead and turn right at the *dacha* of the 'new Russians.'" He smiled ironically. "You do know who 'new Russians' are?" We did, and we also knew to turn right when we saw the large villa up the road.

The sense of not knowing people was commonplace during the early 1990s. It did not only apply to those who had money. There was a general uncertainty about who people really were and who they would become. Viktor described a sense of betrayal as people he had known suddenly became *drugoi*—other, different, new. Viktor, besides being a secondary school history teacher, was a military officer and secret member of the Committee for State Security (KGB). Here he refers to his state security colleagues: "Do you know how hard it is to watch the treason of many? When we were together? We sat together, as we say, at one desk. Together we had those shoulder boards, everything. And suddenly a completely different person. Do you understand? Another [person]. That's it." Employees of the state security agency would have been scrambling to remake themselves in the early 1990s; however, this theme of not knowing other people surfaced in many of the interviews. It was intimately connected to work.

Through work, the Soviet state gave people a place in society and enabled them to know others in society. When Sveta asked Galina if social relations had changed, Galina spoke about the factory, "When I worked there, in the factory, I walked in the whole department and I could paint you a picture [of the people], but now it is very hard for me to say." She thinks this may be due to a "degradation of morals." Margarita also has trouble knowing what people are up to in the new Russia. When I asked her what people did to relieve stress, she said she had no idea. Instead she spoke about neighbors who drink, spit, and do not greet her—"whatever they want they do." Then she turned to the subject of work.

> Before there were the mill operators and the lathe operators [at the meat-packaging plant] and everything, everything worked normally. Lord, and now, I simply don't know. Well, when we worked, even at the institute, we went to the collective farm. We harvested potatoes in the fall. We harvested beets, carrots, cabbage. [. . .] And now nobody does anything. I don't know who does what. I can't imagine. I don't know. They play those automatic casino games.

Margarita finds it difficult to know what people are doing these days, when everyone does "whatever they want." In Soviet times, people knew each other through work. The youth volunteer work brigades she refers to were perhaps the purest, most idealistic version of work under the Soviet system, unremunerated and collective. Even at the factory Margarita knew who did what. "And everything, everything worked normally." But now even her neighbors are strangers. Margarita cannot even imagine what they might do with their time. It seems to Margarita that nobody does anything. It is true that unemployment levels are likely high in the Moscow Oblast' town where she lives, given that the poultry-processing institute is no longer able to provide as many jobs. Margarita claims that now people do "whatever they want," and she gives an example that is the antithesis of socially useful work—gambling. Margarita attributes her loss of bearings to a loss of morals—instead of working for society, people are gambling. Another interviewee concurred:

> Well the communist system was a little better. Well there was a little more
> order there. This new system—we cannot. . . . Now there are neither
> capitalists nor communists. There's nobody. Well, that system seemed to
> keep stable, that form. People worked. They understood more about people.
> Now look! Maybe it will rectify itself. Now there is less respect for people,
> more rudeness. Nobody was rude but they worked then.

For this generation the transformed society is opaque, and that makes the motivations and intentions of others also opaque. "Now there are neither capitalists nor communists. There's nobody." Before, "people worked." But it is not that people are not working in the new Russia. Rather, the meaning of work has changed.

When older Russians speak about the difficulty of knowing other people and what they do, they are commenting on the demise of formal and informal social connections organized through work. These relations positioned people in networks of social exchange.

WORK AND SOCIAL CONNECTIONS

Much has been written from political-economic and historical viewpoints about the transformation of labor relations during the early 1990s in Russia. In Soviet times managers and workers were mutually dependent on each other. Managers needed cooperative workers in a context of a labor shortage, while workers needed managers for housing, healthcare, holidays, and access to consumer goods. It was in the interest of both to set production goals low and fulfill them. Informal relations and loose alliances between different levels of workers and management in Soviet industry were not necessarily sanctioned by the state, but in a capitalist economy these alliances were a real threat to the power and profits of the new elite. Filtzer has written of the robust system of informal "shop floor relations" that had to be destroyed in the early 1990s: "The elite, in order to maintain its political control over society, required the atomization of the population and of the industrial work-force in particular" (1994, 6). This atomization ensured that no viable opposition would emerge. The atomization also meant that people lost a sense of connection.

Blat

Formal and informal workplace relations were important in order to make things happen. According to Ledeneva's *Russia's Economy of Favours*, "*blat* is the use of personal networks and informal contacts to obtain goods and services in short supply" (1998, 1). *Blat*'s origins are prerevolutionary, when *blat* implied criminality. By the 1950s, *blat* enmeshed itself with the official Soviet system, primarily through industry. *Tolkachi* were *blat* dealers who "'pushed' for the interests of their enterprise in such matters as the procurement of supplies. Their 'professional' role was to support the Soviet command economy, to enable it to work, which paradoxically could be done only by violation of its declared principles of allocation" (25).

During the 1960s, the relationship between state industry and *blat* further evolved. *Blat* retained its intimate connections to the workplace but was not located in the workplace. The *blatmeister* secured public resources for personal, not industrial, needs. This variation of *blat* had its heyday under Brezhnev. Because of the dual nature of *blat*, "grounded in both personal relationships and in access to public resources" (3), occupational position organized *blat* networks because occupation "provided access to different kinds of resources—material resources as well as contacts, time and information—which could be involved in informal exchanges" (127). In this way *blat* connected people to each other primarily through their positions in the economy and bureaucracy of the Soviet state. "One's present and past jobs, those of friends, relatives, and others with whom one had blat, and all *those* people's social and kin relations gave one access to commodities and services" (Pesmen 2000, 135). Connections across occupations accessed the widest array of goods, services, and favors. *Blat* networks were also strengthened when they included members of different social strata, or vertical connections. These social relationships "tended to 'colonize' state institutions" (Argenbright 1999, 7) and personalize the bureaucracy (Ledeneva 1998, 85), functioning as conduits of public goods and services. State structure organized the very social connections that served to circumvent the state.

In Soviet times, women generally used *blat* networks to secure daily household needs connected to tasks such as shopping. Men's *blat* networks were more likely to be used for "obtaining a job, acquiring construction materials, or obtaining official permission for a dacha" (Ledeneva 1998, 120), all tasks that required connections in industry or state bureaucracy. While this division of tasks was likely not hard or fast, as a general pattern it had implications for men's and women's experiences in the early 1990s. Ledeneva (1998, 121) also notes that by virtue of their presence in commerce and service sectors of the economy, sectors less affected than manufacturing, women were more likely to have access to consumer goods and services.

Blat was the "proof of one's belonging" (Ledeneva 1998, 84) in society and "rested on individual repertoires built up over lifetimes" (Pesmen 2000, 135). There is some debate in the literature about whether *blat* practices are analogous to gift giving and whether they are different from friendship (Pesmen 2000, 128; Caldwell 2004, 82). A distinction between *blat* and friendship is artificial at best. These practices existed along a continuum and were always open to interpretation. Nielsen recounts an outing with his musician friend Seryozha who asked his friend Volodya to help find some Armenian wine. A friend of Volodya's provided the alcohol. Nielsen asked Seryozha if he gave Volodya records. Seryozha said, "Well, once in a while I bring him an LP. But Volodya's a friend and a good guy. He won't object if he gets nothing in return" (2006, under "B. The Weakness of Money"). Moreover, *blat* exchanges took place between individuals situated in networks. In the above example Volodya's friend did Volodya a favor; in turn, Volodya did Seryozha a favor. Seryozha might not give Volodya anything, but it is also possible that Volodya might ask Seryozha to do a favor for another friend or even a friend of a friend. Thinking of an exchange between individuals is misleading. It makes more sense to think of Soviet *blat* as a chain of exchange that involves a loosely connected group of people. A person might not get anything in return, or she might make something happen for someone else. Through "chains of 'help,'" one might occasionally lose track of for what one owed whom and what one was owed. New friendships were born" (Pesmen 2000, 137). When I use the term *blat,* I use it broadly to indicate a network of social connections that made things happen. Otherwise I simply refer to social connections. These connections were seen as friendships, acquaintances, and even corruption. To distinguish these categories is artificial and strained at best, especially when *blat* was a network with long chains of interaction that might include any of these relationships.

Importantly, *blat* affected inequality in the Soviet system. "There was no equality in what one could get through personal channel, but there was an equality in that everyone enjoyed what his or her personal contacts provided" (Ledeneva 1998, 85). Inequality was linked to sociability instead of money. "In so far as those who had no privileges in the state distribution system could by-pass rationing and queueing it had an equalizing as well as a stratifying effect. It therefore had a bearing on the society's egalitarian claims and its actual inequalities" (36). Ledeneva does not go so far as to suggest that inequalities were tempered through *blat*—rather, it could both equalize and stratify—but the logic of inequality under the Soviet system was complicated by *blat.* Caldwell does contend that *blat* is "geared at evening out inequalities of access" (2004, 82). The most extreme inequalities were based on privileges granted to the *nomenklatura,* or party appointees, but privileges were disseminated through *blat* networks at all levels of society. "Those who did not possess power or privileges to enable them to live according to formal rules were forced to elaborate a network of acquaintances, personal connections, mutual obligations to each other" (Ledeneva 1998, 162–63). In this sense *blat* was a form of alternative power.

Giddens writes of the "two 'faces' of power"—"the capability of actors to enact decisions which they favour on the one hand and the 'mobilization of bias' that is built into institutions on the other" (1984, 15). Power is exercised through the use of "resources"—both material and bodily. Those resources are "drawn upon and reproduced by knowledgeable agents in the course of interaction" (15). This type of power is highly diffuse. For Giddens power is action. *Blat* held power in collective action.

BLAT AND BEING NEEDED

Individuals who were well positioned in *blat* networks and helped solve other people's problems "formed a stratum called 'useful people' (*nuzhnye liudi*), who were in demand when something was needed" (Ledeneva 1998, 115). They were people who entered into friendships easily and cultivated relationships that "consisted of regular access to each other's resources rather than just favour-for-favour exchanges" (115). "Useful people" is the same phrase that I have translated as needed people. Needed people were useful people in that they had something to offer. As one of Ledeneva's informants explained: "It does not matter what you can offer, nobody wants anything extraordinary, it can be just advice or information ('Sugar will be available in that shop at 6 p.m., go and get it' or 'I am going to queue for sausages, do you want half a kilo?') It is important to be useful to the other, in other words, to care" (1998, 148).

None of our informants explicitly referred to *blat.* This is not surprising given Ledeneva's discussion of the "misrecognition" (1998, 59) of *blat* whereby individuals involved did not refer to their own connections as *blat.* Instead of *blat,* interviewees, like Margarita, Galina, and others, talk about knowing people in Soviet times and not knowing people in post-Soviet times. They are referring to the collapse of networks based in large part on position vis-à-vis the Soviet state. These networks were enmeshed with the Soviet state as much as they circumvented it, and so the collapse of the state was also, to a certain degree, a collapse of social relationships. In the words of one interviewee, "Stability crumbled in all relationships." This explains why older Muscovites insist they can no longer fathom who people are when they do not understand what people do for work. Work organized social connections. As Pine and Bridger note, "The combination of policies of full employment, ideologies of collective ownership, and social construction of identity through productive work meant that a job conferred not only a wage but also mediated a set of social, economic and cultural relations between the individual and the wider community" (1998, 8).

Social relations in Soviet Russia were how people made things happen. Needed people were especially capable in this realm. What might happen through these very broad networks was never entirely predictable. It was spontaneous and felicitous, and could produce the unexpected. And yet social relations were intimately tied with order—the order of the state and people's positions in that order. That order gave social relations their efficacy and power. People could get the goods and services they needed because social relations hinged on the state through, primarily, occupation. Order gave shape to spontaneity and made it potent.

WORK AND BEING NEEDED

Informants spoke about the loss of work using the idiom of being unneeded. Below are excerpts from interviews with men, the first with an engineer and the second with an academic, that connect the loss of work to feelings of being unneeded by the state.

> Ira: And what happened in Russia during and after perestroika? How can you describe it? [. . .]
>
> Stanislav: Uncertainty in life, no desire, many did not even have a desire to live.
>
> Ira: From those changes?
>
> Stanislav: A lot of institutes, factories, collapsed. People who had worked there all their lives and knew that they had work, and that this meant that they had the means to survive, were without work. I even had good electricians, who had received the Lenin prize. Afterwards they dug ditches somewhere in order to survive. Zelenograd is an electronics city. If they closed it, then people . . . without that they had nothing, and a lot, well, it is just that I had acquaintances who even committed suicide. They couldn't handle it. This was simply not recorded and not counted.
>
> Ira: So they really suffered. . . .
>
> Stanislav: Well, people sat in one place for thirty years and suddenly they kicked them. They said you aren't needed anywhere [*ne nuzhnyi nigde*]. [. . .] He saw . . . Before he saw that he was needed [*nuzhen*] to the country, that he was in demand [*vostrebovan*], then suddenly people were simply not in demand [*vostrebovannye*] and nobody needed them [*ne nuzhny nikomu*].

And the academic:

> You need to consider that among Russians were so many specialists in the professional system—specialists who were oriented toward government offices, enterprises. They worked there for years and afterwards it was as if they were, as industry was destroyed, they ended up as if they weren't in demand [*nevostrebovannymi*] at all. Not in demand [*nevostrebovannymi*]. And what do you do in that situation? You had to break yourself—

psychologically. [. . .] That means, like soldiers, professional army men, who fought a lot and were indispensable [*neobkhodimy*], needed [*nuzhny*] and suddenly they return to a peaceful life. Some sort of posttraumatic syndrome actually.

It was not simply being without work that made people feel unneeded, but their inability to offer something to others through their work. What they had worked for—the socialist state—was now defunct, as was the place they occupied in that state. Middle-aged workers were particularly vulnerable given the fact that they were close to retirement. They did not have the time to remake themselves, nor were they already retired and shielded from restructuring. They were caught—often forced into early retirements with meager pensions. This was at a time when their experience accorded them something to offer others, particularly younger generations. Consider the following three statements from different interviewees.

It was also that moment when we could have, could have now helped. [. . .] We had already built and done so much.

What rich experience—it just seemed that we would still be needed [*nuzhny*].

Before we knew everything, but now we don't know anything.

Suddenly, when their experience and connections should have been the most needed for the state and for others around them, they were unneeded.

Yuri Ivanovich told me about his younger brother in Murmansk who had worked in a glassmaking factory that supplied parts for airplanes and submarines. He spoke of the exactness of the technology used and the strength of the glass produced. "Those were respected people, including my brother, and suddenly he found himself without work. There weren't orders. There wasn't anything." When he paused, I asked him about how his brother experienced the changes.

Very hard. He was the typical representative of the working men in this country. In that time, the factories . . . and those people. . . . They simply didn't live, but survived. They didn't pay a salary. Many were just dismissed. But he was a good mechanic and in a good division so they kept him a long time. What did they do during that time? From time to time there was suddenly some work. They paid them symbolically. They lived on that or they worked on the side. How does a mechanic or welder work on the side? Well, for example they ask him to make a fence, a fence. When they bury a person, we have that iron fence around [the plot]. So they made those iron fences. And how did they pay? It wasn't always money. They paid in vodka. So it was with my brother, and with many in this country. So he brings home vodka, cooks with his workmates. At the end of the day they drink. So did he. He began to drink. Wherever, however he could find work. And he fell, he fell.

I asked him if his brother were still alive. "He is gone. Drinking people go early." He concluded: "That was perestroika."

Yuri Ivanovich's brother had been respected as a worker under the Soviet state. When industry collapsed, people paid for his services with gifts of vodka and he drank this vodka together with his workmates. It was not clear whether his brother died from alcohol-related causes or not. Yuri Ivanovich also spoke of toxic exposure and lung cancer, and I did not push him to specify the cause of death for his deceased brother.

Many of our interviewees made a connection between the loss of work, or the threat of the loss of work, and drinking. "And now there is also a breakdown. There is no work. The people are quietly drinking themselves to death because there is nowhere to work." Or, "It was hard for husbands because they couldn't bring home money. They didn't have work. They had to apply who knows where. That's why it was as if drinking husbands were suffering." Professor Vladislav told me: "Many men are broken, drinking, having lost the meaning of life. They lose their work now." Referring to men who could not provide, a woman said, "Where did they go? Either they drink or they commit suicide." And: "A lot of [men] felt unneeded, useless, defective." Soviet work was intimately bound to being needed for Russian men.

Work served as both the site at which individuals were incorporated into the Soviet state structure and an identity by which individuals related to each other socially. It is the primary nexus of space and order explored here. But if unemployment mediated between shock therapy and mortality, it is important to turn to shock therapy itself, including the global political-economic context that facilitated it.

CHAPTER 5

Shock

How is it possible to reconstruct the soul and character of people?

—interviewee

I n the late 1980s through 1990, under Gorbachev, there was a brief period of hope before shock therapy. Shock therapy bore the mark of Milton Friedman's neoliberalism and was legitimated in the 1980s heyday of Reaganomics and Thatcherism. This chapter deals with the years of economic shock therapy from the perspective of older Muscovites. Ivan and Lidia introduce the themes of gender and inequality and their relationship to being unneeded.

RESTRUCTURING

Political scientists generally date perestroika from March 1985, when Gorbachev was appointed general secretary, to December 1991, when the USSR was dissolved and Gorbachev resigned. The vast majority of my informants did not think of perestroika in this way, but rather in its simple senses of restructuring or reconstruction.[1] For many of them perestroika had no end date even as late as 2007. Gorbachev started the process and lost control of it, Yeltsin corrupted it, and Putin managed it.

When middle-aged Muscovites became aware of the process of reform they were, for the most part, hopeful. Economic progress had slowed and there were shortages of food and household goods. They realized some change was necessary. Yet they held onto promises such as that made by the 1986 Congress of the Communist Party that each family would be provided with a separate apartment by the year 2000. They thought that reform meant that existing industries would start producing more consumer products. As one interviewee said:

> Yes, yes, yes, there was a moment, when, naturally we all really wanted that those stagnant times would turn into more rapid development. [. . .] First there wasn't enough clothing. There wasn't enough food. There wasn't enough housing. Of course, we wanted everything to be better. We felt that there wasn't enough for everyone, that someone was holding us back. And whether you wanted to or not, we felt the influence of that stagnation on us.

In the political realm, Gorbachev faced increasing opposition. Yeltsin, as the first democratically elected president of the Russian Soviet Republic in June 1991, was riding a crest of popular support. In August 1991 Yeltsin stood atop a tank in front of the Russian parliament building, known as the White House, as the defender of democracy against an attempted coup. In December of that same year, the leaders of Russia, Belarus, and the Ukraine dissolved the USSR, effectively forcing Gorbachev to resign.

Under Yeltsin in January 1992 a number of reforms were introduced as a type of economic shock therapy. They are widely regarded as a social disaster: "inexcusable from a moral perspective" (Chubarov 2001, 200) and "one of the greatest crimes committed against a democracy in modern history" (Klein 2007, 220). In a conversation about this time with Sveta's parents at their *dacha* I mentioned that the logic behind the reforms was a kind of economic shock therapy. Sveta's mother looked at me and simply said, "Nobody needs therapy like that." In the early 1990s the hope that things would improve was replaced by the realization that they would not. "We thought that we'll live better. We'll throw away everything bad and we'll improve everything. [. . .] And then it happened that our generation, especially those in their forties, were simply sacrificed. People weren't prepared at all to completely flip in that way to democracy . . . well to capitalism, because that didn't smell like democracy." They were not prepared for shock therapy. Middle-aged Muscovites, in particular, bore the brunt of the shock.

FREE MARKET MONETARISM

Keynesian economics, which advocates government regulation in the economy, dominated the global scene after World War II. With the economic slowdown of the 1970s the doctrine of the free market came to the fore. The roots of this approach lie in Milton Friedman's free market monetarism. Friedman's work at the University of Chicago spearheaded the Chicago School of Economics and garnered him a Nobel Prize in Economics in 1976. Friedman held that markets operated most optimally when unencumbered by government intervention, setting the stage for Reaganomics and Thatcherism in the 1980s.

Friedman's tenets of deregulation, privatization, and cuts to social spending were first implemented in the latter 1970s as structural adjustment programs in Latin America—in Brazil, Argentina, Chile, and Uruguay. Friedman himself coined the term "shock treatment" on a visit to Chile in 1975 (Klein 2007, 81). The treatment came with side effects: inflation, unemployment, curtailed social services, increased poverty, and new forms of inequality. Harvard economist Jeffrey Sachs applied similar principles to market reform in Bolivia before he moved to Poland and then Russia. Sachs's approach, known as the big bang or shock therapy, was a bit more humane than that of the Chicago School. He believed economic reform should be accompanied by international aid and debt forgiveness. Unfortunately, by the time of shock therapy in Russia, the global community would not commit to anywhere near the amount of international aid necessary to preserve the country from economic collapse.

In the following I try to remain faithful to the perceptions of older middle-aged Muscovites, some of whom spoke about capitalism, the market, and government regulation, if not neoliberalism. Like the scholars Collier (2011) critiques, they employ labels as shorthand for complicated processes that were, in many senses, beyond the control of neoliberal ideologues and technocrats, whether Russian or foreign. I try to stay close to the everyday realities of the early 1990s—loss of work, unpaid salaries, shortages, rising prices, hunger, worthless privatization vouchers, poverty. These were the concerns of middle-aged Muscovites, many of whom were pragmatic. They cared about ideology when they discovered that ideology and its political-economic vehicles informed their social possibilities.

A COLLISION OF LOGICS

The dominant logic of Soviet socialism at the time this generation came of age was a radiant future (*svetloe budushchee*) built over time through Soviet labor. In Soviet ideology, history was progressive. A better life and a better society always lay ahead. It may have been necessary to sacrifice, but the ideology of a radiant future did not account for periods of regression. Regression was the fate of capitalist societies with their never-ending cycles of boom and bust. During their formative years, middle-aged Muscovites saw progress around them. With war as the backdrop, progress was evident in postwar reconstruction, the construction of Moscow, increased consumerism, and the scientific and technological revolution of the 1950s, including the accomplishments of the space program. In the 1960s, the expansion of housing served as further proof of Soviet progress.

The logic of economic shock therapy flew in the face of the Soviet ideal of progress. Neoliberal economics holds that "markets can spontaneously create a new world if the old can first be destroyed. Shock therapy's package of price liberalization, stabilization, and privatization aims to dissolve the past by the fastest means possible. . . . It is neoliberalism's pious hope that destruction is the vehicle for genesis" (Burawoy and Verdery 1999, 5). In order for economic shock therapy to succeed, things had to get worse before they could get better. The fruits of Soviet labor—state industry in particular—had to be destroyed. Destruction, not construction, was the guiding logic, at least in the initial stages of reform.

According to Sachs, the Western author of shock therapy, the reason shock therapy did not succeed in Russia was because Russian technocrats were not thorough enough: "Despite the [*sic*] all of the uproar in recent years about 'shock therapy' in Russia, knowledgeable observers understand that it simply never occurred, an obvious point when one compares Russia's disorganized and partial stabilization efforts with the decisive actions in the Czech Republic, Estonia, or Poland" (1995, 53). The implication is that what happened in Russia was not a Western-prescribed program of reform but a uniquely Russian endeavor. Russians are ultimately held responsible for the chaos of the 1990s.

Middle-aged Muscovites mourn what has been destroyed. At the same time, they contest the discontinuity that destruction projects onto their lives. In the chapter on work, Viktor and Vera, in particular, were adamant that younger Russians were benefiting from the sacrifice and labor of older generations. Vera told Sveta, "You are still living on what our generation built." And Viktor proclaimed that "All of present-day democratic Russia . . . rests on what that [wartime] generation built." This couple refused to accept that their life work had been destroyed, even as they mourned the destruction of Soviet society and its social relations.

SHOCK THERAPY

After the dissolution of the Soviet Union, young Russian and Harvard technocrats, headed by economists Yegor Gaidar and Sachs respectively, wasted no time in transforming Russia's centralized socialist economy. The plan began with price liberalization and the withdrawal of state subsidies. With the end of price controls, the government expected prices to treble. In fact, they rose ten to twelvefold (Chubarov 2001). Inflation of consumer prices, which in 1992 rose 1,490 percent (World Bank 2013), meant that the price of basic necessities jumped steeply upward. People's assets, accumulated over a lifetime, lost practically all of their value within a few months. People lost their savings.[2] Among interviewees, lifelong savings of five, ten, and twelve thousand rubles were lost.

In tandem with these developments, there was a severe industrial contraction whereby production was halved in a matter of years (Chubarov 2001). Many people lost their jobs.

> Even though we worked at those factories, I didn't expect that it would flop. They suddenly failed. Yes, and I never even thought that industry would come to a stop.

> Everyone was really nervous and suffered. Work was up in the air. [. . .] And where would they take you if everything was closed?

> Whoever worked at factories, that was very . . . that was it. Everything was shuttered. [. . .] Everything fell apart into OOO [LLC, limited liability companies] and EEE or something—into those shreds.

Those who kept their jobs often were not paid or were paid in kind. People remembered not being paid for six, seven, and eight months. Official and partial unemployment peaked at 14 percent (Chubarov 2001)—a level that does not account for those working without a salary. In a society where guaranteed employment was a basic tenet of social justice, this was previously unimaginable. Industry was the backbone of the Soviet economy. As the interviewee above said, "I never even thought that industry would come to a stop." In many factories, it did indeed stop as the backbone of the Soviet economy was broken.

The shock of unemployment was not restricted to those who lost their jobs but affected everyone who understood that their work and basic needs were no longer secure and they were expendable. "I think it all happened, in part, uncontrolled. If they had told people that, 'Your enterprise will go bust. You will be left without work. You will live on kopeks. They will even not pay anyone their salary for eight months.' It was as if there was no money in the country. It was terrible." Younger workers moved from one sector of the economy to another hoping to find the elusive higher salaries of a free market. "Many left in all directions. [. . .] But the older ones who were just under fifty [. . .] where would they go? There was a saying: 'Thirty, maximum forty years old and that's it.'" Older workers did not have the time to retrain, change specialties, or wait for industry to recover.

Inflation, unemployment, and salary arrears meant that the majority of Russians struggled to make ends meet, but the situation of the middle aged was especially dire as they saw their expected future evaporate. "I began to fight for my subsistence," said one older man. They stopped eating meat and lived, in some cases, entirely on bread, potatoes, or macaroni. They sold odds and ends on the street for extra income. "There was nothing for people to live on. They began to sell, practically their silverware, all of that." It was not simply that prices were rising and income was not rising to the same degree for the majority of the population. It was also that no one knew if or when it would end. "The hardest times were under Yeltsin when they didn't pay my pension for half a year. They didn't give my husband his salary. I was already [newly] retired. [. . .] If you eat some piece of meat you try to boil it and feed your husband—and myself some edge on a bit of bread. [. . .] Under Yeltsin tomorrow was on the whole a dead end." Uncertainty, even fear, was augmented by an absence of state regulation and control. Levels of crime rose and the Russian mafia appeared on the streets to fill the vacuum, offering protection to businesses for a price. A prominent Moscow State University political scientist involved in polling at the time told me that the catchword was order (*poriadok*)—people simply desired a return to social order and stability. "Many began to look back to Brezhnev's days with nostalgia, realizing that stability in life had its own definite value and that, at times, 'stagnation' was more desirable than reforms and changes" (Chubarov 2001, 149).

Following price liberalization and withdrawal of state subsidies, public assets were privatized. Anatoly Chubais, under Gaidar, was in charge of privatization, which began with "voucher privatization" or "the people's privatization." Every Russian citizen would receive a voucher worth ten thousand rubles—an appreciable sum at the end of 1991 roughly equivalent to the value of a new Lada car. According to the plan, people would be able to cash in their vouchers or purchase shares in newly privatized enterprises in 1993. Unfortunately, by 1993, after a year of rampant inflation, the vouchers were next to worthless. In Chubarov's assessment, "The result of Chubais' voucher privatization was that all Russians for a moment became candidates for property ownership, only to discover the next moment that most of them were effectively excluded from owning a slice of the former state assets" (2001, 205). People sold vouchers for about forty rubles each wherever they found buyers. An early incarnation of the MMM financial pyramid scheme began to collect privatization vouchers in an investment scheme. "MMM invest turns your vouchers into gold!" promised the television advertisements (Hoffman 2003, 219). As one interviewee summarized:

> Then they began to create . . . front men . . . those pyramids. For forty rubles people brought vouchers. You could turn them in there. One person sold them, another waited. Another sold them for a bottle. Everyone did whatever. And afterwards someone collected them and they privatized [state assets]. The result was they privatized all of our energy supply. In sum they fooled us. They lied to us. We never loved Chubais, we don't love him, and we won't love him.[3]

Margarita still has her vouchers; by the time she wanted to redeem them she could not find any organization accepting them. Her experience was not unique. "They gave us vouchers which we could never turn in anywhere." Another interviewee simply said, "They shafted the people."

In another privatization program shares were distributed to employees of enterprises. Management often bought back workers' shares. One woman who had a personal connection to the head accountant of a clothing company received a call from the accountant's assistant. "'Do you want to make a pretty penny?' I said, "Who doesn't want to?' 'Well, come,' she said, 'we'll go tomorrow morning.' So I was on the committee where we enumerated how many shares all of our workers, each one, had." When she sold the stock she had received and purchased, she received three thousand rubles per share while, according to her, all the other "girls" received fifteen hundred. She received seventy-five thousand rubles and used a third of her windfall to buy a refrigerator and stove before putting away the rest for her burial. When she told this story to Ira, fifty thousand rubles were worth close to two thousand U.S. dollars. Ira, incredulous, asked her if she meant fifty thousand in today's rubles. She did. She alluded to an agreement between managers.

Stanislav, a foreman in the electronics industry, described how vouchers were taken from the workers by factory directors and party bosses "who had connections to buy that factory for kopeks. [. . .] Then bigger sharks bought them out or beat them out. Then it developed into whoever had the greatest possibilities, the most connections grabbed and sliced away." In 1995 all pretense of "the people's privatization" was dropped, and remaining state assets were auctioned off under a program dubbed loans-for-shares.[4] Bankers and businessmen with connections to Yeltsin acquired the state's assets for a pittance. This group became Russia's oligarchy. Interviewees reserved much of their acrimony for the oligarchy. "Without any profession, he's a millionaire, and for him you are . . . Who needs anyone anywhere? [. . .] By means of what labor did they achieve it? Deceit! Speculation! And it is permitted—that is the question!" Compared to an increasingly wealthy oligarchy, ordinary workers' social status was diminished. According to more than one interviewee, privatization was a crime. Millionaires stole their riches from the people without any retribution. One middle-aged Muscovite man ominously remembered a time when such people would have been shot.

There is some debate as to how much economic and social inequality actually increased during the years of economic shock therapy, since inequality was officially nonexistent in Soviet times. According to World Bank data, the Gini index, a measure of inequality in society where 0 represents complete equality and 1 complete inequality, was 0.24 in 1988 and reached its zenith in 1993 at 0.48.[5] In 2009 it was 0.40, a value comparable to the United States (World Bank 2013). Of course, it is difficult to assess the validity of 1988 data and the comparability of these two figures. However, there is no doubt that inequality was much more visible.

IN THEIR OWN WORDS

This generation of Muscovites described the early 1990s as a time of collapse, upheaval, disorder, decay, wildness. The period itself was characterized by chaos, madness, mutiny, thievery, the grabbing of power and profit. It was "the organized destruction of a country" or "the crime of wild capitalism against organized socialism." In their evocative phrasing, the fall of the Soviet Union and all that ensued was "a cultural revolution," "the opening of another world," "as if the world had burst open." It meant "the loss of the sense of life," "the loss of a future," and "the decay of the spirit." People experienced it as a radical upheaval of society. It was decidedly not reform. The word *perestroika* was a euphemism for something else—revolution, or worse. "As in one of our songs it is sung 'To the foundation we destroy and then we'll take it and build a new world.'" One Muscovite explained, "And it was . . . it was so-called . . . In my opinion it was not perestroika. It was simply an apocalypse. It was simply all devastation. Perestroika is when we make a new house from our old *dacha,* right? When we know what we want. But then nobody knew what, who, what they wanted." When I told Professor Vladislav my interest in that time he asked me when I had first come to Russia.

> Michelle: The first time was 1993.
> Professor Vladislav: And did you see?
> Michelle: Yes, I saw.
> Professor Vladislav: The year 93 was very . . . the process, you saw it, right?
> Michelle: Yes, I was in Peter [St. Petersburg].
> Professor Vladislav: The feeling of decline, true, yes, even superficially—
> the dark streets, the drawn faces, yes, people poorly dressed, poorly lit
> [*osveshchenny*]. . . .

People's hopes that change would still bring a radiant future were well and truly extinguished by 1993.

As the Russian author of shock reform, Gaidar is widely reviled. Viktor, the secondary school history teacher, said that the country had been betrayed. "Although it was necessary to change—to put a market economy into place. But with government regulation. Name me one government with a market economy where the government relinquishes everything." He referred to an interview in which Gaidar maintained that his program of price liberalization saved Russia from famine, civil war, and extinction. He called that a lie. He thought Gaidar would do better to ask forgiveness of the Russian people. One man said he could not stand to see Gaidar. When he found out that Gaidar had been poisoned, but lived, at the end of 2006, he thought, "'Why didn't they poison him to the death?' No, but [. . .] he grabbed money from the whole country, from each person. He did that and that's why he will still answer for that on the Day of Judgment." That day may have already come. Gaidar died in December 2009 at only fifty-four years of age of complications of cardiovascular disease.

The metaphors used to describe this time are instructive. The country "ran free" and people were "fish in muddy waters," unable to see and easily duped by the government, banks, and schemes. "No leader appeared. No idea appeared. It was as if they sicced a sitting dog. They sicced a dog and all hell broke loose, I think of it like that. And then the country ran loose. And on the sly whoever got their bearings, they started to catch fish in muddy waters." Social norms became opaque. "Horrible, and people still didn't understand anything. They rushed from one extreme to another. One person made a killing. Another didn't. Everyone went their own way." Some were like fish caught in "muddy waters"; some did the fishing. Ivan's and Lidia's accounts of this time highlight particular experiences of this generation in the early 1990s as their lives, along with the state and economy, were painfully transformed.

Ivan

I first met Ivan, an English teacher, at a meeting of the English club I attended in Moscow. He is a tall, lean man with a slight stoop. His dark hair is thinning in the back. He was polite and soft-spoken, but also excitable. On certain topics he became agitated and even angry. Besides teaching English at a secondary school and two institutes of higher education, he gives private English lessons to children from well-to-do families. He is married to a former student, twenty years his junior, and they have two young daughters. The second one was born during my stay in Moscow.

He was apologetic when he first invited me to his home in southeast Moscow. They have two very narrow adjoining rooms in a barrack, or a dormitory originally constructed for workers. When we stepped off the bus he pointed to where a bomb had blown up apartment buildings across the street in September 1999, one of a spate of apartment bombings that month in Russia. The staircase of Ivan's building is wide and would be quite grand were it not in such a state of neglect. There is litter strewn about; drywall and plaster covers the cement floor; graffiti covers the walls. The dank smell of alcohol and urine permeates the dim entryway. As is common in five-story buildings in Moscow, there is no elevator. There is a communal bath-room—where I once saw water running on an enormous pile of unattended laundry—and a communal kitchen on each floor of the building where occu-pants have an electric burner or two. This is where Ivan's wife, Olya, some-times cooks with her baby in a sling and her toddler on the floor nearby, although she prefers to use an electric steamer in one of their rooms.

The first time I visited them, Ivan exchanged words with his neighbor in the broad hallway. Electricity charges from 2004 either had or had not been paid by the neighbor. The cashier at the utility company told Ivan that the debt had not been paid. His neighbor, however, had already collected Ivan's share of 575 rubles and shown him a receipt of payment. As we stepped inside the small private entryway connecting the two narrow rooms, Ivan told me his neighbors were uncultured and he preferred not to interact with them, but they would now need to arrange a time to visit the utility company together.[6]

Before I conducted an interview with Ivan, I had not realized that he had ever been anything but an English teacher. Pointing to a collection of Lenin's works on a shelf above the doorway, he told me that he taught secondary school history until 1991 when he was thirty-eight years old.

> Ivan: But when perestroika began, I observed a lot of incorrect things, a lot
>   of false things and I refused to teach history. I was left without bread.
> Michelle: You refused?
> Ivan: Yes, I refused.
> Michelle: And why?
> Ivan: Because of the many incorrect things, the many lies.
> Michelle: For example?
> Ivan: About the history of our country, and about the history of other
>   countries. About world history. About capitalism and socialism. We
>   already know how socialism ended. But we believed in it—really
>   believed—and now it turns out that we were deceived and I refused to do
>   history because it is lies. Each time history is rewritten under new leaders.

A few minutes later he explained: "I lectured, I taught, and what, it turns out, came out is that I taught lies. That which was written in books, that which they taught us at [the institute], that is what I taught." Ivan felt he couldn't relearn and teach a new history if and when it ever came. "And I couldn't anymore, simply reeducate myself again. Wait until everything is organized and truth is apparent. And I understood that truth would never come to light now. It will not be. Nobody knows that truth—how, what, which was. For that I need one more life to live out, and there is no more time. I was already too old." The head teacher at the school suggested Ivan teach English instead. At first he was only one lesson ahead of his students, but he was motivated by the need to earn a living. He returned to university and received another degree in the department of foreign languages and then stayed on to teach there too.

Before the fall of the Soviet state, Ivan had a savings of ten thousand rubles, which likely represented seven to nine years' base salary. He was waiting to be assigned an apartment. In a matter of a few months Ivan's life savings was worth almost nothing, and there would be no apartment. With his savings, he bought a cheap jacket for two hundred rubles at the market, which still hangs in the closet. When I asked him to describe the early 1990s in two words Ivan said, ruefully, "the fall of the spirit." The phrase is sometimes translated as despondency in English. "The fall of the spirit . . . and an absolute uncertainty about the future. There is no future." I wondered if perhaps now, fifteen years hence, he saw a future for Russia. He raised his voice. "Russia has no future. Russia has no future." Ivan is affronted by new economic inequality:

> It is perfectly understood that a normal person working a full workday even . . . even sixteen hours like I do [. . .] . . . doing any honest work cannot earn billions, millions. It is possible to earn . . . Well how much? I don't know. Well let it be even five thousand [U.S. dollars] per month— more than enough for our country. I would agree that they could earn five thousand. But millions per month is not possible in any normal, honest way. You can only steal that, like they did. They stole enterprises, they privatized. They took away our checks. I gave away a check and millions of people gave vouchers to savings banks. We thought they were specially organized, that we would receive profit. But they stole everything for themselves and consequently got those enterprises, plants, factories from the government.

He began to speak about Potanin, an oligarch who acquired his wealth by first proposing and then profiting from the loan-for-shares program.

> He has a huge nickel production plant. That plant is worth, I don't know, billions. From where does a person, one person, have enough money to buy that? Even if it were a low price. [. . .] It isn't possible for a normal, simple person to get that somewhere and buy that. That is only attainable through theft. And that is how they [. . .] stole for themselves and calmly sit around pontificating about laws, about democracy.

Ivan told me that he did not mind if there were wealthy people as long as others could live "worthily, normally." He thought it was absurd that some people living in poverty could not afford food and others were "swimming in fat." "They do not know what to do with their money. They buy sports teams, yachts, the pyramids in Egypt."

In the summertime Olya and the girls stay at the *dacha* 250 kilometers from Moscow where Ivan is building a modest country home. Ivan says he no longer has time to suffer. He only has time to survive, raise his girls, and construct the *dacha*. "A lot of people lost their spirit, lost their faith. They took to drink. They were unemployed, without food. There was nothing to live on. They were thrown out. Millions of people were thrown out on the street, from their work. They closed companies, factories. . . . What were people supposed to live on?" He told me, "I survived all of these hard years, fifteen years. I haven't taken to drink."

The fall of the Soviet Union represents a real rupture in Ivan's life, and he was perhaps the most embittered person interviewed. Older respondents, while unhappy with their lot, were resigned to it in as far as they were now too old to do much about it. Ivan responded to the changes. He works long hours and is unable to provide as he would like for his family. Ivan told me that teaching was an acceptable career for a woman but not for a man. He claimed that most of his female colleagues were living on their businessmen husbands' earnings.

Living in a barrack without much extra income has taxed Ivan's marriage. More than once Ivan and Olya have separated. Olya feels Ivan is failing her as a husband. She wants a better life for herself and her children. For his part, Ivan doesn't feel Olya fulfills her duties at home as a wife, cooking and cleaning. At one point Ivan's father-in-law told him that perhaps Olya would do more housework if she lived in a decent apartment—a prospect that looks increasingly unlikely given the rising values of Moscow real estate.

Lidia

Lidia's experience was, in some sense, more harrowing than Ivan's, but she was much less embittered. Lidia lived on the same plot of land where she was born, about thirty kilometers to the northwest of Moscow in the Moscow Oblast' that surrounds the city. Lidia's parents built the house in the 1960s. An electric train line ran behind the back fence of Lidia's yard and stopped at a station about a kilometer away. A dirt road along the train line led the way back to the house.

The dark green wooden house was in the Russian country style with decoratively carved white window frames and white lace curtains. The yard was left to nature except for a small garden during the summer. In rain or during the spring thaw the yard filled with mud and visitors walked over wooden planks until they reached the front steps, which led up to a mudroom, full of shoes, boots, overcoats, and assorted Russian house slippers (*tufli*) available for anyone. Beyond the entryway, there was a small kitchen, sitting room, and two bedrooms off the sitting room. During the year I visited, new wallpaper with green vertical vines was hung in the sitting room and a new dresser installed in the corner as part of preparations for the marriage of Lidia's son. A few years earlier, pipes were installed for running water in the kitchen. There was an outhouse in the back.

Lidia was not in good health. In her twenties, she spent half a year hospitalized and was officially disabled.[7] She has been married twice to men who drank. Her second husband died of alcohol poisoning in 1990 when their second child was three years old. She worked at home for twelve years, often until two in the morning while her children were sleeping, knitting and sewing for a local factory that employed the disabled. In the early 1990s, the factory for the disabled was closed. When food coupons were issued for basics such as bread, meat, butter, and eggs, Lidia would leave her nine-year-old son in the bread line, which extended across the market square, while she took her five-year-old daughter shopping for other groceries. They went without meat.

Yet Lidia said, "Well, generally that perestroika time, because I am a homebody, it didn't touch me very much. Because I'm like in my own little world, in my circle. [It was] as if I were defended, in this shell, my house, my fortress." She thought that women with families were protected to some extent. "If a woman has a family then, of course, it was easier for a woman. If she was without a family and a business woman, like they say now, then of course it was also hard because industry, everything completely changed." Lidia described perestroika in terms of a loss of belief.

> A person should always have belief in something, because only belief makes a person strong. And if during the Great Patriotic War only belief made a person strong—belief in meeting one's loved ones—so in the times, so to say, before the Great October Revolution, belief was the foundation. There are those ideas like Old Believers, right? It is the fortress of the soul, spirituality. Belief, that is. They were united around this belief. Throughout time it was the foundation of a person's life. So here, when there was no more socialist government and no belief in stability [. . .] everyone ran about [*kidalis'*]. And throughout time, man searches for somewhere to run [*kinut'sia*].

While *kidat'sia* (in the form *kidalis'* above) has the sense of running amok, *kinut'sia* implies movement in a purposeful direction. Belief in a future— after the war, in the afterlife, in socialism—"makes a person strong" and gives a person "somewhere to run."

Lidia was philosophical about the changes.

> Well, it is like it always is in Russia. We destroy the old world. [. . .] And of course there are those who take advantage of the destruction. As always, when some try to do something and others try to pocket it all, to pilfer as much as possible. It is like that. Well, simply a collapse occurred and that's it, nothing else, I think, a collapse—everything disordered. Before there was some sort of radiant future to hold on to, some sort of faith, although not in God. But something, in something, if only in a radiant future. As if we waited for something, especially in the year 2000 when they promised to give each person a separate apartment. [. . .] Yes, generally we all, yes, aspired to a better future, created that better future. And then we stopped aspiring to anything. The old values disappeared. Like in the beginning we had no God. Now that socialism, radiant future didn't happen and nothing else has appeared on the horizon. And it has simply been a full collapse.

While society has changed around her, she thinks she herself has remained the same, struggling to make ends meet and care for her children. She prefers "everything *sovkovoe*," or Soviet-style. "I have not yet restructured myself. And my kids also grew up without perestroika, still with that *sovkovym* mentality also. And that is why now it is very hard for them to integrate." She and her family lived modestly, not far from the first Russian IKEA and a grandiose MEGA mall, which she had never seen.

GENDER AND BEING NEEDED

Ivan and Lidia both told me about difficult times in the early 1990s. Ivan lost savings, an expected apartment, and his career as a history teacher. Lidia lost her second husband and then her work. Yet they had very different reactions. Ivan is bitter about his losses and feels he cannot adequately provide for Olya and the girls despite his best efforts in the new economy. Lidia feels she was protected at home and has remained the same. Lidia receives some meager state support due to her disabled status, but this support does not do much to ease the poverty of her family. While these are but two individuals, their stories illustrate something about gender and being unneeded in the Russian context.

In Soviet times needed people were engaged in state work and social practices of redistribution of favors and goods. Thus they had something to offer the state and others around them. In the early 1990s this feeling may have been particularly compromised for men, who found themselves peripheral to state, industry, and family. Women, at least, were still needed to hold their families together. In a sense, Ivan is still needed, in that he is the sole breadwinner in his family. But it is also true that he feels he cannot offer Olya and his girls what he should be able to. He is still needed because he is still giving, but he is not giving enough. The threat of unneededness was palpable. He took solace in the things he could do—build a *dacha,* raise and protect his daughters.

In Russia, women are often regarded as more flexible, pragmatic, and long-suffering. Interviewees told me that Russian women were better equipped to confront hardship and social change. Russian women, they said, are resilient and hardy. Under the Soviet system, women's double or triple burdens (LaFont 2001; Verdery 1996) meant that they worked outside the home and were also responsible for housework, children, and husbands.

They were used to the daily struggle to feed and clothe their families. Many interviewees felt that women's central role in the family preserved them in the early 1990s. Interviewees disagreed whether this made the early 1990s harder for men or women. One woman claimed that it was harder for men in the early 1990s because it had always been easier for them. "It seems to me it was harder for men than women. Why? Because the harder yoke has always fallen to women." Women were used to hardship. According to another woman, a man might drink and forget everything else, even his responsibility as breadwinner. Women's cares were less easily forgotten. In this sense the early 1990s were harder for women because "she is the master at home." "A man hopes his wife will figure it out," said another interviewee. Vera, who described herself and her husband as children of the war, said: "The family hearth—everything depends on the woman, Sveta, and don't believe anyone [else]. Everything, the happiness of the family, peace, quiet—that depends on the woman. However bad a man is, a woman can make anything out of him." As Professor Vladislav said, women were now the saviors. Women were expected to fight for their family. "You always need to fight, always need to fight, most of all for your loved ones."

The responsibility for children was central to the explanations of why women did better in the early 1990s. As one woman said, "A woman always, even if she loses her husband, she is still with her children and she doesn't give up. She doesn't give up. But a man somehow quickly loses interest in life." Interviewees thought that family responsibilities gave women's lives purpose and direction. "So a woman tries to be needed in whatever situation—to find herself somewhere where she is really needed. A woman keeps herself in hand. More so women who have children." A woman is needed because others depend on her. One academic told me that women give and preserve life, and that is why they live longer than men. Rephrasing a verse from the Bible he explained, "Whoever saves the life of another shall live long." Especially in the chaos of the early 1990s, women were needed more than ever.

Men, on the other hand, might lose themselves in times of difficulty. "With men it is more complicated of course. It is hard for a man to find himself." In the early 1990s more men were peripheral to the state, industry, and daily family life; they were more likely to go adrift when they were not able to fulfill their role as breadwinner. "They closed factories, right, and something like that. And men . . . as changes [occurred] in the family life, a man lay on the sofa and began to drink. That's it. He lost his bearings and lost himself, and what was a woman to do? She conquered and began to hustle." Even if men retained their work and their salaries, their paychecks were no longer worth what they had been, in monetary or moral terms. Their status as breadwinner was diminished, especially in an environment where, by the mid-1990s, income inequality was glaringly obvious.

In the quotations above, women "find themselves" while men "lose themselves." A woman tries "to find herself somewhere where she is really needed." But, "It is hard for a man to find himself." He loses "his bearings and [. . .] himself." In one case "finding herself" is explicitly linked to being needed: "So a woman tries to be needed in whatever situation—to find herself somewhere where she is really needed." Finding oneself, in English, has a connotation of realizing who one truly is and what one truly wants to do—to be in touch with a unique self, separate and apart from others. Here, the meaning is quite different. Finding oneself is tied to finding one's place of neededness among others—having a sense of how others depend on oneself and knowing how important one is to others, especially family. People who have nothing to offer others are not connected to others and are in danger of being lost. The self here is constituted through relationships with others and thus can be lost without these relationships.

Women find themselves in their ability to give to others. In its most fundamental formulation this is about women's ability to give and preserve life—by giving birth, of course, but also by raising children and sometimes by saving men from themselves. Men's neededness—being needed by others—is more tenuous.

This talk, of course, portrays gender difference as natural, and reflects the particulars of Russian patriarchy and feminism. The point here is that women were still needed in the early 1990s because they had something to offer others. They could still make things happen for themselves and others. It is probable that the collapse of the economy compromised men's social networks more than women's, given the contraction of the industrial sector and the expansion of the service sector, where men and women, respectively, were disproportionately employed in Soviet times. Women's access to consumer goods and services was particularly important during shock therapy. In addition, women may have been more likely to use their social connections during Soviet times to fulfill daily needs whereas men were more likely to have secured favors through state bureaucracy (Ledeneva 1998, 119–21).

In the early 1990s the state was defunct, but daily needs—food, clothing—still had to be satisfied.

Russian women have long found refuge from politics and the state in the family (Gal and Kligman 2000; Kürti 2000; Rivkin-Fish 2004; Watson 1993). Family-oriented traditionalism has been offered as an explanation for women's relative resilience in terms of mortality (Palosuo 2000; Saburova et al. 2011; Watson 1995). Western feminism lacks appeal among many Russian women (Boym 2001; Bridger, Kay, and Pinnick 1996; Gal and Kligman 2000; Hemment 2004b; Kürti 2000; Verdery 1996; Watson 1993) who see it as a threat to the family (LaFont 2001). Russian women want more male participation in the family (Gal and Kligman 2000; Rivkin-Fish 2004) and are prepared to help their husbands achieve success (Meshcherkina 2000). To many Russian women a men's movement makes more sense than a women's movement (Boym 2001; du Plessix Gray 1989).

While women worked even harder to hold their families together, men were unable to financially support their families as before. In her ethnography of homelessness in St. Petersburg in the late 1990s, Höjdestrand found that "many homeless men seemed to think that the incapacity to perform the conventional breadwinning functions justified a total abandonment of family life as such, even in cases involving motherless children" (2009, 127). Women's responsibility of caring for others may have preserved them even as it burdened them. Men lost themselves without much to give to others—when they felt unneeded.

INEQUALITY

Another theme explicitly emphasized in Ivan's account is increasing social inequality. As we have seen in the previous chapter, this generation struggled to make sense of new wealth and blatant socioeconomic inequalities. Vast personal fortunes were amassed during the years of shock therapy. To a generation raised with the ethic of socially useful work, this seemed criminal and immoral. In 1992, Russians began to refer to the "nouveaux riches," but this early inequality was mild compared to the class of elite businessmen, bankers, and oligarchs that emerged in 1994 and 1995.

Older Muscovites struggled to make ends meet during the early 1990s. Their struggle took place in a city of increasingly ostentatious inequality. The inequality may have been just as important as the struggle itself. Although social inequality had existed in Soviet society, the logic of inequality had changed from access to goods and favors to the accumulation of wealth for conspicuous consumption. This new logic asserted itself most forcefully in the urban space of Moscow where power has long been concentrated. New wealth was flaunted, maligning Soviet ideals, especially for the generations that had come of age after the Great Patriotic War at the height of the Soviet state. Referring to Brezhnev's time, a time of growing cynicism, one man said:

> At least then during the stagnation we all lived roughly alike. Of course the managing workers, especially in the communist branch, all the party organizers and so on and higher . . . but then we didn't have . . . not large-scale, not large-scale. All the rest were roughly living the same. When someone had a good profession, he received more. But now the people have just lost their conscience.

Professor Vladislav told me about a sense of estrangement or alienation that arose between people with the advent of the "cult of money."

Wilkinson's work on inequality (Wilkinson and Pickett 2009; Wilkinson 1994, 1996, 2005) proposes that relative deprivation is more important than absolute deprivation in predicting life expectancy in industrialized countries. Income inequality explains health disparities between developed countries as well as within those countries. This position, while not without its detractors (Deaton 2003), emphasizes the deleterious effects of inequality on social relations, eroding trust, respect, and reputation.

Income inequality is but one form of inequality that affects health. Status goes beyond income. Michael Marmot headed the Whitehall studies in the United Kingdom which demonstrated graduated differences in mortality among civil servants according to employment grade. Since then, evidence for a social gradient of health has accumulated from around the world. In his book, *The Status Syndrome,* Marmot (2004) points to the importance of autonomy and social participation in explaining the gradient.

The World Health Organization's Commission on Social Determinants of Health, chaired by Marmot, reports: "Poverty is not only lack of income. The implication, both of the social gradient in health and the poor health of the poorest of the poor, is that health inequity is caused by the unequal distribution of income, goods, and services and of the consequent chance of leading a flourishing life" (CSDH 2008, 31). The final report of the commission identifies material circumstances, social cohesion, psychosocial factors, behaviors, and biological factors as mediators between socioeconomic status and health (CSDH 2008).

In epidemiology, social cohesion and psychosocial factors go by many different names. Social cohesion includes social capital, or civil society (Solar and Irwin 2007). Psychosocial factors include life events, job strain, job insecurity, perceived control, locus of control, coping style, social support, and social exclusion. Many of these variables have been used in studies on mortality in Russia. However, in an interim report of the WHO commission Solar and Irwin identify a key weakness of this literature: "It has become commonplace among population health researchers to acknowledge that the health of individuals and populations is strongly influenced by SDH [social determinants of health]. It is much less common to aver that the quality of SDH is in turn shaped by the policies that guide how societies (re)distribute material resources among their members" (2007, 21). In other words, the variables mentioned above become attributes of individuals and their communities rather than attributes of political economy. It is also true that, in an era of globalization, policies are situated in the global economy. Shock therapy in Russia is an especially good example of how political and economic policies result from a particular global history.

SHOCK THERAPY AND MORTALITY

No account of excess deaths in Russia would be complete without the historical backdrop of the rise of neoliberal capitalism on the global stage from the 1970s onward. The collapse of the Soviet Union only served to further the arguments for a free market economy with less government regulation. By the early 1990s shock therapy was considered a proven strategy of economic reform.

Mortality increased most steeply in 1992 and 1993 (Shkolnikov, Cornia et al. 1998). In a recent study, mass privatization—the transfer of at least 25 percent of large state-owned industries to the private sector—was associated with mortality among working-age men across countries of the former Soviet Union (Stuckler, King, and McKee 2009). The authors estimate three quarters of the increase in Russian adult male mortality between 1992 and 1994 may be attributable to mass privatization. During these years over half of all state-owned enterprises were privatized. The authors address the Western architect of economic shock therapy directly.

> In a famous essay, and a series of other papers setting out the shock therapy package, Jeffrey Sachs argued that, "the need to accelerate privatization is the paramount economic policy issue facing Eastern Europe. If there is no breakthrough in the privatization of large enterprises in the near future, the entire process could be stalled for years to come. Privatization is urgent and politically vulnerable." Did slow privatization hurt the prospects for capitalism? Is Slovenia—one of the most gradual privatisers—any less capitalist than is Ukraine? In fact, by approaching transformation rapidly and radically, prospects for western-style capitalism might have been seriously impaired in countries like Russia. Countries that privatized more slowly managed to reach a capitalist endpoint but did not absorb nearly the same amount of social costs along the way. (Stuckler, King, and McKee 2009, 406)

Stuckler, King, and McKee suggest unemployment mediated the relationship between shock therapy and mortality, noting that unemployment meant more than the loss of a job "in view of the wider parts played by firms from the former Soviet Union in provision of housing, education, childcare, and preventive health care" (2009, 405). Other studies also point to unemployment as a driver of mortality. Walberg and colleagues (1998) use regional data to propose a model of increased mortality in areas with a combination of high labor-force turnover, crime, and inequality. Perlman and Bobak (2009) use statistical models to test the associations between mortality and self-reported unemployment, wage arrears, compulsory leave, payment in goods, and job insecurity. But only compulsory leave among women was significantly associated with mortality during the study period from 1994 to 2003.[8] It seems that unemployment, while undoubtedly important, is only one part of the story.

New forms of social inequality undercut a Soviet generation's identity with roots in the shared sacrifices of war and reconstruction. It also marked Soviet achievements as misguided, worthy of abandonment or destruction. By extension, Soviet workers did not feel valued. There is a holistic story that ties together global, Soviet, and Russian political economy and Soviet and Russian social relations; ideas about sacrifice and collectivity; socially useful work and social connections; and gender and inequality. The position of not having anything to give, of being unneeded, is central. In the early 1990s Russia the country itself had nothing to offer the world; in fact, it was desperately in need of foreign aid. The destruction of the state and its economy compromised social relations, which were enmeshed in the organization of the state. Changes in the global political economy, then, resulted in the most intimate and fatal repercussions for individuals.

It is one thing to describe social turmoil and another to delineate how this results in disease and death of individuals. Clearly, an epidemiology that restricts risk factors to the attributes of individuals or their communities is necessary but insufficient to tell the story of Russian mortality. In the next chapters we return to mortality and an anthropological reading of the epidemiology of the mortality crisis.

CHAPTER 6

Mortality

The historical divergence in life expectancy between Eastern and Western Europe since the 1960s has been called the East-West divide (Vàgerö and Illsley 1992). Whereas life expectancy in the West continued to steadily improve, in the East it remained the same or worsened. Figure 1 shows three former Eastern bloc countries' male life expectancies against that of France and the United States from 1960 through 2011. Life expectancy in the United States steadily increased by almost ten years to seventy-nine years. In France, it increased by twelve years to eighty-two years. Generally, male life expectancies in the East and West differed by no more than five years in the 1960s. These differences grew larger until the mid-1990s, when male life expectancies in the East began a slight recovery. Likewise, differences in female life expectancies (see Figure 2) widened between the East and West from the 1960s to the 1990s, when the gap begins to decrease slightly. As much as the general pattern of an East-West divide holds, the Russian Federation, represented by a thicker line, is clearly distinct from the Czech Republic and Romania, which roughly represent the range of life expectancies among Eastern bloc countries over this time period. Russian life expectancies are strikingly lower and more volatile. Russia's life expectancies are lowest and have not recovered as much. In 2011 male life expectancy in France was more than fifteen years longer than in Russia; female life expectancy was ten years longer.

As might be expected, looking at selected countries of the former Soviet Union (Figures 3 and 4), the Russian Federation data are not as distinct (note

FIGURE 1. Male life expectancies at birth, Czech Republic, Romania, Russian Federation, United States, and France, 1960–2011.

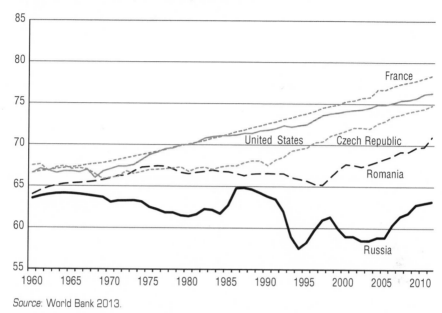

Source: World Bank 2013.

FIGURE 2. Female life expectancies at birth, Czech Republic, Romania, Russian Federation, United States, and France, 1960–2011.

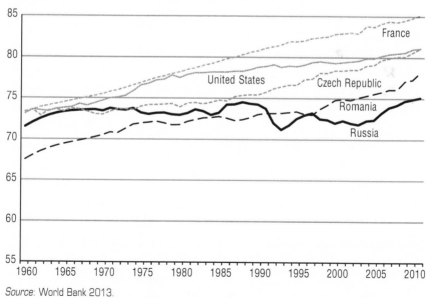

Source: World Bank 2013.

that the values on the vertical axes have changed). Among many of these former Soviet Union countries, life expectancy improved from 1985 to 1987. This is widely attributed to Gorbachev's antialcohol campaign and, less frequently, to the reforms of perestroika, which some have surmised may have "inspired hopes for a better future" (Notzon et al. 1998, 795; Watson 1995). Men's life expectancy suffered a precipitous drop in the early 1990s in most of the former western Soviet republics (not all of them shown). The Georgian data plateaued during this time period, but Armenia represents the only real exception to the trend. The data are more complicated for women's life expectancy, but again most countries registered substantial declines in the early 1990s. Nonetheless, only in the Baltics (Latvia, Lithuania, and Estonia) and the Ukraine did the declines approach those of the Russian Federation (Latvia and the Ukraine are shown in Figures 3 and 4). The sex difference in Russian life expectancies reached its greatest measure in the early 1990s. In 1992 women's life expectancy exceeded men's by ten years; in 1994 it exceeded men's by fourteen years.

Importantly, Russian life expectancy suffered another drop from 1998 through the mid-2000s, which is attributed to the 1998 financial default. This drop was not as severe but was more prolonged than the drop in the early 1990s. Russian male life expectancy was sixty-three years in 2011; female life expectancy was seventy-five years. In 2011 the Russian and Belarussian sex differences in life expectancies, at twelve years, were the largest in the world.

Even against the preceding and succeeding trends, the drop in life expectancy from 1990 to 1994 is dramatic, particularly in Russia. Figure 5 illustrates the crisis even more starkly using data on Russian adult mortality, or the probability of a fifteen-year-old dying before reaching age sixty. Included in the figure are lines for Latvia and the Ukraine, two former Soviet Union countries with comparable increases in mortality. As seen, the spike in working-age male mortality in the early 1990s is striking—so much so that initially there was some concern as to whether the increase in mortality was an artifact of better death recording. It is now well established by epidemiologists that the data represent a real phenomenon (Leon et al. 1997; Notzon et al. 2003; Notzon et al. 1998). Latvia has a striking spike in mortality among both males and females in the early 1990s, although it is exceeded by Russian mortality. Similar spikes, albeit less pronounced, are seen in Estonia and Lithuania (not shown in the figure). The Ukrainian data (and to a lesser extent the Belarussian data, not

FIGURE 3. Male life expectancies at birth, selected former Soviet Union countries, 1960–2011.

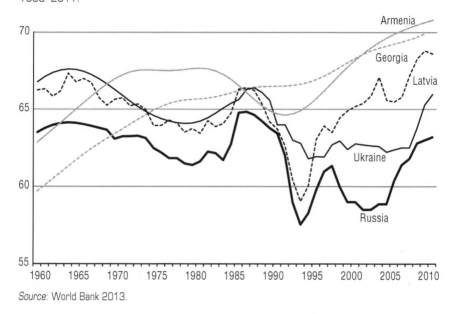

Source: World Bank 2013.

FIGURE 4. Female life expectancies at birth, selected former Soviet Union countries, 1960–2011.

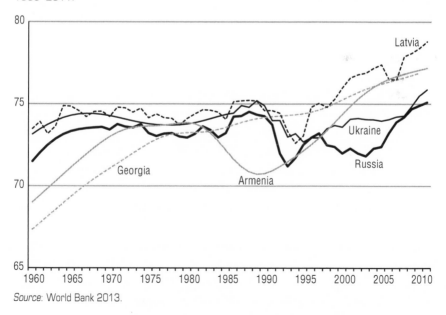

Source: World Bank 2013.

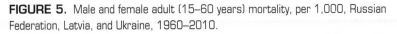

FIGURE 5. Male and female adult (15–60 years) mortality, per 1,000, Russian Federation, Latvia, and Ukraine, 1960–2010.

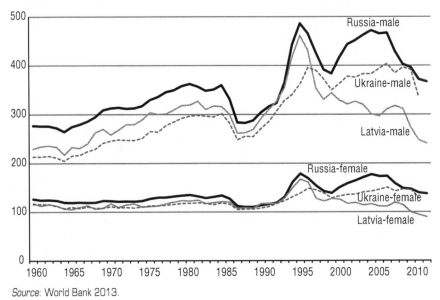

Source: World Bank 2013.

shown) show an increase in mortality in the late 1990s and early 2000s that shadows the Russian increase, but in 2009 adult mortality rates were below those in Russia.[1] In sum, the Russian mortality crisis is the most severe of any country in Eastern Europe or the former Soviet Union.

Some observers treat the early 1990s as a continuation of the trend begun in the mid-1960s. Shkolnikov and colleagues describe mortality as increasing steadily, "interrupted only by a short-lived improvement in 1985–1987." "In the early 1990s," they write, "deterioration resumed" (2004, 31). Field (2000) argues that these are two phases of the demographic crisis with different patterns of mortality. It is also possible to see a distinct and acute crisis of mortality in the early 1990s from which Russia is only beginning to recover. The interpretations are not mutually exclusive, although they are a source of debate because of their implications about Soviet society, neoliberalism, and global political economy.

CAUSE OF DEATH

The excess mortality is driven by three causes: cardiovascular disease, injuries, and alcohol-related deaths. Table 1 shows the contribution of each cause of death to excess mortality in the early 1990s. According to these data, from recorded cause of death on Russian death certificates, cardiovascular disease (diseases of the heart and cerebrovascular diseases in the table) and injuries are the main determinants of the drop in life expectancy in the early 1990s, representing 36 and 29 percent of the change, respectively. "Chronic liver disease and cirrhosis" and "other alcohol-related causes" together account for 12 percent of the change. In data not seen here, death rates from alcohol-related causes, followed by homicides, registered the greatest relative increases (Notzon et al. 1998). Because cardiovascular deaths are much more common, a slight change in the death rate results in a larger impact on life expectancy.

TABLE 1. Contribution of change in mortality from each cause of death to the change in life expectancy, Russia, 1990–1994

Cause	Total		Male		Female	
	Years	%	Years	%	Years	%
Infectious diseases	−0.12	2.4	−0.17	2.8	0.02	−0.5
Diseases of the heart	−1.35	26.1	−1.56	25.9	−0.85	26.9
Cerebrovascular diseases	−0.49	9.6	−0.45	7.5	−0.46	14.7
Malignant neoplasms	−0.04	0.7	−0.00	0.0	−0.02	0.8
Pneumonia and influenza	−0.17	3.4	−0.24	3.9	−0.06	2.0
Chronic obstructive pulmonary disease	−0.06	1.2	−0.09	1.5	−0.01	0.3
Chronic liver disease and cirrhosis	−0.12	2.4	−0.13	2.1	−0.10	3.3
Other alcohol−related causes[1]	−0.49	9.6	−0.61	10.2	−0.27	8.4
Motor vehicle crashes	−0.01	0.1	0.00	−0.1	−0.01	0.3
Other injuries[2]	−0.92	17.8	−1.17	19.3	−0.46	14.7
Suicide	−0.27	5.2	−0.40	6.7	−0.05	1.6
Homicide and legal intervention	−0.33	6.3	−0.42	6.9	−0.17	5.2
Remainder	−0.79	15.2	−0.80	13.2	−0.70	22.3
All causes	−5.16	100.0	−6.05	100.0	−3.16	100.0

Source: Notzon et al. 1998, table 5.

[1] Deaths attributable to alcohol intoxication, namely alcohol poisoning and alcohol dependence syndrome.

[2] External causes of death such as occupational injuries, drownings, falls, injuries due to operations of war, and injuries of undetermined intent. This category does not include the external causes of death of motor vehicle crashes, alcohol poisoning, suicide, homicide, and legal intervention.

SOCIAL DETERMINANTS OF MORTALITY

Although a decline in life expectancy from 1990 to 1994 has been found for every age group, it is particularly pronounced among the middle aged. Table 2 shows the contribution to the change in life expectancy for five- and ten-year age groups among the total, male, and female population. Numbers (almost entirely negative) represent how many years each age group contributes to the total fall in life expectancy over the five-year period from 1990 to 1994. Percentages reflect the proportion of the total decline contributed by each age group. As seen, most of the change in mortality comes from ages thirty-five through sixty-four for both males and females. In the literature, ages forty to fifty-four, or those born between the years 1936 and 1954, have been identified as those most at risk of dying excess deaths (Leon et al. 1997; Notzon et al. 1998; Walberg et al. 1998). A greater proportion of deaths among the middle aged signals that absolute impoverishment is not a primary causal factor. When it is, death rates tend to increase among the very young and elderly (Leon and Shkolnikov 1998).

TABLE 2. Contribution of change in mortality from each age group to the change in life expectancy, Russia, 1990–1994

Age	Total		Male		Female	
	Years	Percent	Years	Percent	Years	Percent
0	−0.09	1.7	−0.09	1.4	−0.09	2.7
1–4	−0.02	0.4	−0.02	0.3	−0.03	0.9
5–14	−0.01	0.3	0.00	0.0	−0.03	0.9
15–24	−0.27	5.1	−0.36	5.9	−0.12	3.8
25–34	−0.59	11.4	−0.80	13.2	−0.25	7.9
35–44	−1.01	19.5	−1.32	21.8	−0.46	14.7
45–54	−1.26	24.5	−1.55	25.6	−0.70	22.0
55–64	−1.03	19.9	−1.17	19.4	−0.65	20.4
65–74	−0.58	11.2	−0.57	9.5	−0.43	13.7
75–84	−0.24	4.6	−0.16	2.7	−0.30	9.5
≥85	−0.07	1.4	−0.02	0.3	−0.11	3.5
All ages	−5.16	100.0	−6.05	100.0	−3.16	100.0

Source: Notzon et al. 1998, table 4.

Education, occupation, and marital status are also implicated in the mortality crisis, especially for alcohol-related deaths, and the patterns are similar to those found in the West, where more education, white-collar occupation, and marriage are protective (Chenet, Leon et al. 1998; Malyutina et al. 2004; Plavinski, Plavinskaya, and Klimov 2003; Shkolnikov, Leon et al. 1998). Income, however, does not appear to be associated with mortality in Russia, which is not surprising given the lesser importance of income as a marker of status in Soviet society and the difficulties of its assessment in the immediate post-Soviet period. In the early 2000s it remained a poor predictor of mortality in post-Soviet Russia (Perlman and Bobak 2008).

Epidemiology identifies a population at risk—unemployed, unmarried, working-class, middle-aged male Muscovites with less education. Next we turn to cardiovascular and alcohol-related deaths. Social scientists have pointed to a lack of social capital and psychosocial stress as the drivers of cardiovascular and alcohol-related deaths.

CARDIOVASCULAR MORTALITY

Cardiovascular mortality mirrors the general East-West mortality divide. Cardiovascular deaths rose in most industrialized countries until the 1960s, when they began to decline in the West. The Soviet bloc countries were an exception to this pattern—cardiovascular death rates continued to rise from the 1960s onward. By 1990, rates in Russia far exceeded those in Western Europe and the United States, especially for cerebrovascular disease, or stroke. Age-adjusted mortality rates per 100,000 for stroke in 1990 were 51 in the United States and 246 in Russia (Notzon et al. 1998). The difference in rates increased with a stark upswing in the cardiovascular death rates in Russia during the early 1990s. From 1990 to 1994 cardiovascular deaths increased by over 30 percent (Notzon et al. 1998). Although cardiovascular deaths account for a substantial proportion of excess deaths in Russia during the early 1990s, the literature specifically addressing cardiovascular deaths during this time is relatively sparse compared to the literature on alcohol-related deaths.

Cardiovascular behavioral risk factors include smoking, poor diet, and lack of exercise—all long-standing problems in Russian society. Furthermore, these problems may have increased during the early 1990s. However, these risk factors are not thought to have an immediate effect on cardiovascular health, but rather a long-term effect. Intermediate risk factors for cardiovascular death and disease include raised blood pressure, raised blood glucose, raised blood lipids, and obesity. Epidemiologists estimate that less than half of cardiovascular mortality in Russia is explained by these classic behavioral and intermediate risk factors (Averina et al. 2003; Ginter 1995; Koek, Bots, and Grobbee 2003).

The World Health Organization's MONICA (Multinational Monitoring of Determinants and Trends in Cardiovascular Disease) Project from the mid-1980s to the mid-1990s is the world's largest prospective study of cardiovascular disease in thirty-eight populations in twenty-one countries of Europe and Asia. Using the data from Russia, Stegmayr and colleagues (2000) find that blood pressure, cholesterol, and obesity all declined from1987 through 1994 in the Siberian city of Novosibirsk, Russia's third-largest city. Smoking rates largely remained stable, only increasing slightly among women. Yet the stroke rate increased markedly during this time. The authors conclude: "It is evident that changes in socioeconomic determinants of stroke may have played a major role in the alarming increase in stroke rates in Novosibirsk. If so, it is evident from the present results that such socioeconomic determinants are not mediated by the most well-established biological risk factors" (Stegmayr et al. 2000, 7). In other words, socioeconomic factors are important determinants of excess cardiovascular deaths in Russia during the early 1990s. Moreover, these factors may have unique, as yet poorly understood, physiologic pathways. New longitudinal studies like the Stress, Aging, and Health in Russia (SAHR) and the Health, Alcohol, and Psychosocial Factors in Eastern Europe (HAPIEE) studies are investigating the relationship between psychosocial risk factors and mortality, but the results will only indirectly comment on the early 1990s (Shkolnikova et al. 2009; Peasey et al. 2006).

The World Health Organization (WHO) recognizes low socioeconomic status and psychosocial stress—chronic life stress, social isolation, and anxiety—as psychosocial risk factors for cardiovascular disease. Starting with Berkman and Syme's (1979) study of mortality in Alameda County, evidence has accumulated for the effects of social support on cardiovascular disease and death. Reviews of the literature on psychosocial factors and cardiovascular disease identify the following risk factors in Western populations: little social support, acute and catastrophic life events, depression, and work demands and perceived control (Bunker et al. 2003; Eller et al. 2009; Everson-Rose and Lewis 2005; Krantz and McCeney 2002; Lett et al. 2005;

Rozanski, Blumenthal, and Kaplan 1999; Tennant 1999). A recent study suggests that perceived control is especially important for those without classic cardiovascular risk factors (Surtees et al. 2010). It is also a hallmark of psychological stress across species (Sapolsky 2004). Again, these social risk factors may act on physiology in ways that are distinct from behavioral risk factors of smoking, poor diet, and lack of exercise.

In another seminal study of psychosocial risk and cardiovascular disease, low incidence of heart disease in the Italian American town of Roseto, Pennsylvania, up until the mid-1960s was attributed to high levels of social cohesion, dubbed the Roseto effect. When social cohesion began to unravel, the rate of heart disease increased (Bruhn and Wolf 1979; Lasker, Egolf, and Wolf 1994). In part because of differences in definition and measurement, epidemiological evidence that social cohesion or social capital influence cardiovascular mortality is equivocal. The effects may vary by population, gender, economic status, and age (see Franzini and Spears 2003; Hyyppä et al. 2007; Islam et al. 2008; Kelleher et al. 2004; Lochner et al. 2003; Scheffler et al. 2008; Sundquist et al. 2006). In the literature on Russian mortality in the early 1990s, however, a decline in social capital is repeatedly proposed as a key determinant of the rise in cardiovascular mortality.

ALCOHOL-RELATED MORTALITY

Alcohol-related mortality is the primary focus of the social science literature on the mortality crisis. As early as 1993, Okólski writes, "It seems that of all plausible determinants of adult male mortality increase in Eastern Europe, the most widely accepted underlying factor is growing alcohol consumption" (177). In 1995, Ryan comments: "a favourite national pastime is proving fatal" (647). Epidemiologists agree: alcohol "plays a central role" (Leon and Shkolnikov 1998, 790) and "evidence demonstrates the importance of alcohol" (McKee 1999, 824). "It is important to note that the analyses by cause of death strongly support the argument that alcohol has played a major part in the decline in life expectancy in Russia" (Walberg et al. 1998, 317).

The earliest articles on the Russian mortality crisis stressed cardiovascular and violent deaths (Shkolnikov, Meslé, and Vallin 1995). Quickly the literature turned to an almost exclusive focus on alcohol—its production, availability, cost, quality, proof, and consumption (Cockerham 1997; Leon et al. 1997; McKee 1999). When Notzon and colleagues (1998) wrote their seminal article detailing the contributions to mortality by cause of death (see Table 1 earlier in the chapter), they concluded that a number of factors were at play. Commentary on the article by Leon and Shkolnikov directed the focus to alcohol: "Notzon and colleagues conclude that the steep decrease in life expectancy in the 1990s is the result of many factors, including 'economic and social instability, high rates of tobacco and alcohol consumption, poor nutrition, depression, and deterioration of the health care system.' However, alcohol appears to be a proximal risk factor and plays a central role in the recent crisis" (Leon and Shkolnikov 1998, 790). Since then, the literature has moved from the amount and type of alcohol consumed (Khaltourina and Korotayev 2006; Nemtsov 2002; Nemtsov 2000; Nemtsov 1998; Popova et al. 2007; Rehm et al. 2007; Treml 1997) to binge drinking (Bobak et al. 2004; Bobak et al. 2003; Britton and McKee 2000; McKee and Britton 1998; Nicholson et al. 2005; Pridemore and Kim 2006) and surrogates—alcohol-based liquids such as medicinal tinctures and colognes (Gil et al. 2009; Lachenmeier, Rehm, and Gmel 2007; Leon et al. 2007; McKee et al. 2005).

Public health scholars have also made a case that some cardiovascular deaths are attributable to alcohol. A number of articles suggest that the pattern of binge drinking common in Russia may lead to hemorrhagic stroke, sudden cardiac death due to arrhythmias, and cardiomyopathies—which may also explain why cardiovascular deaths increase over the weekends in Russia (Chenet, McKee et al. 1998; Leon et al. 1997; Leon and Shkolnikov 1998). In 1999, Bobak and Marmot cautioned that the evidence for alcohol as the major determinant of the mortality crisis was circumstantial and insufficient given the tenuous relationship between alcohol and cardiovascular mortality. They called for more general research on the relationship between binge drinking and cardiovascular mortality in Russia. In response, Britton and McKee (2000) performed a systematic review of the literature on patterns of drinking and cardiovascular mortality and found evidence that problem drinking (definitions of binging are not standardized) was associated with cardiovascular death, especially sudden cardiovascular death, in cohort studies in Norway, Finland, Sweden, Bosnia, Croatia, and the United States.

Surrogates are ethanol-based liquids such as cleaning agents, eau de colognes, and medicinal tinctures. In Russia, these are widely available and are significantly cheaper per unit of ethanol than vodka (Leon et al. 2007). Using a case-control design based on the population of Izhevsk, a city in the Udmurt Republic, the consumption of surrogates was strongly associated with all-cause mortality among working-age men. According to these data, fully 43 percent of mortality among working-age men is attributable to hazardous drinking, defined as the consumption of surrogates or problem drinking[2] (Leon et al. 2007), although prospective cohort data has shifted this estimate downward to 26 percent (Tomkins et al. 2012).

Evidence on the relationship between alcohol and mortality from prospective cohort studies—the gold standard of epidemiology—in Russia is still thin. There are methodological challenges to studying sudden deaths related to recent alcohol use (Tomkins et al. 2007). There is also concern that individuals generally underestimate the amount they drink (Nemtsov 2004; Nemtsov 2003). Existing prospective cohort datasets do not necessarily include adequate information on binge drinking or the use of surrogates.

The Russian prospective cohort studies that do exist report contradictory results. Deev and colleagues (1998) found no relationship between alcohol and cardiovascular mortality in a prospective cohort study, although estimates of alcohol consumption were mostly based on data collected many years before death. Plavinski, Plavinskaya, and Klimov (2003) focus on two cohorts of men in St. Petersburg recruited in the mid-1970s and mid-1980s. Among men with less than secondary education, mortality in the 1990s increased 60 to 80 percent, but alcohol consumption only explained up to a 22 percent increase in mortality. They conclude that "the increase in mortality in Russia was socially determined, and though alcohol may play a part in this process it is not the sole factor" (1242).

Perlman and Bobak (2008) used data from the Russia Longitudinal Monitoring Survey, a prospective cohort study, and found that more than once a week drinking (19 percent of males in the sample; 4 percent of females) significantly increased mortality risk. However, abstention from alcohol in the previous month, which represented a much larger proportion of the total study population (27 percent of males in the sample; 53 percent of females), also increased mortality risk. There was no significant relationship between binge drinking and mortality. They summarize:

> Our findings did not fully support the hypothesis that binge drinking is of particular importance. . . . Frequent drinking, however, predicted mortality in the full models and may reflect heavy drinking better in this study. The reasons for higher mortality among non-drinkers are uncertain, but, as elsewhere, it is plausible that this group includes former heavy alcohol consumers who stopped drinking because of ill health. (98)

The finding that nondrinkers are at increased risk of death is not unique to this study. Malyutina and colleagues (2002) report that men in Novosibirsk who were frequent heavy drinkers, but not binge drinkers, were at increased risk for all-cause and cardiovascular mortality in the early 1990s. Equally striking is the increased risk of dying among nondrinkers. Table 3 is a simplified version of some of their results, showing that nondrinkers are at increased risk of dying from all-cause, cardiovascular, and coronary heart disease deaths. There are four other significant findings, two indicating that drinking decreases risk and two indicating that drinking increases risk. Table 4, which includes only drinkers, shows that those who drink 120 grams or more of alcohol three or more times per week (frequent, in the table) are at significantly increased risk of all-cause and cardiovascular mortality. These drinkers represent less than 10 percent of the total study population. In their discussion the authors note, "we need to clarify the reasons for excess mortality in non-drinkers" (2002, 1453). The authors find that adjusting for health selection bias—"by which drinkers with poor health stop drinking and thus artificially increase mortality in non-drinkers" (2002, 1451; which is also the explanation given by Perlman and Bobak [2008])—attenuates increased risk of dying in nondrinkers, but the increase in cardiovascular mortality remains significant. Although they suggest that an appreciable 16 percent of cardiovascular deaths in the 1990s might be attributable to alcohol, they are cautious, writing that "alcohol is unlikely to provide the universal explanation for the mortality trends and fluctuations in Russia" (Maltutina et al. 2002, 1453).

The most comprehensive prospective cohort study comes from Izhevsk starting in 2003. Data over six years on two thousand men aged twenty-five to fifty-four years suggest that hazardous drinking (as reported by proxy) is responsible for 26 percent of total mortality among men in that age group (Tomkins et al. 2012). Abstainers had twice the mortality of nonproblematic drinkers. The authors explain that former drinkers who stopped drinking due to illness, "sick-quitters," drive mortality up among abstainers (Tomkins et al. 2012, 8). Nonproblematic drinkers represented almost three quarters of the study population. Hazardous drinkers and abstainers both represented 13 percent.

Overall, evidence from these prospective cohort studies (Perlman and Bobak 2008; Malyutina et al. 2002; Tomkins et al. 2012) indicates that most drinkers are less at risk of dying than nondrinkers are. For a smaller proportion of men, drinking confers risk; for a greater proportion of men, it confers protection. It is misleading to refer to alcohol as the cause of the mortality crisis since it is also associated with *reduced* mortality among a majority of men.

TABLE 3. Adjusted relative risks of death from all-cause, cardiovascular, coronary heart, stroke, and external causes by alcohol intake during previous week and by typical dose per occasion

Mortality	Adjusted relative risk				
	All–cause	Cardio-vascular	Coronary heart	Stroke	External causes
Alcohol intake					
None	1.0	1.0	1.0	1.0	1.0
Nondrinkers	*1.26	*1.55	*1.63	1.29	1.27
<40 g	*0.66	0.71	0.58	1.03	0.62
40–70 g	0.85	0.78	0.76	0.80	1.00
80–119 g	0.90	0.85	0.86	0.80	1.38
120–159 g	*1.38	1.25	1.13	1.69	0.90
≥160 g	0.93	0.91	1.00	0.61	1.26
Typical dose					
<80 g	1.0	1.0	1.0	1.0	1.0
Nondrinkers	*1.32	*1.72	*1.81	1.47	1.37
≥80 g	1.00	1.02	1.13	0.86	1.50
≥120 g	0.94	0.97	1.17	0.52	1.60
≥160 g	1.05	0.99	1.27	*0.36	*2.08

Source: Malyutina et al. 2002, table 5.
* Statistically significant.

TABLE 4. Adjusted relative risks of death from all-cause and cardiovascular disease by frequency of drinking, stratified by typical dose per drinking occasion (drinkers only)

Mortality	Drinking frequency			
	Rare	Occasional	Weekly	Frequent
All–cause				
<80 g	0.89	1.0	0.98	1.23
80–119 g	0.63	1.0	1.15	1.25
≥120 g	0.86	1.0	1.08	*1.61
Cardiovascular				
<80 g	0.92	1.0	1.16	1.34
80–119 g	0.60	1.0	0.93	1.07
≥120 g	1.07	1.0	1.22	*2.05

Source: Malyutina et al. 2002, table 5.
* Statistically significant.

It is probably fair to say that loyalty to the alcohol risk factor among epidemiologists exceeds the evidence from prospective cohort data, even though other evidence, based on proxy data (retrospective data from siblings or relatives), is increasing (Bobak et al. 2003; Nicholson et al. 2005). Nonetheless, with more than a decade of research on the topic, epidemiologists conclude "there is now compelling evidence that alcohol directly and indirectly plays a major role in both the high underlying mortality in Russia and, in particular, the fluctuations that have occurred in the period since the 1980s" (Shkolnikov et al. 2004, 59). "Alcohol provides the most plausible, proximal explanation for the massive fluctuations in Russian mortality" (Leon, Shkolnikov, and McKee 2009). Its central role "cannot be denied" (Peck, Shankar, and Bangdiwala 2007, 151). Over time, estimates of alcohol's contribution to the crisis have increased from 12 percent overall (Notzon et al. 1998) to 52 percent among working-age men (Zaridze, Brennan et al. 2009).

It is clear that frequent heavy drinking and the consumption of surrogates are indeed related to excess mortality in Russia, including deaths from cardiovascular disease and from external injuries. It is not as clear that alcohol should eclipse other causes of death.

PSYCHOSOCIAL STRESS

The literature on alcohol and mortality in Russia is divided into two camps. One camp emphasizes continuity with an unhealthy Russian lifestyle that was exacerbated during the Soviet period. Drinking is "a particularly self destructive health practice within the overall configuration of Russian health lifestyles" (Cockerham 2000, 1314). Cockerham writes: "During the Soviet period, heavy alcohol consumption became common throughout the year, which most likely fostered a lifestyle characterized by consistent binge drinking. This situation suggests that it is the normative demands of a particular lifestyle, rather than health policy or stress, that is primarily responsible for the pattern of male drinking in Russia" (1997, 126). He concludes, "Although more research is needed, the strongest evidence to date suggests that unhealthy lifestyles are the principal social determinant of increased mortality in the region" (127). If lifestyle has been and continues to be unhealthy, it holds little explanatory power in terms of an increase in mortality. Why did the unhealthy lifestyle suddenly prove so lethal?

The other camp emphasizes that drinking is a result of psychosocial stress. Referring to an increase in alcohol consumption, Ryan explains: "It is hardly fanciful to adduce a felt need to seek escape of a sort from the increasing harshness and bewildering uncertainties of daily life. For many people exogenously created changes may well seem to have threatened the social, political, and economic collapse of their country and, in a sense, of the world as they knew it" (1995, 646). Twigg writes, "Of course, the most well-known and visible manifestation of Russians' inability to cope with the stresses of the post-Soviet transition is the vodka bottle" (2001, 312). Leon and Shkolnikov comment: "It seems plausible that the increase in alcohol consumption in the 1990s was driven by the stress of economic and political transformation" (1998, 791). And:

> Obviously, the often chaotic political and socio-economic transition of the 1990s created high levels of psychosocial stress, resulting in many premature deaths. . . . This stress can be a direct cause of ill-health and even death but, more often, its effects are indirect, leading to heavy drinking and other health damaging behavior as a way to cope with it and so to "escape" from the grim reality that is life for many people in Russia today. (Shkolnikov et al. 2004, 70)

Scholars have proposed complex models linking socioeconomic transformation, stress, and alcohol. Walberg and colleagues (1998) postulate that alcohol mediates the association between mortality and labor-force turnover, crime, and inequality. Siegrist (2000) links the loss of social roles, such as work, marital, and family roles, to prolonged stress. Prolonged stress, in turn, leads to stress-relieving behaviors such as alcohol consumption. These two articles do not present data on alcohol consumption in Russia. Other articles, using data on alcohol use, yield unexpected results.

Perlman and Bobak (2009) propose alcohol as a mediator between unemployment and mortality, yet they find alcohol consumption does not account for the association. Cook et al. (2013) propose alcohol consumption and drinking patterns as a mediator between education and alcohol-related dysfunction, an association that would seem self-evident. Yet they find that drinking behavior does not fully explain the association. They conclude, "the results illustrate the challenge in formulating statistical models that convincingly identify the pathways that link educational differences to health-related behaviours and outcomes, even when the universe of potential explanatory pathways is by definition restricted, as is the case with alcohol-related dysfunction" (10). The same drinking behavior has worse effects among less-educated men.

As described above, in the psychosocial camp alcohol is seen as an escape, used by men as a maladaptive coping mechanism. This understanding, while intuitively sensible, is unsatisfactory, perhaps foremost because most alcohol use, even high levels of alcohol use, is not necessarily associated with poorer health. Rather, alcohol use is often associated with better health.

As will become clear, being unneeded is a more distal driver of the mortality crisis. Being unneeded translates social collapse to bodily death from cardiovascular and alcohol-related causes. It helps explain findings in the epidemiological literature. Why are certain social connections associated with poorer health, while others are associated with better health? Why is alcohol drinking often associated with better health? Why do the effects of drinking vary among men?

In the next chapter, I will turn to a discussion of what one interviewee called the "death of society." In Russia it was first and foremost the death of society—that which exists between individuals—that led to the death of individuals. The emic view contests assumptions about Russian social relations and drinking, solving puzzles in the epidemiological literature.

CHAPTER 7

Death of Society

We all perfectly understand where the death of society leads. The death of society is at first spiritual [*dukhovnaia*], then physical [*fizicheskaia*].

—interviewee

Vasilii, a former alcoholic and member of the sobriety society Sober Russia, attended the 2007 Moscow alcohol policy seminar. After the seminar I arranged to meet him at the salon where he gives massages. A polite, soft-spoken man, Vasilii told me that sickness of the soul leads to sickness of the body.

> A person has a soul, spirit. And there is the body. So, in the beginning the soul is hurt, and through the hurt of the soul the body is hurt. At first a person's soul is sick, and then the body begins to get sick. And then he dies and that's it. And why? Because first the soul . . . the soul sickened. The soul was harmed and only afterwards the body.

He described the soul as emanating outward from the body, an "energetic envelope." As he spoke, he told me to close my eyes and then he reached out toward me, "I can reach out to you, not touching you. But you sense that I am somewhere close." He explained how breaking laws—he gave the examples of fighting, stealing, and hooliganism—compromises the energetic field, rendering the body vulnerable. "When you break a law [. . .] then your energetic envelope breaks. You continue further, now the body. If you are already sick there . . . There is sick. [He waved his hand near the side of my body without touching me] . . . *Here* [he touched my side] is sick." Vasilii's soul is located around the body. An envelope suggests enclosure and protection, but energy suggests flexibility and movement.

This is not an inner, individualized soul, but a soul that is constituted beyond the individual, between individuals. The Russian soul is social. This view is also represented in other ethnographies of Russia. Pesmen, who takes the Russian soul as her central object, reports that someone told her the soul "isn't in individuals but in their union" (1995, 71). Paxson describes a soulful person as one who gives to others, while a soulless person holds back (Paxson 2005, 78–80). Wierzbicka notes that the Russian soul comes into being through communion with others. She quotes from Pasternak's Doktor Zhivago, "you in others, that's what your soul [duša] is" (Wierzbicka 2003, 427).

Vasilii spoke of transgressions that violate social norms and make the body vulnerable. Breaking social norms ruptures the soul, which is located between people. And a ruptured soul can no longer protect the body from hurt. This understanding of the soul lying between people recognizes that society protects the body through norms of social interaction—an interpersonal order. It follows that the body is vulnerable to societal ills. It is a very Durkheimian way of thinking about the relationship between individual and society. In his work on suicide, Durkheim writes that "individuals share too deeply in the life of society for it to be diseased without their suffering infection" (1979, 213).

The soul protects through order but it also allows individuals to transcend the self and extend into space—*prostor.* The soul is the site of authenticity and truth—what really matters. Again Pesmen writes about the Russian soul as "having a tendency to 'expand' itself and 'broaden' other things, and is opposed to what was often called 'this' or 'everyday' life, considered to be less alive, deadening, not *life*" (2000, 307). The Russian soul sets people free to overcome the banality of everyday life, but it does this through tight social bonds. "It was the dusha that drew people together to create a specific kind of communion that . . . 'you value more than anything else in the world'" (Pesmen 172). Through the tightness of social bonds, the soul offers space. It enlarges the individual. Space could potentially be dangerous if the soul wanders too far, but social bonds hold the soul back from being lost. Paxson

(2005) describes a fear of "being led away" in moments of wonder, but social belonging prevents this.

Middle-aged Muscovites did not talk about "psychosocial determinants" of mortality. They spoke about a soul that exists between people. It is a soul that conveys bonds and order but also expansiveness and space—an existence beyond the borders of the individual body. How then does the Russian soul with its characteristics of order and space help explain cardiovascular and alcohol-related deaths? How does a rupture in the soul weaken the physical heart and drive Russians to drink? First I establish how middle-aged Muscovites connected cardiovascular death and alcohol consumption with being unneeded. Then I stretch beyond my ethnographic data to suggest how being unneeded affects bodily health. I also contrast the emic view with etic views in the epidemiological literature that attribute cardiovascular deaths to a lack of social capital and alcohol consumption to a need for escape.

THE HEART AND BEING NEEDED

On a cloudy February day I boarded a crowded bus at a metro stop with directions and address in hand. A woman whom I had previously interviewed had asked a friend, Natasha, if she would also speak with me. Natasha was at home with her five-year-old granddaughter, who watched cartoons in the main room while we talked. Natasha, like Lidia and Margarita in earlier chapters, assured me that nothing much had changed for her. "You know, for me somehow, it didn't touch me at all. I have my problems, I had my affairs. Somehow the politics . . . I, I don't give a damn about the politics." I tried to clarify that I was interested in her daily life, not politics. "No, no. It was the same as how it had been for me. [. . .] It didn't touch me." She told me that in the early 1990s she received her salary—"my *kopeiki*" (pennies)— as before. There were no salary arrears at the hospital where she worked in housekeeping. The head doctor distributed food packages on Fridays. Since she had three children she received fifteen kilograms of milk a week, which she gave away or used to make chocolate truffles. Natasha was adamant that she personally was not hurt by the changes in the early 1990s, but she was also adamant that society *was* hurt.

Natasha told me that people live and die alone now. She spoke of a friend who died of a heart attack at seventy years old in the hospital where they both worked. "Right at work she had a heart attack and that's it. That's it.

Forgotten." And then she said: "Who needs us? Who is needed now? Now no one needs anyone else. The world has become terrible." After talking about how children no longer help parents, she added, "I also don't help anyone. I only help my granddaughter."

Natasha connects her friend's death with being unneeded and she makes it clear, when she talks about children helping parents and grandparents helping grandchildren, that being needed is helping others. In the epidemiology of Russian mortality, social capital—and its presumed relationship to civil society—is an important psychosocial determinant of cardiovascular death. However, the literature does not recognize how a culturally specific form of social connection was destroyed in the early 1990s. Moreover, the concept of social capital is more about receiving from others, while being needed is more about giving to others.

SOCIAL CAPITAL

Political scientist Robert Putnam, whose work on civic engagement in Italy and the United States popularized the concept of social capital (1993, 1995, 2000), defines social capital as "features of social life—networks, norms, and trust—that enable participants to act together more effectively to pursue shared objectives" (1995, 664) and more simply as "social networks and the norms of reciprocity and trustworthiness that arise from them" (2000, 19). In his book *Bowling Alone* (2000) Putnam documents a decrease in civic engagement in the United States over the course of the past half century. He details declines in voter turnout, labor unions, church attendance, and membership in parent-teacher associations, women's groups, fraternal organizations, Boy Scouts, and Red Cross. Although Americans still bowl, they do not bowl in leagues.

Wilkinson introduced the concept of social capital to public health. In his book *Unhealthy Societies* (1996) he argues that income inequality destroys social cohesion and social capital and this contributes to differences in mortality among more developed societies. In a review article on social capital, income inequality, and mortality Kawachi and colleagues concur: "disinvestment in social capital appears to be one of the pathways through which growing income inequality exerts its effects on population-level mortality" (1997, 1495).

Measurements of social capital often incorporate elements of social support and social networks. In the first instance, social capital is commonly measured by what individuals receive from interactions with other individuals—for example, emotional, instrumental, or material social support. When social capital is treated as an attribute of social networks, measurement may include number, frequency, and type of social contacts. A third sense of social capital is an attribute of a group of people, not an individual. Societies, regions, and neighborhoods have social cohesion; individuals do not. This requires a higher-order level of analysis, using indicators such as the number of voluntary associations in a community. However much mutuality and reciprocity are emphasized as hallmarks of social capital by Putnam and others, in the hands of epidemiologists reciprocity is rarely measured (Abbott and Freeth 2008). Even when social capital is considered as social cohesion, the concept concerns what individuals receive from living in certain places.

Francis Fukuyama, famous for having declared the end of history after the fall of the Berlin Wall (Fukuyama 1992), defines social capital as "an instantiated informal norm that promotes co-operation between two or more individuals" (Fukuyama 2001, 7). However, it seems that social capital assumes more than this. Indeed, a Western model of civil society is considered an epiphenomenon of social capital (Fukuyama 1999). This model requires the existence of voluntary associations, independent of the state, that serve to mediate between citizens and state. Therefore, societies without Western civil society must not have social capital—or they have "distorted" social capital.

DISTORTED SOCIAL CAPITAL

More than one social scientist has attributed the Russian mortality crisis to low social capital in Soviet and post-Soviet society, although a few have also raised questions about the usefulness of the term (Twigg 2003). Kennedy, Kawachi, and Brainerd (1998) find that a lack of social capital in post-Soviet Russian society—which they measure as mistrust in government, crime, poor quality of work relations, and low civic engagement in politics—is related to higher mortality rates, particularly cardiovascular mortality, across regions. In their discussion, though, the authors move from the characteristics of post-Soviet society to the characteristics of Soviet society. Based on the association of crude death rates in 1980 and 1994, they see continuity in mortality rates across time, suggesting "a key consequence of Soviet society was the distortion of social relations, and subsequently the erosion of civil society which may have made populations of certain regions more vulnerable to economic and social transformations" (1998, 2038). In other words, Russia could not withstand economic shock therapy because of long-standing distorted social relations that eroded civil society.

According to Rose (1999), Russia is an "anti-modern" society that lacks the rule of law to curb state authority. Related to this, links between citizens and the state are constricted, resulting in an "hour-glass" society.

> In an hour-glass society there is a rich social life at the base, consisting of strong informal networks relying on trust between friends, relatives, and other face-to-face groups. . . . At the top of the hour-glass, there is a rich political and social life, as elites compete for power, wealth, and prestige. . . . [T]he result is not a civic community but an hour-glass society, because the links between top and bottom are very limited. (Rose 1995, 35)

Rose calls Russian citizens "anticitizens." They "protect their well-being by keeping the center of the hour-glass as narrow as possible in order to limit what the state can do to them" (1995, 41). Rose refers to the "culturalist approach" to support the claim that today's unmodern Russia is deeply rooted in "the premodern folkways of unreformed czarist rule" (1999, 68).

> From a cultural perspective, events of the past half-dozen decades, and even more so, of the past half-dozen years, are assumed to make little difference to the relationship that Russians have to life, nature, work, and vodka. While the truth of this culturalist perspective may be exaggerated, its relevance to us is clear: that the distinctly unmodern past of Russia still exists as an unacknowledged legacy, and one with which the country must still come to grips. (Rose 1999, 68)

Against this background, Rose (2000) empirically investigates the relationship between social capital and health in Russia using 1998 data. He finds an association between participation in informal networks and poorer self-rated emotional health in post-Soviet Russia. That is, individuals who use informal connections to find a flat or get medical treatment, for example, have poorer emotional health. Rose interprets this as an indication that informal networks in the Russian context are "an indirect measure of individuals retreating from formal organizations of an 'anti-modern' society that has left them with emotional scars" (2000, 1428). Rose perhaps means that Russians who rely exclusively on friends and family for help do so because they no longer trust formal institutions.

These findings are at odds with those in an earlier article coauthored by Rose (Bobak et al. 1998). Here the authors, using 1996 data, report an association between reliance on formal institutions (employer, state, public organizations, charities, or church) and poorer self-reported health. In this case, individuals who first relied on institutions for help when they had a problem felt less well. The authors call this finding "difficult to explain" but propose that, given the importance of informal social networks in Soviet Russia, "those who are forced to rely on formal institutions do so because they are socially isolated" (1998, 277).

In sum, both informal and formal measures of social capital have been found to be associated with *poorer* reported health in Russia. In contrast, Rose (2000, 1428) reports a "striking" relationship between better reported health and reliance on "anti-modern networks"—using money or connections to get officials to grant favors. He does not attempt to interpret this finding, and indeed it does not make much sense in an "hour-glass" society where citizens try to restrict connections with the state "to protect their well-being" and "limit what the state can do to them" (Rose 1995, 41).

In the research discussed above, poor health is attributed to the legacy of the Soviet past. The roots of the mortality crisis lie in a long-standing distortion of Russian social capital. At best, the mortality spike in the early 1990s reflects the inability of the Russian population to withstand painful but necessary reforms. Shock therapy in Russia is treated as normal, while the mortality crisis is an exotic complication. At worst, shock therapy simply drops out of the picture. In Rose's stark prose, "The legacy of the Soviet era is that of social failure" (1999, 70). Either way, Russians bear ultimate responsibility for the mortality crisis.

SOCIAL CAPITAL-ISM

In the Western literature the concept of social capital is as much influenced by Western capitalism as the concept of being needed is influenced by Soviet socialism. Fine (2001) and Navarro (2004) have stressed the intellectual history of social capital as intimately bound to the history of economics and a turn to Friedman's free market monetarism. The logic of the free market is the accumulation of capital, broadly defined as resources—be they natural, physical, financial, or human—used for production. Cash is capital; assets are capital; even labor may be capital. Social capital, then, "properly refers to productive value that can be extracted from social networks and organizations" (Doug Massey in Muntaner 2004, 675). Fundamentally, social capital is about what individuals receive. This is especially evident when epidemiologists measure social capital as help received in buying a home, making house repairs, seeing a doctor, getting hospital treatment, entering university, or getting a permit (Rose 2000). Or social capital is measured using the answer to the question, "On whom do you rely first of all when having problems?" (Bobak et al. 1998, 271). These variables measure what people get from others. Russians used their social connections to make things happen for themselves, certainly, but, even more importantly, for others. In this sense, social connections granted status and power.

Social capital is presumed to result in a level of organization in society that is necessarily separate from the state—civil society. In Fukuyama's (1999) treatment, civil society is an epiphenomenon of social capital. If a society has norms that promote cooperation, then civil society—voluntary associations separate from the state—will develop. Post-Soviet scholars have considered the concept of civil society extensively, contesting the assumption that there was no civil society in Soviet times and throwing doubt on the usefulness of the term (Hann and Dunn 1996; Hann 1998). Buchowski (1996), among others, troubles the assumption that civil society is necessarily separate from the state. Civil society is both used to govern and to "exert pressure on the power of state" (1996, 82). It "cannot be defined in terms of the opposition of society to the state, but should be seen as a dialectic of these two elements" (82).

Soviet social relations were complexly intertwined with the state. They were organized through Soviet structures, namely occupation, and served economic purposes, such as the distribution of goods and services. In addition, social relations infiltrated the political realm, secured political favors, and "softened the rigid constraints . . . of the Soviet political system" (Ledeneva 1998, 182). In contrast to "anticitizens" of an "hour-glass" society (Rose 1995, 1999, 2000) who attempt to limit their contact with the state, Soviet citizens were preoccupied with establishing connections inside the state apparatus to render the state more human and thereby secure favors. Soviet social relations were a culturally specific form of civil society.

It is not surprising that epidemiologists find that individuals who rely only on formal institutions or only on informal connections report poorer health. Rose finds that using so-called "anti-modern networks" (2000, 1428)—using money or connections to get officials to grant favors—is associated with better health. In Soviet times, informal connections included personal contacts within formal institutions. The combination of formal and informal, horizontal and vertical connections secured goods and services not provided through official channels of the state and its bureaucracy. Individuals with only one source of help—formal assistance or informal connections—have lost the critical combination of formal and informal. Without this, what they are able to do is limited. Without a personal connection, there is no guarantee that official institutions will respond to individuals. Without a link to official institutions, what personal connections can accomplish is also limited.

Fukuyama writes that "if the state gets into the business of organizing everything, people will become dependent on it and lose their spontaneous ability to work with one another" (2001, 18). In late Soviet Russia people honed their ability to spontaneously work with one another. Russians co-opted the organization of the state to facilitate collaboration and meet needs. In Russia it was the collapse of the state and the restructuring of the economy that compromised the ability to cooperate with others. Russians lost those "features of social life" that enabled them "to act together more effectively to pursue shared objectives" (Putnam 1996). In that sense they lost social capital, but it makes little sense to call it social capital in a society with a currency of favors. Middle-aged Muscovites call it being needed— being in the position to make things happen through the allocation of favors.

For useful or needed people in Soviet Russia, "controlling events" came not through acquiring goods and services, but through the redistribution of goods and services. Katherine Verdery writes of "allocative power" as socialism's most basic "law of motion"; power is located in redistribution instead of accumulation (1991, 420–21). While Verdery is writing of bureaucracy, the logic played out in all social relations. As one of Ledeneva's informants explains in her book on *blat,* a *blatmeister* "realized that socialist society is a huge distribution system, and one just needed to find as many wires of this system as possible and stay near the socket" (1998, 172). Needed people were able to redistribute resources precisely because they were entangled within webs of state power. As Ledeneva points out, Soviet *blat* networks were "interwoven with other forms of power—both economic and political" (1998, 2); they were "rooted in institutions of power" (68).

Social capital reflects Western ideals and the political economy of neoliberal capitalism. Being needed reflects Russian ideals and the political economy of Soviet socialism. The mortality crisis in the early 1990s is a result of the collision of two cultural logics that left a certain generation of Muscovites isolated and disempowered—unneeded—in the new Russia.

If an important component of cardiovascular risk is psychosocial, then it is also cultural and political-economic. In different populations, different psychosocial factors may exist. This does not necessarily mean that receiving support is not important for heart health in Russia. Neither does it necessarily mean that giving is not important for heart health in the West. It does suggest that certain risk factors may be more culturally salient or more culturally visible and that their effects could be heightened or muted depending on culture.

How then does being unneeded result in increased cardiovascular mortality? Why is being unneeded unhealthy for the heart? There is Western literature suggesting that giving—altruism and pet ownership—improves cardiovascular health (Arhant-Sudhir, Arhant-Sudhir, and Sudhir 2011; Das and O'Keefe 2006; Post 2005). A few studies among the elderly have suggested that receiving support is not always beneficial when it leads to indebtedness and dependency (Silverstein, Chen, and Heller 1996; Stoller 1985). The specific relationship, condition of need, expectation of long-term reciprocity, cultural norms, and life-course position all act as modifiers on the effects of receiving social support. In some cases, giving may be more important for health and well-being (Liang, Krause, and Bennett 2001; Batson 1998).

Giving is also active, while receiving is passive. In Soviet Russia giving was a form of control over circumstances. Perceived control is a well-established cardiovascular risk factor. In his article on social capital in post-Soviet Russia, Rose writes, "Among all the indicators of social capital, however defined, a sense of controlling events has the largest Beta for physical and emotional health" (2000, 1429).[1] Other data support the link between perceived control and health in post-Soviet Russia (Bobak et al. 1998; Bobak et al. 2000). Barrett and Buckley (2009), using data from 2003, find that women report less perceived control than men in Russia, as elsewhere. Perhaps the effects of perceived control on morbidity and mortality vary by gender. Measurements of perceived control do not measure being needed. Being needed may attenuate the effects of low perceived control among women.

Some middle-aged Muscovites might insist that Russians have had little control over their lives throughout history and that they themselves are no exception. Nonetheless, social connections in Soviet times served as a minor corrective by which individuals, in collaboration, could displace the weight of history and politics. Through these connections Russians felt a sense of space apart from the prevailing order of their time. In the early 1990s,

unneeded people were not able to push against order to create a bit of undetermined space. Unneeded people did not have recourse to the logic of social
relations because they could not offer anything to others. Therefore, they
were subject to the whims of history and politics.

The logic of being needed is about giving, but its importance for health
may come from the way it fosters social integration. A study comparing
middle-aged men in Lithuania and Sweden finds that psychosocial factors
such as social integration may be more important than classic risk factors
for cardiovascular disease (Kristenson et al. 1998). Moreover, these differences may also explain socioeconomic differences in cardiovascular health
in Sweden (Kristenson et al. 2001). Intriguingly, Stone (2000, 1733) notes
research that finds Estonian women who felt "less valued" had higher heart
rates, a risk factor for cardiovascular damage. The logic of social integration is culturally specific, and yet culturally specific logic may reveal roots of
poor health in other places too.

ALCOHOL

In the epidemiology on alcohol use, puzzling research findings show that
alcohol use in Russia is not related to psychological distress (Cockerham,
Hinote, and Abbott 2006), anxiety sensitivity (Zvolensky et al. 2005), alienation (Palosuo 2000), or poor self-reported health (Cockerham 2000; Perlman
and Bobak 2008). In fact, some studies report that alcohol use is associated
with better indicators of health, both psychological and physical (Rose 2002;
Bobak et al. 1998). Bobak and colleagues (1998) find that individuals con-
suming more alcohol report better physical functioning. They find this "difficult to interpret," simply commenting, "the direction and magnitude of this
association are not plausible and most likely reflect reverse causation" (1998,
275). In other words, sick individuals stop drinking; the association between
alcohol consumption and better health is spurious. The article focuses on perceived control as a predictor of reported health, but the relationship between
alcohol and perceived control is not reported. Cockerham (2000) does not
report on the relationship between alcohol and reported health but does consider that men are both more likely to drink and more likely to report better
health. He attributes this finding to men's "lack of knowledge or awareness
about the implications of their health lifestyle, or a disregard that may ultimately prove fatal" (2000, 1318). McKeehan (2000) finds that individuals who drink report better physical health in Moscow. It seems that for a

majority of Russian men, alcohol may improve health—certainly self-reported health, but perhaps even objectively measured health.

Self-reported health and mortality are not the same outcome, but they are often correlated (Idler and Benyamini 1997). The fact that they show significant relationships with alcohol in *opposite* directions—drinkers report better health and frequent heavy drinkers are more likely to die—is intriguing and may help to explain why uncovering a strong epidemiological association between alcohol consumption and mortality has not been straightforward. McKeehan's (2000) article uses sophisticated multilevel modeling to show that while an individual who drinks is more likely to report better health, individuals living in areas of the city where more alcohol is consumed report poorer health. It is possible to once again interpret this as reverse causation—sick drinkers stop drinking. Another interpretation is that drinking improves health for individuals living in areas of the city where health is poor. In this case alcohol would serve as protection in an environment of risk.

In a recent article Leon, Shkolnikov, and McKee write:

> We are still lacking an adequate account of what underlying mechanisms may have transmitted the shocks of the collapse of communism and the succeeding convulsions that affected all aspects of Russian society, to the behaviours of individuals, inducing many to change their drinking and thereby altering their risk of premature death. . . . [A] complete explanation for the role of alcohol in the Russian mortality crisis has to go beyond this to examine the social and psychological mechanisms involved. Pathways are going to operate both through the effects of ethanol on physiology as well as through the effects of social deprivation, impoverishment and isolation that are a result of drinking. (2009, 1634)

This quotation begins with a call for ethnography. Ethnography has the potential to reveal "underlying mechanisms" that connect large-scale social change to the experiences and behaviors of individuals. The mechanisms hinge on an understanding of Soviet and post-Soviet social relations and their embeddedness in larger ideological, political, and economic configurations. Leon, Shkolnikov, and McKee conclude by highlighting social deprivation, impoverishment, and isolation as a result of drinking. Certainly, frequent binging and the use of surrogates will contribute to these. But drinking is also a reaction to social deprivation, impoverishment, and isolation.

DRINKING AND BEING NEEDED

When Natasha's three children were young and she was not working in the hospital, her husband drank. "He crawled, like a cockroach on all fours," she told me, as a description of his low state. She would take her children with her to meet him as he left work and collect his salary, but he would sometimes leave through another exit, disappearing for three or four days at a time. They have since separated, although they are not divorced. He has stopped drinking and they now share responsibility caring for their granddaughter during the week. Natasha has her granddaughter until five in the afternoon. When he comes home from work as a lathe operator, her husband looks after Katya until ten at night. When I asked if it was hard for her husband to stop drinking, she spoke about his various past treatments. She also spoke of his relationship with his granddaughter: "He can now drink a bottle of beer or something else, but he has a granddaughter, he helps out really well, he buys what . . . he buys her everything. He loves her. He teaches her everything. They even do drawing and everything." Her husband doesn't need to drink now because he is needed as a grandfather.

Unneeded men drink. As one interviewee told me: "And what to do? . . . Everywhere you go, whatever you say they push you away, and say 'Go away, who needs you?' He drinks, there isn't another option." In the early 1990s, men struggled to maintain a sense of being needed, but women were more needed than ever in the family. My friend Tatiyana, who took Margarita back to Novyi Arbat street after fifteen years, explained:

> Because, for a man it is very scary to not be needed. Yes, really scary, because for a woman it is all the same. She is always needed because she is in the family. So, she is in the family and she must care for someone. But a man must feel needed, if you will, his . . . well, some sort of significance. And when that collapsed. . . . Well, what I mean is my generation, the men of my generation, because those drops in [earnings]. [. . .] The working pay of those people fell very low. Why? Because all of industry was ruined. That's why. [. . .] And a person who suddenly sees that not only can he no longer provide for his family, but even for himself, in general, feed himself. He loses himself. And that is why for many men it was a simply a catastrophe. Because of this they began to drink more.

While women do drink in Russia, they are much less likely to drink than men (Bobrova et al. 2010). Women are more likely to sit together over tea in the kitchen. Nonetheless, in the early 1990s women also turned to drink. In fact, deaths among women attributable to alcohol dependence and alcohol poisoning registered one of the largest percentage increases from 1990 to 1994 of all causes of death (Notzon et al. 1998). Tellingly, middle-aged Muscovites considered women drunks an especially ominous sign. Interviewees thought that drinking women must not have children. One woman explained:

> A woman, she doesn't let herself go. More often than not a woman . . . well those who have children, those who . . . I am saying, we are not talking about those. . . . There are those [who drink] among women. Those are the worst drunks and that's it. But in general, women have children. There are some grandchildren. So a woman already gets something, do you understand? One or two children to raise.

I let her continue.

> I was at the sanatorium and I said that . . . I said, "Well, something happened and it is as if I am not needed as a mother." Like that. And they said to me, "What are you on about? You say such things!" So, to raise [children], that is over all, that is already over and above. So there. So I calmed down.

At some point in her life, this woman lost the sense that she was needed. But she was a mother and the others at a sanatorium (I assume these were women, but they could have been men) were shocked that she would even entertain the thought that she was not needed. "What are you on about? You say such things!" The others might not have had to say much more. She understood what they meant. Women get something "over and above" from raising children—a sense of neededness.

What do Russian men do when they confront being unneeded? Older Russian men traditionally do not have the same relationship with their children or grandchildren as Russian women do. If they are not able to provide for women or children and do not feel valued at work, there is not much to prove that they are needed in society. Drinking may be one way men are able to experience a sense of neededness. Drinking in Russia is a culturally sanctioned mode for men to experience, as Tatiyana said, "some sort of significance." It does this by satisfying a yearning for social belonging. Pesmen quotes a man who explained why drunks talk so much about respect. "They are really saying 'Do you feel that I am an absolutely related, dear person to you?'" (1995, 72). Another woman told her that respect is "awareness of others" (1995, 72). Drinking is also tied to social belonging and status through giving and generosity (Pesmen 1995, 2000). At the alcohol policy seminar Vasilii, the former alcoholic, mused on drinking as a threesome: "Thee people and one half-liter bottle. How do you divide five hundred [milliliters] by three? Yet there were never any fights." Drinking together is status leveling (Koester 2003), creating a sense of social equality and belonging. People who refuse to drink with others may be accused of thinking themselves superior. In the early 1990s, a sense of social equality among drinkers would have been especially important for men whose status in the new Russia was the least secure. In Moscow unemployed middle-aged men with less education were exposed to the emergence of the nouveaux riches as they themselves became unneeded.

Drinking also relates to the ideas of order and space in Russia. As far as order, drinking is a ritualized practice that is primarily undertaken with others and tightens social bonds. As far as space, drinking is a practice that flouts authority and social responsibility—a bit of space free from the state, work, or family.

DRINKING AND SPACE

On the first day of the 2007 Moscow alcohol policy seminar, a Russian man who did not identify himself stood after a panel on alcohol mortality to make a comment. He began by talking about how hard liquors are referred to as "spirits" in English. In Russia, he said, drinking was also related to spirit and soul. "It is happiness," he continued, "and you are not talking about that side of it." His comments, while acknowledged, met with little response. Later I was in on small talk where some of the social scientists commented on the man's ruddy skin tone and insinuated that he might be "one of those"—which I took to mean an alcoholic. When I found this man at the seminar reception he had been drinking. I wanted to ask about what he meant by happiness, but he was soon diagnosing the peculiar characteristics of my unborn child. The topic made me intensely uncomfortable and I left. Despite my failure to elicit more from him, I think his reaction to the presentations connecting alcohol exclusively to mortality is crucial to understanding why Russian men drink and why they might have drunk more in the early 1990s.

Another man told me that men are the warriors and hunters, the risk takers. "If I am alive or not . . ." He didn't finish his thought but continued with a story from Pushkin's historical novel *The Captain's Daughter* (1957). When Pugachev, the leader of the Cossack Rebellion under Catherine the Great, is reminded of his impending mortality, he recounts the story of an eagle and crow. The eagle asked, "Crow, isn't it unjust somehow that you live three hundred years and I only thirty? Why is that?" The crow said, "Everything depends on diet, on food." The eagle said he would feed on what the crow did and they flew off. The crow found a dead horse and pecked at the decaying flesh. The eagle pecked once, pecked twice, and spit it out, declaring, "It is better to live thirty years and feed on living blood, than to live three hundred on carrion." This man then interpreted the story:

> In that is the heart of the matter, of all stories about our men. At the heart
> of it we end our own lives, with our arrogance, our pretension, our drive
> somewhere, to certain heights. [. . .] And what is more, it is considered
> almost culture, if I want to weasel out of something, I must [. . .] sit a bit.
> Related to this, it isn't a shot, a taste of whisky[2] for example, but by the
> glassful. We are avid smokers, all of us, and a multitude of other excesses.

Men "weasel out" of their responsibilities through drink. What is more, they transcend the banality of their everyday lives through drinking and other excesses. In their article using life stories to illustrate different patterns of drinking, Zdravomyslova and Chikadze write about one man who drank "to alleviate the unbearable boredom of his existence. He says, 'All my adventures take place when I am drunk'" (2000, 46). Sokolov writes, "In Russian culture, intoxication is seen as a state that temporarily places individuals outside the moral boundaries of the moral community—and then admits them back in" (2006, 17–18). Individuals are able to maneuver between society's conflicting claims and alternative moralities (Sokolov 2006; Koester 2003). Men, in particular, can feed on living flesh and never fully lose themselves.

Russian men crave the fresh, the real, and the spontaneous. Like the eagle feeding on living blood, Russian men would rather experience the thrills and extremes of life even if they die young. A Russian cardiologist told me that he had trouble convincing his male patients to take their medication. He tried to tell them that taking their medication would lengthen their lives. That did not move them. "Think of your grandchildren," he would say. It did not seem to matter. Middle-aged men did not seem to care if they lived five more years. They wanted to live life to the fullest and if that meant a shorter life, so be it. Drinking opens up space beyond mere existence.

At the same time, moments of release into this unbound space are ordinarily held in check by the very limits they flout. Order and responsibility demarcate space for spontaneity and excess, and even yield as men push against them, but they do not fully give way. In Soviet times, the drive to excess was limited, to greater or lesser degrees, by responsibility to family and state. As my landlord told me, if a man needed to work during the week, he better sober up after the weekend. On the other hand, if men lost their work or were idle at work, there was little reason to stop drinking come Monday. Over time, as Soviet ideology and state control waned, and work was no longer imbued with the same sense of significance, it no longer held men back. This may be why mortality started to increase in the 1960s.

In the early 1990s when the Soviet state was defunct and the contours of the new Russia still hazy, men's risk taking was not sufficiently counterbalanced by any order. In the context of a failed state, drinking could spin out of control and become excessive. When the Soviet state fell, men turned to drink to experience a lost sense of social belonging, as well as a sense of power to push against what bound them. Unfortunately, not much bound them. Responsibilities that ordinarily served to limit excessive drinking were diminished. Men pushed further and further before finding limits. Working-class men suddenly rendered unneeded by the state would have been most at risk, especially if they were also unneeded at home. Feeling unneeded may even have led to increased negative effects from problematic drinking.

Drinking binds people together at the same time as it sets them free. Initially this seems contradictory—a paradox. But if we think of Vasilii's soul, the energetic envelope around the body, the soul allows the self to escape the atomism of the body and venture out into the spiritual space of society. Individuals can push against the borders of the envelope and, in so doing, enlarge their souls.

REMEDY FOR THE SOUL

Drinking in the early 1990s was a logical response to what one interviewee called the "death of society." Russian drinking ties individuals together in soulful communion. It is true that drinking can also be destructive. Drinking among Russian men is often binge drinking, so even normal drinking behavior, if done frequently enough, will drive up death rates from alcohol poisoning and cardiovascular deaths related to repeat binging, especially among men who are unneeded. Further, as men increasingly rely on drinking as one of a diminished set of social practices that are soulful—that is, social—drinking eventually turns on them to become a mark of soullessness and social isolation.

Kideckel's (2008) ethnography of working-class Romanians describes drinking as part of identity, work-team solidarity, and masculinity. In postsocialist Romania more men drink alone. Furthermore, "stress-related drinking . . . magnifies alcohol's negative effects on body, health, and spirit" (2008, 203). In Zdravomyslova and Chikadze's article on drinking patterns, Vlad's drinking "became excessive and self-destructive when other masculine characteristics, i.e. a well-paid job, independence, and a stable family life, deteriorated" (2000, 43). Sometimes, though, drinking among Russian men is facilitated by their work and workplace, "embedded in social norms related to particular industries and the reproduction of the masculine 'worker' identity" (Saburova et al. 2011, 8). As long as men remain employed, this may protect them to a degree by containing drink within a framework—giving drinking a space without letting it spin out of control.

Medical anthropologist Merrill Singer and colleagues' article "Why Does Juan García Have a Drinking Problem?" illustrates how one man's drinking problem bears the imprint of global political economy. Analysis that remains at the level of the individual is deeply misleading. In this case, expanding wage labor in Puerto Rico created a relationship between masculinity and alcohol, wherein alcohol was reward for labor. When Juan García immigrated to Brooklyn and subsequently lost his factory work there, "drinking was all that was left for Juan that was manly in his understanding" (Singer et al. 2010, 316). Similar historical analyses trace the effect of industrialization on masculinity and drinking in Russia (Hinote and Webber 2012; Transchel 2006).

Some epidemiologists dismiss the finding that alcohol use is associated with better indicators of reported health, calling it "not plausible" (Bobak et al. 1998). If drinking serves to connect individuals, repair a sense of neededness, or reassert masculinity and social equality, this finding should be expected. In the early 1990s drinking provided Russian men a sense of being a part of something larger—society—at a time when society itself was in question. Alcohol use is not always associated with indicators of psychosocial stress because drinking is what real, soulful Russian men do. Drinking men are socially connected men with social status. Thus, drinking is often associated with better health.

Drinking in Russia during the early 1990s was not only an attempt to escape problems but perhaps primarily an attempt to address them, with sometimes tragic consequences. Alcohol in Russia improves men's health—both perceived emotional and physical health—before it ever kills them. Much drinking in Russia is *resilience,* a culturally sanctioned means for men to express their masculinity, neededness, and social significance.

A focus on alcohol as a behavioral risk factor leads to a preoccupation with the individual and draws attention away from the larger political-economic context. Alcohol is part of the mortality crisis, but the behavior of individuals reflects broader social logics, themselves reflections of political economy at the local, national, and global levels. In its attempt to identify risk factors, epidemiology strips these factors of their cultural context.

So why were certain Russians more likely to die in the early 1990s? The destruction of the state and the socialist economy was also the destruction of certain Soviet social connections that granted Russians a limited means of control over their lives. Social connections and perceived control are known to be associated with cardiovascular health. Alcohol-related deaths are also related to the destruction of social connections. Russian men sought social connection through drink—the traditional means by which men bond. Coupled with Russian men's predilection for extremes, men drank harder and more frequently. In Soviet times responsibilities to the state and family served to hold men back. With these defunct or diminished in the early 1990s, men ventured further away, losing themselves. It was the death of Soviet society and a sickness in the soul—that soul which lies between people—that made the individual body vulnerable. "The death of society is at first spiritual, then physical."

CHAPTER 8

Freedom

I don't understand what freedom [*svoboda*] is. I don't understand that word.

—interviewee

In the West, many people originally saw the undoing of the Soviet state as the beginning of political freedom in Russia. "Russia Free" optimistically proclaimed Brisbane's *Courier-Mail* after the failed August 1991 coup against Gorbachev (Anderson 1991). Soon thereafter, the headlines were less sanguine. The *Washington Times* ran the headline, "Russia's Needs Go Beyond Freedom" (Sieff 1991). In December Adelaide's *Advertiser* cautioned about the "High Price of Russia's 'Freedom.'" Newspaper headlines in 1992 and 1993 echoed the sentiment that Russian freedom came at a cost.

When Soviet bureaucracy and industry unraveled in 1992 and 1993, so did the rules and resources that individuals used to make things happen. In that sense, when Margarita and Tatiyana say "there is no more of that space," they meant that their ability to maneuver through and against the state was constricted. That type of space felt like freedom precisely because it was held apart from the state and often circumvented or pushed against the state. Thus, individuals had a social freedom based on their ability to connect with others and cooperate to overcome problems. Margarita and Tatiyana, among many other middle-aged Muscovites, did not experience the early 1990s as freedom. In fact, in the absence of a stable order they felt socially disempowered.

Connections were compromised. Besides, chaos and confusion meant there was nothing much to act against. The early 1990s was disorienting and life threatening. Individuals, especially men, were free from the state and free from social relations grounded in the state. Free to die.

Not surprisingly, among this older generation, talk about freedom is highly ambivalent. When Sveta asked Lyudmila about freedom she responded, "What freedom?" Sveta gave the example of being able to go abroad. "Freedom, yes, now go ahead, wherever you want. Yes, freedom. But how will you go? There is nothing [no money] to go with." "And how do you understand freedom?" Sveta asked. "We don't have freedom. We are now all forgotten." Real freedom is social relevance—being needed, not forgotten. In Russia, freedom is predicated on participation in social practices that give the individual a sense of social relevance and a sense of social power—the ability to intervene in the world and make a difference. In addition, freedom implies carving out space that is not fully determined by the official order. Just as the space of the soul ideally exceeds the individual body, the space of the social transcends societal structures. The Soviet system unwittingly granted that space. Russian capitalism may, in fact, be no different in this wise. However, especially in the early 1990s, Russian capitalism had not solidified to the extent that it could offer ordinary people any sense of a transcendent space.

Western political philosophy has long defined freedom as either negative or positive (Berlin 1969): negative freedom is the absence of constraint and positive freedom the ability to act toward self-realization. Years ago, MacCallum (1967) proposed that freedom is a triadic relationship between constraints, agent, and actions. Thus, freedom is the absence of constraints so that an agent may act. The way middle-aged Muscovites spoke of freedom differs from these formulations. The notions of structure and soul complicate seemingly natural categories such as constraint, agent, and action.

A different freedom evolved with the Soviet state. Sveta, who would have been only ten in 1991, told me, "We used to have such literature and films. Now we are free and nobody has a use for them." Freedom needs constraint to frame it, to give it something to play with, and something to push against. In this analysis freedom is not the absence of constraint so that an agent may act (MacCallum 1967) but the presence of constraint so that an agent may act against it. It is only in pushing against constraint that agents experience true freedom. True freedom is found in undetermined spaces, framed by the rules that govern our lives and that keep us from losing ourselves entirely.

Bespredel—Freedom without Limits

The Russian word *bespredel* literally translates as "without limits." In the Russian-English dictionary it is translated as "license" or "unbridled freedom" (Katzner 1994). When I asked my two young female research assistants to define *bespredel,* they related it to chaos, when there are no laws and when moral norms are unclear—"there are no clear models for what is good and what is bad." *Bespredel* is when people do things that do not fit within legal, moral, or ethical frameworks or norms. "That is when people do what is good for them and don't consider anything else."

Middle-aged Muscovites mourned the loss of the Soviet framework. A woman told Ira: "Of course it has become, well before under communism, you could say, somehow it was all ordered [*po polochkam*], do you understand? But now it is some sort of license [*bespredel*]. Well, where . . . and you don't know to whom. . . . Look if something happens, you don't know whom to turn to. You don't know. Well I don't even know how to express it." Ira started to ask a question: "Well, how do you think that . . ."

> What's to think? I know that now there is unbridled freedom [*bespredel*]
> from every side [. . .] from every side, wherever you turn, well, how
> everyone is dismissed [*chto tak raspustit' vsekh liudei*]. Now even adults
> are not what they once were and even at work they spit. And they spit on
> everything. Oh! I don't like that. There, I don't like this order. Let there be
> Stalin or whomever, under Stalin didn't we also live? Well there wasn't such
> unbridled freedom [*bespredel*] there wasn't.

Po polochkam, which I have loosely translated as "ordered," comes from the root word for shelf, *polka*. But *polka* also has the connotation of compartment or cubbyhole, so *po polochkam* here might be translated as "in a frame." The connotation of compartment or cubbyhole also conveys space. Bounded space, but space nonetheless. Space within order.

This woman thought that the loss of order meant "you don't know whom to turn to." The loss of order disrupts social relations. People are embedded within a partially known political and economic social landscape that enables them to know, again partially, others embedded in that same social landscape. When the framing is transformed, people are no longer held by the expected, taken-for-granted structures through which they are known and know other people. Social interactions suffer. There is no one to turn to because it is hard to know who people are. What kind of person are they? What will they do? The framework that normally helps answer those questions is missing.

In the early 1990s, individuals had unbridled freedom (*bespredel*) and space without limits. "Everyone went their own way." A taxi driver explained it thus:

> Here is what I want to tell you, in the 1990s they said there was freedom, democracy, but the freedom was bad. The democracy was bad. We don't need that kind. It was, you know it's called "no limits" [*bespredel*]. Whatever they want, they do. And the main thing, everywhere it was "no limits," completely "no limits." You know in the nineties I had this impression: that we were all like a dog that had been on a leash [and] then broke away. And everybody . . . that was how it was: people broke away from leashes. [. . .] Everyone was off their leashes, everyone. Everyone was fierce to each other. Everyone was dissatisfied because, well, because it was obscure what was happening. First of all, the power of the law wasn't active. The power of the law which should be followed for order, it was gone. It was like that.

I asked him if things were less obscure now. "Well, people have already cooled down a little, cooled down. They began to think a little. It's like that in my opinion. They began to reflect, began to reflect, what and how. [. . .] They began to put a stay on something." The fundamental problem in Moscow in the early 1990s was not that Soviet socialism was defunct, but rather that rules and resources of social practice, those that derived from state bureaucracy and economy, were undergoing transformation. The rules by which individuals came to know and interact with other individuals were being rewritten. "Everyone went their own way." *Bespredel* is freedom without constraint.

Svoboda

Russian-informed considerations of freedom have recently appeared in the literature. *Svoboda,* the most common Russian translation for freedom, comes from the root word *svoi* (self/ours). "Its etymological load is . . . telling. Its Indo-European root is *se- or *sue, the same root that forms the term for the social category, 'svoi,' or 'one's own.' Svoboda's linguistic burial grounds yield symbolism that takes us far from [*sic*] Western sense of the term for anarchical, self-centered acts. This freedom is one that is seemingly rooted in society and social intercourse" (Paxson 2005, 96). According to Caroline Humphrey, in medieval times *svoboda* meant something akin to "the security and well-being that result from living amongst one's own people"; "an agglomeration of practices of our own way of life" (2007, 2). "It suggests an image of a social kind of freedom, one that was not centred on the singular individual" (2).

Living among one's own people, though, relies on constraint and restraint. One interviewee explained: "It doesn't mean, of course, that freedom is everything permitted, everything. No, I don't think like that. Above all there should be some sort of own internal censure so that it [lies] in rational limits. In limits so that my freedom does not become bondage for someone." Another said, "Freedom is responsibility. You answer [for others]." In *From Under the Rubble,* Solzhenitsyn proclaims, "Freedom is self-restriction! Restriction of the self for the sake of others!" (1981, 136). Freedom must involve limits and constraint if it is conceived as social. *Svoboda* is inflected with social order.

Humphrey and Boym consider the Russian word *volia* as another variant of freedom. "*Volia* is sensation, emotion, and action. It is both the conscious willing and the active exercise of boundless release, something that one experiences away from society or any kind of limitation. It is direct and unpretentious" (Humphrey 2007, 6). Boym writes, "*volia* is usually a liberation from social ties for oneself only" (2010, 78–79). If *svoboda* is social in nature, *volia* is individual. In its most dangerous form *volia* is freedom to act against the social self—the soul. "It is not just that the volya of another person may be harmful to one's self, it is that the psychic consequences of unrestrained volya are likely to be destructive to the very person holding it" (Humphrey 2007, 6). *Volia* is commonly translated into English as "will." While *svoboda* intimates order and constraint, *volia* is more aligned with unbound space.

In one interview a woman explained that men had a harder time in the early 1990s even though, "there are . . . those among men who are strong with *volia.* They, of course, on the other hand, get up, fight, organize their affairs. It is as if for them it is *prostor, volia,* it is like opportunity." Here boundless space is only ever navigated by a strong will. Only someone who knows exactly where they are going can risk spinning off into space and losing himself. Flirting with that type of extreme risk may be especially seductive to Russian men.

After I had known Ivan awhile, he asked if I would visit some of his English classes to chat with his students. At the end of these classes, I asked the students to write, anonymously, the answer to three questions. One of the questions was "What, in your opinion, is freedom (*svoboda*)?" One young man wrote:

> Real freedom is when a person has lost absolutely everything, when he already has nothing to lose. A free person doesn't fear death because it is inevitable. He doesn't depend on anything. I have arrived at this based on my personal experience. Here is the model of a person not free: choose work, family, choose a car, choose a television, a refrigerator, furniture, choose good health and sport, etc. A free man does not choose.

In the margin next to an asterisk he wrote, in English, "see 'Fight Club.'"

Fight Club is a 1996 novel by Chuck Palahniuk, later turned into a cult film about secret male fight clubs that evolve into an anticonsumerist, anarchic, terrorist organization. In the book freedom is glossed as "losing all hope" (Palahniuk 1999, 14). At the same time, the book is about male belonging. Men fight each other as part of the club. The fight club is a society of men united against consumer society. The student wrote that "a free man does not choose." Indeed, each of the choices he lists—work, family, car, television, refrigerator, health, sport—could be seen as a surrender to consumer society. Conformity is disguised as free choice, and each choice serves to further entrap individuals in prevailing political-economic arrangements.

This young man's vision of freedom is a freedom from society. As such, it is unbound and risky. "A free person doesn't fear death." Indeed, many men insufficiently bound, faced with *prostor,* and without the *volia* to navigate it did meet their deaths. Freedom is only safe when it is social.

FREEDOM IN CONSTRAINT

In Paxson's ethnography, informants are nostalgic for freedom, in a way that makes little sense for Westerners. "During the time of Stalin, we lived better than we live now. Everyone was free" (2005, 96). Nielsen's ethnography of St. Petersburg in the early 1980s highlights an authority-freedom duality. In his account freedom demands an anchor in authority, or rather multiple anchors in different forms of authority. Like the layers of an onion, the anchors start with the state and proceed inward toward the intimate circle of friends and relatives where moral responsibility reigns. At its purest, freedom is individual and "a dissolving, anarchic force from within, undermining all order and self-restraint" (Nielsen 2006, under "C. The Free Outpouring of the Soul"). Authority protects against this anarchic freedom (under "D. Faith and the Weakness of Authority"). In Boym's evocative *Another Freedom* she writes, "Freedom is only possible . . . with concern for boundaries" (2010, 4). Each of these accounts introduces some element of order and constraint to the concept of freedom—Stalin, authority, boundaries. Boym likens freedom to an adventure: "It explores new borders but never erases or transcends them. Through adventure we can test the limits but also navigate—more or less successfully—between convention and invention, responsibility and play" (5). Freedom is space for the unknown, the possible, the "what if."

For middle-aged Muscovites, individuals are free when they have the space (*prostor*) to act through and against order. The structure of order is a necessary condition because certain structures are used to bend and circumvent others. In Soviet society, such space was found within the order of the state. Social relations in this space often collectively pushed against the power of the state, although they were not always successful in doing so. In this analysis, freedom is not the absence of constraint but the presence of constraint. If there are few rules to wield and to bend, there is little freedom.

SPIRITUAL FREEDOM

In her account of the Russian concept of freedom Boym uses two examples from Dostoevsky. In *The Brothers Karamazov* the monk Elder Zosima considers the monastic life as a source of freedom. "People may ridicule the vows of obedience, fasting, and prayer, yet these are the only way to attain true freedom. . . . Who is more likely to conceive a great idea and serve it: the isolated rich man or the man *freed* from the tyranny of habits and material goods?" (Dostoevsky 2003, 420). In Dostoevsky's novel *The House of the Dead* the prisoner in a Siberian penal colony thinks, "In consequence of our day dreaming and our long divorce from it, freedom appeared to us here, somehow freer than real freedom, that exists in fact, in real life" (1985, 355). To a Westerner, the monastery and the prison are unexpected locations of freedom.

Dostoevsky, along with other Russian philosophers, interprets freedom as an inner, spiritual state that cannot be quenched by confinement. In fact, freedom is only truly known in confinement. Confinement bears down on freedom, putting it under pressure and distilling it. In turn, this "freer freedom" puts pressure on the borders around it, bending them back. The very friction between freedom and the order that delineates its space serves as proof that freedom exists. I am free because I struggle with what binds me. I am free because I recognize the frame around my life. I cannot remove it, but I can nudge it further away, at least momentarily. What at first glance seems nonsense—that freedom can reside in the monastery and the prison—makes more sense if freedom is found in the relationship between order and space.

The Western account of freedom and constraint is different. In Foucault's *Discipline and Punish: The Birth of the Prison* (1995), the monastery is the birthplace of dominion. In the monastery, disciplinary methods such as cloister, cell, exercise, and timetable render docile bodies without the use of overt force or violence. Modern institutions such as prisons, barracks, schools, factories, and hospitals all inherit methods of monastic discipline. Disciplinary methods enclose and partition space, but the space is so finely partitioned that individuals occupy their own space. The space they are granted is not a space of collectivism, indeterminacy, possibility, and spontaneity—the soulful space in between people—but a space of individualism, observation, control, and rank—the space of a single physical body. In Foucault's account, freedom hardly exists at all. If it does exist, it is experienced by exercising existing disciplinary techniques. Freedom does not challenge constraint as much as maintain constraint. Constraint, therefore, determines the limits of freedom and is a threat to freedom.

THE PRISON OF THE INDIVIDUAL

Some older Muscovites think of life now as narrower, not broader. Some of this is due to poverty and inequality, but some of it is due to capitalism's insistence on a different sense of freedom, one in which dominant political-economic logics colonize individual bodies and desires. Some describe younger generations as different people and their lives as narrower. Professor Vladislav told me: "Now I look at the young new generation. They strive more for comfort, for stability. They want a quiet life. In that sense the mentality is becoming more Western, more modern. They simply want to organize their small individual life and big projects don't worry them." As Sveta and I sat on the park bench with Valentina, our first interviewee, she spoke about Russian's wide nature and emotional richness. "For us Europeans, some of them . . . are somehow narrow, [going] from this to that." She thought European children were more obedient than Russian children. Russians were less disciplined. "Freedom and democracy," she said, and paused. "In Russia these things are somehow never simple."

For many middle-aged Muscovites, individual freedom is an oxymoron. Freedom lies in society, in the space of the soul outside of the body. A monastery is a collective of monks; even a prison is a collective of prisoners. Dostoevsky thought that true freedom was no stranger to the monastery or the prison. Perhaps he might also have thought that a true individualism is no stranger to the prison. Individualism imprisons the soul.

STRUCTURE AND AGENCY

At a seminar on post-Soviet mortality in Kiev in October 2006, I overheard an exchange between two sociologists, one American and one Russian. The American had presented a paper that used Max Weber's concepts of life choices and life chances, drawing a distinction between agency and structure. The Russian sociologist made the comment that those born in poor families did not have many choices. The American responded, "Sometimes structure is more important." The Russian paused and said that structure was not operating for those in the lowest socioeconomic statuses.

It became clear that structure meant something entirely different to these two social scientists. According to the Russian, social structure enabled agency. According to the American, social structure constrained agency. The conversation reflected different conceptual relations between freedom and constraint. In the one telling, structure is manipulated by individuals. Structure may impose on individuals but it does not penetrate them. In the West, structure manipulates individuals. Structure fashions individuals in its own image. Surely both of these dynamics are at work in every society—to greater or lesser degrees.

The generation of older Muscovites will soon pass away. Fewer Russians will be nostalgic for the space (*prostor*) that existed in Soviet times. Russians will find space in the structure of Russian capitalism, although the quality of the space will be different. People will learn new rules and wield new resources. As long as Russians are brought further into the fold of global capitalism, they will be sufficiently restrained. And, for that, they will be less likely to die untimely deaths.

Conclusion

Middle-aged Muscovites connected freedom to constraint. In pushing against constraint—bending or breaking the rules, playing with the System—middle-aged Muscovites had a sense of nudging the weight of culture and history. Constraints are necessary to be a part of society, but, by playing with those constraints, people show that they know what binds them and that they have some power to loosen the binds.

Others see freedom as essentially unconstrained—unencumbered by government, unencumbered by society. There are two ways to understand these differences in the idea of freedom. The first would be to assert that freedom is a particular experience. That is, there are cultural differences in the experience of freedom, although it may be a universal ideal. In this sense, perceived freedom reflects differences in the relationship between the individual and society. Another way to understand these differences is to say that cultures recognize and emphasize certain aspects of freedom over others. In this sense, both constraint and agency are implicated—two sides of a coin—but certain accounts reveal more about constraint while others reveal more about agency. I do not think that these two possibilities—freedom as particular or freedom as universal—necessarily contradict one another. Senses of freedom could exist along a continuum. At some distance, depending on the observer, they will look like two different things.

Seeing freedom as universal or particular, however, has practical and political implications. I might conclude this account with a classically ethnographic point: concepts that are taken-for-granted truths are actually products of the cultural configurations we live by. America's self-proclaimed role as the guardian of freedom around the world is less about freedom and more about the exportation of a certain configuration of American ideas and practices. Fighting for others' freedom is actually fighting for others' acceptance of American political economy. This is one conclusion.

Another possible conclusion assumes that aspects of freedom are universal, although differently perceived. This, I think, is the more sophisticated argument, although it is vulnerable to co-option by those who believe that certain people are freer than others and should be liberated. This is not what I mean or intend. This conclusion also has a classically ethnographic point: understanding how others live their lives helps us to see more clearly how we live our own. Middle-aged Muscovites spoke about being free in the time of Stalin, clearly eliding the overt oppression of those times. They also spoke of unbridled freedom, *bespredel,* in post-Soviet Russia. Perhaps the only reason they were so clear and forceful on these points was because they understood there was another sense of freedom—a freedom that, ironically, was imposed through neoliberal economic reform and then structured by Russian capitalism.

With the knowledge that more than one account of freedom exists, middle-aged Muscovites endeavored to express their own understanding and experience of freedom. "Freedom is responsibility." "We don't have freedom, we are now all forgotten." "We work day and night. What kind of freedom is that?" Or they stopped trying: "I don't understand what freedom is. I don't understand that word." They saw the ridiculousness in an idea of freedom where individuals are free to do whatever they like. They said, "There will be freedom in the grave." And, laughing, "Freedom is only our dream." For in Russian capitalism, as in Soviet socialism, freedom comes into being through political economy. Older Muscovites were, in a sense, all participant observers of the new Russian order. They saw how freedom was predicated on submitting to the logic of a capitalist political economy. They also saw that this submission was less possible and more painful for some.

What might we learn about ourselves from all this? Our own freedom depends on being bound by norms and logics that enable us to live together in society. Beyond this, those norms and logics grant us traction to act and friction that makes our actions seem purposeful and free from determination. Certain political-economic configurations may have different "emancipatory potential" (Dunn 2004), but this likely varies for individuals and groups within societies.

Toward the end of my fieldwork, Ira, Sveta, and I started to interview young men and women about fertility decisions. As a way of familiarizing Ira with the questions I was interested in, I asked her to interview me. Over tea in her kitchen, the interview evolved into a conversation, with both of us asking and answering questions. The topic of housing came up, as it did in many of the interviews on fertility. She asked if James and I owned a house. "Yes," I said, and then clarified, "We and the bank both own the house." We talked about mortgages. "How long will you have to pay the bank?" she asked. "Thirty years." She gasped. "That's like slavery."

Owning a house is part of the American dream. Some of us, lucky enough to have a house, do not think twice about saying we are homeowners even as we pay the bank every month. Owning our own house is having a place where we can do our own thing. In our own house we are free from the government, free from a landlord, free from meddlesome neighbors. And yet owning a house is also responsibility and constraint.

The American dream is a beguiling bit of ideology. As we do things like buy a house, we feel we are getting ahead in life and buying a bit more freedom. Yet if we accept the logic that people with more money are freer to do what they like and embark on that quest, we are increasingly embroiled in the consumer capitalist logic undergirding our own society. We are increasingly constrained to live in certain ways and pursue certain goals. Moreover, in a society where money is supposed to buy freedom, it follows that people who do not succeed are less free. They are, we are told in countless ways, fettered by their own fear and indolence. This belies the fact that people have different access to structures—education, rewarding well-paid work, assets, social connections—that enable them to succeed in a consumer capitalist society.

Fortunately for some and unfortunately for others, ideology and political economy penetrate bodies. When we further entangle ourselves in the dominant logic of our society, at least up until a certain point, there are psychological and material benefits that improve our bodily health. Loosening the binds that tie us to others and to institutions in our society sometimes comes at a bodily cost, especially if we feel that unboundedness was not our choice. Individuals who are more free-floating, as it were, are less able to mobilize and wield the rules and resources of social structure. This was true of a generation of Muscovites during the early 1990s.

BEING NEEDED

One concrete example of Russians pushing against constraint and experiencing freedom was when individuals allocated favors and resources through their personal contacts. They were able to siphon from larger resource flows in society, altering a given course of events. This conferred a sense of agency. In Giddens's (1984) language, individuals intervened in the world and made a difference.

People were able to push against constraint precisely because they were held by it. Work was the principal means by which Soviet citizens were incorporated into the state. Yet work was also the means by which Soviet citizens circumvented the state. Work determined what people had to offer others. Someone in the Soviet bureaucracy could arrange permission to build a *dacha* but could not provide a good cut of meat. A friendly butcher could set aside a good cut of meat but not construction supplies. People were needed for different reasons. In the early 1990s wealth, not work, became the currency of value. Now everyone needed the same thing, and some people were more needed than others.

In Moscow where people had fewer kin, work was the principal means by which social relations were structured. It was the means by which people understood and interacted with others. The workplace, of course, was a site of camaraderie. But people interacted with others outside the workplace using work as a framework for social interaction.

Forms of sociability are tied to political economy. In Soviet times, social relations reflected the fact that power lay in allocation, not accumulation. Individuals did not necessarily have resources themselves. Status came not to persons who secured goods or services through contacts, but to those who arranged this for others. Giving was often more important than getting because the ability to give was an indication of social connections. Those that gave to others were needed people in a shortage economy. They themselves were in demand.

Being unneeded communicates a sense of irrelevance. Middle-aged Muscovites said that nobody needed them. They asked, rhetorically, "Who needs us?" They were unneeded by others around them and they were unneeded by the state. "I became unnecessary to the state." Being needed by the state was tied to work. "People sat in one place for thirty years and suddenly they kicked them. They said you aren't needed anywhere." And, referring to the state's workers: "They ended up as if they weren't in demand at all."

Men in particular were unneeded by the state and by others around them. Work, for the first time in their lives, was no longer certain. In the context of hyperinflation, salary arrears, forced retirements, and layoffs in the early 1990s, men were unable to fulfill their role as breadwinners. Women might not have been needed by the state, but they were needed, as always, in the family. "For a woman it is all the same, she is always needed. [. . .] She must care for someone." Many men had long been divested of broad responsibilities in the domestic sphere.

Being needed or being unneeded is a set expression that opens a window on Russian agency, sociability, and gender. Like the Russian sense of freedom, neededness may also tell us something about ourselves. We, too, need to feel we have something to offer others. What we have to offer may vary, but we offer things in order to impact the lives of others and see proof of our worth in the lives of others. Developmental psychologist Philippe Rochat writes that "humans experience themselves through the eyes of others" (2009, 16). He believes that the human preoccupation with reputation is a by-product of our fear of being rejected and ostracized. The foundation of sociability is a drive for mutual recognition, to be "visible rather than invisible, recognized rather than ignored" (Rochat 2008, 308). In this light it makes sense that middle-aged Muscovites said, "We are all forgotten." Giving something to another proves that we matter. Giving eases existential angst, and there is evidence that it is good for health.

GENERATION OF VICTORS, GENERATION OF LOSERS

When I first developed the proposal for this research, one of the critical comments I received was that I would only be speaking to "the losers," or those who had lost out. At the time I thought that things were not so simple. Even during fieldwork, things seemed more complicated. One cold October day I stood along the heavily policed route of a youthful anti-Putin demonstration. As National Bolshevik Party youth chanted angry nationalist slogans ("Russia without Putin"; "Glory to the nation, death to enemies"; "Russia—all the rest is nothing"; "Nation-homeland-socialism"; "Nation and freedom"), an older woman, perhaps seventy years old, saw me taking pictures and came over. "They don't know sorrow. They didn't live through it. They have a voice but they don't have experience."

It remains true that older Muscovites overwhelmingly spoke of their losses. Even those who were happy to see the end of the Soviet state were not thrilled with what had replaced it. Moreover, in the early 1990s the majority of the Russian population found themselves living in poverty. It is naive to think that there were many winners during this time. Almost everyone lost something in the early 1990s. All Russians were "losers," at least momentarily, in that sense. Young Russians also mourn the loss of a radiant future. Twenty-nine-year-old Ira openly admitted being envious of the security her mother described—a job, an apartment, education, and health care. She worried over her future and the ability to provide for a child.

Ethnography in Romania explicitly deals with the "losers of socialism" who are plagued by insecurity, illness, and stress. Weber (2009) describes an epidemic of stress among pensioners, or the "forsaken generation." Kideckel (2008) focuses on the disenfranchised working class. Stillo, writing about tuberculosis patients, explains:

> The losers of socialism are experiencing a loss of place at multiple levels—
> within one's family, community, workplace, and within society and the
> economy as a whole. These are obsolete human beings. . . . When Mircea,
> the former miner, talks about not mattering, he is talking about all of these
> levels. He is no longer valued as productive; he is a burden and a threat to his
> family. He will never be able to provide for them. These men told me many
> times that they are "lost." They mean this in multiple senses as well—alone,
> unwanted, uncertain, out of control, and afraid. . . . They are the dying, but
> not dead yet. (2013, 23)

Stillo argues that these losers of socialism claim rights to health care based on their past socialist labor. I see this as further evidence of the importance of being needed and giving. These ill Romanians need help, but they do not ask for it without reminding others of what they have given. They are entitled because they gave. They reassert that social logic to the very end.

Older Muscovites were born into hardship and famine, but they began life as victors—"our fathers were victorious and we are the generation of victors." Western Russia was devastated by the war, but Russia had secured the Allied victory. This generation made sacrifices to rebuild their country and regarded its scientific and technological achievements in the 1950s and 1960s with youthful awe. With war as the backdrop, their lives were on a trajectory toward a more radiant future, if not *the* radiant future of communism. Things steadily improved until at least the 1970s. "Yes, we really believed in that radiant future. We believed, we believed." "We believed in [socialism]— really believed." When the Soviet economy collapsed, so did the dreams of their youth.

DEATH

Excess mortality in Russia during the early 1990s was but the biological end-point of political-economic processes that have psychosocial consequences. History and culture must be the starting points of a holistic analysis of the crisis—certainly the history and culture of Russia, but also the history and culture of global political economy. This includes post–World War II economic expansion, the rise of neoliberalism, structural adjustment programs in Latin America, the collapse of the Soviet empire, and "shock therapy" in Eastern Europe and Russia.

Epidemiology identifies risk factors—most commonly of individuals, but sometimes of places or communities. The central epidemiological question is this: who is at risk? Applied to the Russian mortality crisis, this question becomes slightly perverse. What made economic shock therapy so harmful in Russia? Responsibility for the crisis moves away from shock therapy to Russian society. What is it about Russia? Economic shock therapy is normalized, and the Russian mortality crisis exoticized.

Deaths from cardiovascular disease were linked to Russia's lack of social capital or civil society. Alcohol-related deaths were blamed on the Russian predilection for drink. But a lack of social capital, if that is the right term for it, was a result of economic shock therapy, not a Soviet legacy. The logic of social relations and social status was being rewritten from being needed to something different—the ability to mobilize resources, human and otherwise, to aid in the accumulation of wealth. Yes, Russian men have always drunk. But they have not always died at such high rates from alcohol-related causes. Something drove them to drink more harmfully. And something made drinking more harmful when they did it. Alcohol use was not merely an escape from stress but a search for social limits, connections, and equality. Men who were unneeded paid a heavier price for their drinking. Ethnography throws light on the epidemiology of mortality.

Ethnography also suggests that remedies are tied up with morality and social connections. It remains to be seen how, as older Russians die and younger Russians embrace the logics of Russian capitalism, ideas about morality and social connections are more fully transformed. The logics of capitalism will appear more natural; alternatives will fade from view. This may ease distress for some, or it may simply render the source of distress less visible. But some younger Russians, including those marching for the

National Bolshevik Party, are not embracing capitalism. If Russian capitalism continues to disenfranchise a substantial proportion of its population through social inequality, it courts more tragedy. A number of our interviewees thought that Russians were prone to revolution and that the future, as always, was unknowable. Maria spoke of a coming "golden age" where Russia would be the savior of a lost world. More prosaically, Russia might find a middle way between Soviet socialism and Russian capitalism, resulting in less social inequality, more work, and a greater sense of neededness.

Western feminists decry the remasculinization of Russian society in its transition to capitalism (Attwood 1996; Watson 1993), but many Russian women would welcome masculinization in the domestic sphere, whereby men would find new meaning and purpose in family responsibilities and family communion. Utrata, Ispa, and Ispa-Landa (2012) suggest that newer discourses about involved fatherhood are emerging, although practice lags behind.

Epidemiology is also able to render the source of distress more visible. Increasingly, psychosocial factors are recognized as important to health, particularly cardiovascular health. In a letter in *Nature,* psychologist Weidner points out that there is little difference in classic cardiovascular risk factors among men in Western and Eastern Europe. The difference lies in psychosocial risk factors, such as social integration. She suggests "a more productive approach to prevent premature death among Eastern European men might be to strengthen social relationships, decrease social isolation and depression, and to increase adaptive coping skills" (1998, 835). There need to be a greater variety of social spaces for male communion, especially for working-class men. In 2006 Russia implemented a comprehensive alcohol policy, but more could be done (Gil et al. 2010; Khaltourina and Korotayev 2008; Levintova 2007; Neufeld and Rehm 2013).

LIFE

I, too, began this research with that perverse question: Why did Russians die? I found I could not answer the question without asking another question first: How do Russians live? What things make life worth living for Russians? This work deals with the paradoxical desire for space and order—"two opposing thoughts or propositions"—and with freedom (*svoboda*)—"a more imposing, illuminating, life-related, or provocative insight into truth" (Nuckolls 1998, 273). Freedom resolves the paradox of space and order. Freedom (*svoboda*) is space (*prostor,* the expanse of possibility) within order (*poriadok*)—the constraint of society. Political philosopher Hannah Arendt writes of "automatic processes," natural, cosmic, and historical, by which we are driven and, yet, "within which and against which [man] can assert himself through action" (2006, 67). For this generation of Muscovites, asserting themselves through action was possible through social connections that hinged on the state. Constraint gives birth to a sense of freedom from constraint. It is only by using and pushing against constraint that we feel ourselves free from the "automatic processes" by which all of us are bound as human beings. And only when we do this collectively are we kept safe as social beings.

CODA

One rainy, cold spring day Anya and I decided to go to the State Tretyakov Gallery. In one of the rooms, I stopped in front of Isaak Illich Levitan's *Above Eternal Peace* (1894), a landscape painting. The painting seems enormous. (It is 1.5 by 2.1 meters.) From a bird's-eye view, gray water stretches toward the horizon, where it meets the sky—dark and gray with thick clouds. The sky lightens slightly above the clouds, but the overwhelming impression is of a vast, gray expanse. In the foreground, on a green hill "straining forward" (State Tretyakov Gallery), is a cemetery marked by a scattering of Orthodox crosses, a cluster of trees bent in the wind, and, partially behind the trees, a wooden church with an onion dome. In one small window of the church is an orange glow. The lake and sky are dramatic, and the church seems so small and insignificant, except for that glow which asserts itself against the gray. The text on the gallery's website refers to the "world's mysterious incomprehensibility." It continues, "It is only the cliff, straining forward as it does, with a wooden church on top, that provides evidence of the human soul, fragile but full of faith, being present in the world. The confrontation between the human spirit and the infinity of the creation is represented in the picture on an epic, universal scale" (State Tretyakov Gallery). As James and I were preparing to leave Moscow, our friend Sergei from the English club gave James a beautiful book of Russian art. James mentioned Levitan's painting and together they found it in the book. James said, "It almost captures how big Russia is." That is the conversation where Sergei told James that Siberia—the last preserve of *prostor* and the collective—was the only place in Russia where one could be free.

Levitan captures the dialectic of Russian *svoboda:* the vast expanse (*pro-stor*) and the collective (*sobornost'*). The Russian word *sobor* refers both to a cathedral, the external walls of institutional order, and the assembly, or the interpersonal order. Without the *sobor,* space and freedom are boundless and dangerous. Freedom needs constraint—in the form of social order and social responsibility—to make it meaningful, powerful, and safe.

Notes

INTRODUCTION

1. I follow the U.S. Library of Congress system for Russian transliteration, except where spellings of certain words or names are already familiar to Westerners.
2. In all cases, I use pseudonyms for friends and interviewees. Russian names include a first, patronymic, and last name. By custom I would have referred to almost all of my interviewees by first and patronymic names, given that they were not close friends. I did address some of my older friends by first name only. In order to simplify for the reader, I refer to many of my interviewees by first name only in the text.
3. *Sovkovii* denotes the quality of being Soviet. A person might be *sovok,* often used derogatorily in reference to someone who still behaves in a Soviet fashion. I once complained to a friend about the surly cashier at the store nearest my apartment building. "You could call her *sovok,*" my friend said.

CHAPTER 1

1. Since 2009 the casinos have disappeared with the enforcement of legislation restricting gambling in Russia.
2. Prospect Kalinin was renamed Novyi Arbat.
3. All translations of quotations from interviews are my own. When I use these quotations, internal ellipses (. . .) reflect a pause or incomplete thought. Bracketed internal ellipses ([. . .]) indicate that I have excluded some of the speaker's words. In written sources, I revert to common usage of internal ellipses to indicate an omission.
4. Rüthers (2006) focuses on the nightlife of the younger generation, namely the *stiliagi,* who emulated Western lifestyle in taste and fashion.
5. The seminar was sponsored by the Institut national d'études demographiques (INED), Institute for Demography and Social Sciences (IDSS), Max Planck Institute for Demographic Research (MPIDR), Center for Demography and Human Ecology (CDHE), International Union for the Scientific Study of Population (IUSSP), and United Nations Fund for Population Activities (UNFPA).

6. Organizers included the Health Protection Committee of the Russian Parliament, Centre for Human Ecology and Demography of the Russian Academy of Sciences, Centre for Civilizational and Regional Studies of the Russian Academy of Sciences, and the journal *Narcologia.*

CHAPTER 2

1. This is also noted by Paxson (2005) when she describes the preponderance of the verbal prefix *raz-* as her informants described the chaos following the fall of the Soviet Union. She writes, "This is the clearest image of raz- that I have configured: *It signals something that begins as a whole and moves or spirals outward*" (2005, 104).

CHAPTER 3

1. Japan had two to three million war dead, about 3 to 4 percent of the population. The United States and Great Britain had under half a million war dead. France had just over half a million. None of these three figures exceeded 2 percent of the national population.
2. The military parade, a tradition since 1965, was cancelled from 1991 through 1994.
3. "Complete secondary education," or ten class years, was made compulsory only in 1981.
4. This is a reference to Khrushchev's Virgin Lands Campaign, intended to increase agricultural production by expanding cultivation in Kazakhstan and other areas of the Soviet Union.
5. Du Plessix Gray (1989) refers to martyr-heroines, a play on the mother-heroines of Stalin's years.

CHAPTER 4

1. Technically the Soviet Union never achieved communism. According to later Marxist-Leninism it was in a state of mature or developed socialism.
2. Less than 200 U.S. dollars a month.
3. From 1992 to 1994 the Russian government began a deliberate process of selling off its assets. During this stage of privatization, free vouchers representing shares of state wealth were distributed to the population. They were then able to convert these to shares in privatized enterprises. Theoretically this strategy would keep assets from being concentrated in the hands of a few. It did not work out that way.
4. Iosif Kobzon is a Russian oligarch of Jewish descent who is famous for his Frank Sinatra–style singing. He served as a member of parliament. There are suspicions that he is connected to the Russian mafia.
5. Abramovich, Khodorovsky, and Fridman are all Russian oligarchs. Abramovich and Fridman are still worth billions, but Khodorovsky served a sentence in prison camp

and his fortune has reportedly dwindled. Khodorovsky was imprisoned on charges of fraud, and the oil company he controlled, Yukos, was forced into bankruptcy over purported tax evasion and seized by the state. The state-sponsored attack on the company was widely interpreted as Putin's attempt to reassert power over the oligarchs and business elite.

6. For more on the terms "nouveau riche" (the French term is used in Russian) and "new Russian" (*novyi ruskyi*) and their evolution, see Balzer 2003; Graham 2003; and Humphrey 2002.

CHAPTER 5

1. Political scientist Archie Brown makes a distinction between these translations, suggesting that reconstruction is preferable, "for it can carry the connotation of building a new edifice on the same land as well as the alternative and more limited meaning of no more than a modest updating of the existing building" (Brown 2007, 18).

2. Savings were not unusual among Soviet citizens, given that there were limited goods and services on which to spend money.

3. This is a play on the phrase, "Lenin lived, Lenin is alive, Lenin will live!" which was used on a well-known 1965 Soviet propaganda poster with Lenin standing in front of the Soviet flag.

4. Technically these were loans to the state from the oligarchy. Once the state paid back its "creditors," the shares would be returned to the state. The state simply never repaid these "loans."

5. Country values range from 0.20s in Northern Europe to the 0.50s and 0.60s in Africa and Latin America. In 2000 it was 0.41 in the United States (World Bank 2013).

6. Conflicts over the division and payment of electric bills are legion in Russia. They are a familiar subject of satirical short stories and films on communal living.

7. Disability is a recognized civil status that confers government benefits depending on the degree of disability.

8. Self-reported unemployment among men approaches statistical significance, but the 95-percent confidence interval includes 1.0 (1.00, 1.93), indicating that there is a better than 5-percent chance that random variation produced the association.

CHAPTER 6

1. The 2009 rates are 372 per 1,000 males in Russia versus 334 per 1,000 males in the Ukraine; 139 per 1,000 females in Russia versus 128 per 1,000 females in the Ukraine.

2. Problem drinking is defined as having one or more episodes of *zapoi* (a period of time marked by drinking and drunkenness, often lasting for days or weeks) in the past year or twice a week or more frequent occurrences of excessive drunkenness, hangover, or going to sleep at night clothed because of being drunk (Leon et al. 2007).

CHAPTER 7

1. The question used to measure perceived control was: "Some people feel they have completely free choice and control over their lives while others feel that what they do has no real effect on what happens to them. How about yourself?" (Rose 2000, 1429).

2. Here he is probably referring to a perceived Western pattern of drinking—cowboys drinking a shot of whisky.

References

Abbott, Stephen, and Della Freeth. 2008. "Social Capital and Health: Starting to Make Sense of the Role of Generalized Trust and Reciprocity." *Journal of Health Psychology* 13 (7): 874–83.

Advertiser (Adelaide). 1991. "High Price of Russia's 'Freedom.'" December 27.

Anderson, Barbara A., and Brian D. Silver. 1989. "Patterns of Cohort Mortality in the Soviet Population." *Population and Development Review* 15 (3): 471–501.

Anderson, R. 1991. "Russia Free." *Courier-Mail* (Brisbane), August 27.

Arendt, Hannah. 1970. *On Violence.* Orlando, FL: Harcourt.

———. 2006. "What Is Freedom?" In *Between Past and Future: Eight Exercises in Political Thought,* 142–69. New York: Penguin Books.

Argenbright, Robert. 1999. "Remaking Moscow: New Places, New Selves." *Geographical Review* 89 (1): 1–22.

Arhant-Sudhir, K., R. Arhant-Sudhir, and K. Sudhir. 2011. "Pet Ownership and Cardiovascular Risk Reduction: Supporting Evidence, Conflicting Data and Underlying Mechanisms." *Clinical and Experimental Pharmacology and Physiology* 38 (11): 734–38.

Ashwin, Sarah. 2000. "Introduction: Gender, State, and Society in Soviet and Post-Soviet Russia." In *Gender, State and Society in Soviet and Post-Soviet Russia,* edited by Sarah Ashwin, 1–29. London: Routledge.

Attwood, Lynne. 1996. "The Post-Soviet Woman in the Move to the Market: A Return to Domesticity and Dependence?" In *Women in Russia and Ukraine,* edited by Rosalind Marsh, 255–66. Cambridge: Cambridge University Press.

Averina, Maria, Odd Nilssen, Tormod Brenn, Jan Brox, Alexei G. Kalinin, and Vadim L. Arkhipovsky. 2003. "High Cardiovascular Mortality in Russia Cannot Be Explained by the Classical Risk Factors: The Arkhangelsk Study 2000." *European Journal of Epidemiology* 18 (9): 871–78.

Barker, David J. P., ed. 2001. *Fetal Origins of Cardiovascular and Lung Disease.* New York: Marcel Dekker.

Barrett, Jennifer, and Cynthia Buckley. 2009. "Gender and Perceived Control in the Russian Federation." *Europe-Asia Studies* 61 (1): 29–49.

Batson, Daniel C. 1998. "Altruism and Prosocial Behavior." In *The Handbook of Social Psychology,* edited by Daniel T. Gilbert, Susan T. Fiske, and Gardner Lindzey, 282–316. 4th ed. Boston: McGraw-Hill.

Bazylevych, Maryna. 2010. "Negotiating New Roles, New Moralities: Ukrainian Women Physicians at a Post-Socialist Crossroad." PhD diss., State University of New York at Albany.

Berdahl, Daphne. 2000 "Introduction: An Anthropology of Postsocialism." In *Altering States: Anthropology in Transition,* edited by Daphne Berdahl, Matti Bunzl, and Martha Lampland, 1–13. Ann Arbor: University of Michigan Press.

Berdahl, Daphne. 1999. *Where the World Ended: Re-Unification and Identity in the German Borderland.* Berkeley: University of California Press.

Berkman, Lisa, and S. Leonard Syme. 1979. "Social Networks, Host Resistance, and Mortality: A Nine-Month Follow-up Study of Alameda County Residents." *American Journal of Epidemiology* 109: 186–204.

Berlin, Isaiah. 1969. *Four Essays on Liberty.* London: Oxford University Press.

Bledsoe, Caroline. 2002. *Contingent Lives: Fertility, Aging and Time in West Africa.* Chicago: University of Chicago Press.

Bobak, Martin, and Michael Marmot. 1999. "Alcohol and Mortality in Russia: Is It Different than Elsewhere?" *Annals of Epidemiology* 9 (6): 335–38.

Bobak, Martin, Michael Murphy, Richard Rose, and Michael Marmot. 2003. "Determinants of Adult Mortality in Russia: Estimates from Sibling Data." *Epidemiology* 14 (5): 603–11.

Bobak, Martin, Hynek Pikhart, Clyde Hertzman, Richard Rose, and Michael Marmot. 1998. "Socioeconomic Factors, Perceived Control and Self-Reported Health in Russia: A Cross-Sectional Survey." *Social Science and Medicine* 47 (2): 269–79.

Bobak, Martin, Hynek Pikhart, Richard Rose, Clyde Hertzman, and Michael Marmot. 2000. "Socioeconomic Factors, Material Inequalities, and Perceived Control in Self-Rated Health: Cross-Sectional Data from Seven Post-Communist Countries." *Social Science and Medicine* 51 (9): 1343–50.

Bobak, Martin, Robin Room, Hynek Pikhart, Ruzena Kubinova, Sofia Malyutina, Andrzej Pajak, Svetlana Kurilovitch, Roman Topor, Yuri Nikitin, and Michael Marmot. 2004. "Contribution of Drinking Patterns to Differences in Rates of Alcohol Related Problems between Three Urban Populations." *Journal of Epidemiology and Community Health* 58 (3): 238–42.

Bobrova, N., R. West, D. Malyutina, Sofia Malyutina, and Martin Bobak. 2010. "Gender Differences in Drinking Practices in Middle Aged and Older Russians." *Alcohol and Alcoholism* 45 (6): 573–80.

Bourdieu, Pierre. 2004. *Outline of a Theory of Practice.* Translated by Richard Nice. Cambridge: Cambridge University Press.

Boym, Svetlana. 1994. *Common Places: Mythologies of Everyday Life in Russia.* Cambridge: Harvard University Press.

———. 2001. *The Future of Nostalgia.* New York: Basic Books.

———. 2010. *Another Freedom: The Alternative History of an Idea.* Chicago: University of Chicago Press.

Bridger, Sue, Rebecca Kay, and Kathryn Pinnick. 1996. *No More Heroines? Russia, Women, and the Market.* New York: Routledge.

Britton, Annie, and Martin McKee. 2000. "The Relation between Alcohol and Cardiovascular Disease in Eastern Europe: Explaining the Paradox." *Journal of Epidemiology and Community Health* 54: 328–32.

Brown, Archie. 2007. *Seven Years that Changed the World: Perestroika in Perspective.* New York: Oxford University Press.

Bruhn, John G., and Stewart Wolf. 1979. *The Roseto Story: An Anatomy of Health.* Oklahoma City: University of Oklahoma Press.

Bucher, Greta. 2006. *Women, the Bureaucracy and Daily Life in Postwar Moscow, 1945–1953.* Boulder, CO: East European Monographs.

Buchowski, Michal. 1996. "The Shifting Meanings of Civil and Civic Society in Poland." In *Civil Society: Challenging Western Models,* edited by Chris Hann and Elizabeth Dunn, 79–98. New York: Routledge.

Bunker, Stephen J., David M. Colquhoun, Murray D. Esler, Ian B. Hickie, David Hunt. V. Michael Jelinek, Brian F. Oldenburg, Hedley G. Peach, Denise Ruth, Cristopher C. Tennant, and Andrew M. Tonkin. 2003. "'Stress' and Coronary Heart Disease: Psychosocial Risk Factors; National Heart Foundation of Australia Position Statement Update." *Medical Journal of Australia* 178: 272–76.

Burawoy, Michael. 1994. "Industrial Involution: The Dynamics of a Transition to a Market Economy in Russia." Paper presented to the SSRC Workshop on Rational Choice Theory and Post Soviet Studies, New York, December 9.

Burawoy, Michael, and Lukács, János. 1994. *The Radiant Past: Ideology and Reality in Hungary's Road to Capitalism.* Chicago: University of Chicago Press.

Burawoy, Michael, and Verdery, Katherine, eds. 1999. *Uncertain Transition: Ethnographies of Change in the Postsocialist World.* Lanham, MD: Rowman and Littlefield.

Buyandelgeriyn, Manduhai. 2008. "Post-Post-Transition Theories: Walking on Multiple Paths." *Annual Review of Anthropology* 37: 237–50.

Caldwell, Melissa. 2004. *Not by Bread Alone: Social Support in the New Russia.* Berkeley: University of California Press.

———. 2009. "Introduction: Food and Everyday Life after State Socialism." In *Food and Everyday Life in the Post-Socialist World,* edited by Melissa Caldwell, 1–28. Bloomington: Indiana University Press.

Carlson, Per. 2000. "Educational Differences in Self-Rated Health during the Russian Transition: Evidence from Taganrog 1993–1994." *Social Science and Medicine* 51: 1363–74.

Carter, Ian. 2007. "Positive and Negative Liberty." In *The Stanford Encyclopedia of Philosophy,* edited by Edward N. Zalta. Stanford University, Fall 2008 edition. Article revised October 7, 2007. *plato.stanford.edu/archives/fai12008/entries/liberty-positive-negative/.*

Chenet, Laurent, David Leon, Martin McKee, and Serguei Vassin. 1998. "Deaths from Alcohol and Violence in Moscow: Socio-economic Determinants." *European Journal of Population* 14 (1): 19–37.

Chenet, Laurent, Martin McKee, David A. Leon, Vladimir Shkolnikov, and Serguei Vassin. 1998. "Alcohol and Cardiovascular Mortality in Moscow: New Evidence of a Causal Association." *Journal of Epidemiology and Community Health* 52 (12): 772–74.

Chubarov, Alexander. 2001. *Russia's Bitter Path to Modernity: A History of the Soviet and Post-Soviet Eras.* New York: Continuum.

Clarke, Simon. 1993. "The Contradictions of 'State Socialism.'" In *What about the Workers? Workers and the Transition to Capitalism in Russia,* edited by Simon Clarke, Peter Fairbrother, Michael Burawoy, and Pavel Krotov, 5–29. New York: Verso.

Clarke, Simon 1992. "The Quagmire of Privatization." *New Left Review* 196: 3–28.

Clarke, Simon, and Peter Fairbrother. 1993. "Trade Unions and the Working Class." In *What about the Workers? Workers and the Transition to Capitalism in Russia,* edited by Simon Clarke, Peter Fairbrother, Michael Burawoy, and Pavel Krotov, 91–120. New York: Verso.

Clements, Evans Barbara. 1991. "Later Developments: Trends in Soviet Women's History, 1930 to the Present." In *Russia's Women: Accommodation, Resistance, Transformation,* edited by Barbara Evans Clements, Barbara Alpern Engel, and Christine D. Worobec, 267–78. Berkeley: University of California Press.

Cockerham, William C. 1997. "The Social Determinants of the Decline of Life Expectancy in Russia and Eastern Europe: A Lifestyle Explanation." *Journal of Health and Social Behavior* 38 (2): 117–30.

———. 1999. *Health and Social Change in Russia and Eastern Europe.* New York: Routledge.

———. 2000. "Health Lifestyles in Russia." *Social Science and Medicine* 51 (9): 1313–24.

———. 2007. "Health Lifestyles and the Absence of the Russian Middle Class." *Sociology of Health and Illness* 29 (3): 457–73.

Cockerham, William C., Brian P. Hinote, and Pamela Abbott. 2006. "Psychological Distress, Gender, and Health Lifestyles in Belarus, Kazakhstan, Russia and Ukraine." *Social Science and Medicine* 63 (9): 2381–94.

Cockerham, William C., Brian P. Hinote, Geoffrey B. Cockerham, and Pamela Abbott. 2006. "Health Lifestyles and Political Ideology in Belarus, Russia and Ukraine." *Social Science and Medicine* 62 (7): 1799–1809.

Cohen, Sheldon, and S. Leonard Syme, eds. 1985. *Social Support and Health.* New York: Academic Press.

Collier, Stephen J. 2011. *Post-Soviet Social: Neoliberalism, Social Modernity, Biopolitics.* Princeton: Princeton University Press.

Connerton, Paul. 1989. *How Societies Remember.* Cambridge: Cambridge University Press.

Cook, Sarah, David A. Leon, Nikolay Kiryanov, George B. Ploubidis, and Bianca L. De Stavola. 2013. "Alcohol-Related Dysfunction in Working-Age Men in Izhevsk, Russia: An Application of Structural Equation Models to Study the Association with Education." *PLOS ONE* 8 (5): e63792.

Creed, Gerald W. 2011. *Masquerade and Postsocialism: Ritual and Cultural Dispossession in Bulgaria.* Bloomington, IN: Indiana University Press.

CSDH. 2008. *Closing the Gap in a Generation: Health Equity through Action on the Social Determinants of Health.* Final Report of the Commission on Social Determinants of Health. Geneva: World Health Organization.

Das, S., and J. H. O'Keefe. 2006. "Behavioral Cardiology: Recognizing and Addressing the Profound Impact of Psychosocial Stress on Cardiovascular Health." *Current Atherosclerosis Reports* 8 (2): 111–18.

Deaton, Angus. 2003. "Health, Inequality and Economic Development." *Journal of Economic Literature* 41 (1): 113–58.

Deev, A., D. Shestov, J. Abernathy, A. Kapustina, N. Muhina, and S. Irving. 1998. "Association of Alcohol Consumption to Mortality in Middle-Aged U.S. and Russian Men and Women." *Annals of Epidemiology* 8: 147–53.

Dostoevsky, Fyodor. 1985. *The House of the Dead.* Translated by David McDuff. London: Penguin.

———. 2003. *The Brothers Karamazov.* Translated by Andrew R. MacAndrew. New York: Bantam.

Dunham, Vera. 1976. *In Stalin's Time: Middleclass Values in Soviet Fiction.* Cambridge: Cambridge University Press.

Dunn, Elizabeth. 2004. *Privatizing Poland: Baby Food, Big Business, and the Remaking of Labor.* Ithaca, NY: Cornell University Press.

Durkheim, Émile. 1979. *Suicide: A Study in Sociology.* New York: Free Press.

Eberstadt, Nicholas. 1994. "Health and Mortality in Central and Eastern Europe: Retrospect and Prospect." In *The Social Legacy of Communism,* edited by James R. Millar and Sharon L. Wolchik, 196–225. New York: Woodrow Wilson Center Press.

———. 2009. "Drunken Nation: Russia's Depopulation Bomb." *World Affairs* 171 (4): 51–62.

Eller, Nanna H., Bo Netterstrøm, Finn Gyntelberg, Tage S. Kristensen, Finn Nielsen, Andrew Steptoe, and Töres Theorell. 2009. "Work-Related Psychosocial Factors and the Development of Ischemic Heart Disease: A Systematic Review." *Cardiology in Review* 17: 83–97.

Everson-Rose, Susan A., and Tené T. Lewis. 2005. "Psychosocial Factors and Cardiovascular Diseases." *Annual Review of Public Health* 26: 469–500.

Farmer, Paul. 1999. *Infections and Inequalities: The Modern Plagues.* Berkeley: University of California Press.

Field, Mark G. 1994. "Postcommunist Medicine: Morbidity, Mortality, and the Deteriorating Health Situation." In *The Social Legacy of Communism,* edited by James R. Millar and Sharon L. Wolchik, 178–95. New York: Woodrow Wilson Center Press.

———. 1995. "The Health Crisis in the Former Soviet Union: A Report from the 'Post-war' Zone." *Social Science and Medicine* 41 (11): 1469–78.

———. 2000. "The Health and Demographic Crisis in Post-Soviet Russia: A Two-Phase Development." In *Russia's Torn Safety Nets: Health and Social Welfare during the Transition,* edited by Mark G. Field and Judyth L. Twigg, 11–42. New York: St. Martin's Press.

Field, Mark G., David M. Kotz, and Gene Bukhman. 2000. "Neoliberal Economic Policy, 'State Desertion,' and the Russian Health Crisis." In *Dying for Growth: Global Inequality and the Health of the Poor,* edited by Jim Yong Kim, Joyce V. Millen, Alec Irwin, and John Gershman, 154–73. Monroe, ME: Common Courage.

Field, Mark G., and Judyth L. Twigg. 2000. Introduction to *Russia's Torn Safety Nets: Health and Social Welfare during the Transition,* edited by Mark G. Field and Judyth L. Twigg, 1–9. New York: St. Martin's.

Filtzer, Donald. 1994. *Soviet Workers and the Collapse of Perestroika: The Soviet Labour Process and Gorbachev's Reforms, 1985–1991.* Cambridge: Cambridge University Press.

———. 2002. *Soviet Workers and Late Stalinism: Labour and the Restoration of the Stalinist System after World War II.* Cambridge: Cambridge University Press.

———. 2006. "Standard of Living versus Quality of Life: Struggling with the Urban Environment in Russia during the Early Years of Post-War Reconstruction." In *Late Stalinist Russia: Society between Reconstruction and Reinvention,* edited by Juliane Fürst, 81–102. London: Routledge.

Fine, Ben. 2001. *Social Capital versus Social Theory: Political Economy and Social Science at the Turn of the Millennium.* New York: Routledge.

Fitzpatrick, Sheila. 2006. Conclusion: Late Stalinism in Historical Perspective. In *Late Stalinist Russia: Society between Reconstruction and Reinvention,* edited by Juliane Fürst, 269–82. London: Routledge.

Forest, Benjamin, and Juliet Johnson. 2002. "Unraveling the Threads of History: Soviet-Era Monuments and Post-Soviet National Identity in Moscow. *Annals of the Association of American Geographers* 92 (3): 524–47.

Foucault, Michel. 1995. *Discipline and Punish: The Birth of the Prison.* Translated by Alan Sheridan. New York: Vintage Books.

Franzini, Luisa, and William Spears. 2003. Contributions of Social Context to Inequalities in Years of Life Lost to Heart Disease in Texas, USA. *Social Science and Medicine* 57 (10): 1847–61.

Fukuyama, Francis. 1992. *The End of History and the Last Man.* New York: Avon.

———. 1999. "Social Capital and Civil Society." Prepared for delivery at the IMF Conference on Second Generation Reforms, Washington, D.C., November 8–9, 1999. *www.imf.org/External/Pubs/FT/seminar/1999/reforms/fukuyama.htm.* Accessed October 5, 2013.

———. 2001. "Social Capital, Civil Society and Development." *Third World Quarterly* 22 (1): 7–20.

Fürst, Juliane. 2006a. "Introduction—Late Stalinist Society: History, Policies and People." In *Late Stalinist Russia: Society between Reconstruction and Reinvention,* edited by Juliane Fürst, 1–19. London: Routledge.

———. 2006b. "The Importance of Being Stylish: Youth, Culture and Identity in Late Stalinism." In *Late Stalinist Russia: Society between Reconstruction and Reinvention,* edited by Juliane Fürst, 209–30. London: Routledge.

Gal, Susan, and Gail Kligman. 2000. *The Politics of Gender after Socialism: A Comparative-Historical Essay.* Princeton: Princeton University Press.

Giddens, Anthony. 1984. *The Constitution of Society: Outline of the Theory of Structuration.* Berkeley: University of California Press.

Gil, Artyom, Olga Polikina, Natalia Koroleva, David A. Leon, and Martin McKee. 2010. "Alcohol Policy in a Russian Region: A Stakeholder Analysis." *European Journal of Public Health* 20 (5): 588–94.

Gil, Artyom, Olga Polikina, Natalia Koroleva, Martin McKee, Susannah Tomkins, and David A. Leon. 2009. "Availability and Characteristics of Nonbeverage Alcohols Sold in 17 Russian Cities in 2007." *Alcoholism: Clinical and Experimental Research* 33 (1): 79–85.

Ginter, Emil. 1995. "Cardiovascular Risk Factors in the Former Communist Countries: Analysis of 40 European MONICA Populations." *European Journal of Epidemiology* 11 (2): 199–205.

Gorer, Geoffrey, and John Rickman. 1962. *The People of Great Russia: A Psychological Study.* New York: Norton.

Greenhalgh, Susan. 1995. "Anthropology Theorizes Reproduction: Integrating Practice, Political Economic, and Feminist Perspectives." In *Situating Fertility: Anthropological and Demographic Enquiry,* edited by Susan Greenhalgh, 3–28. Cambridge: Cambridge University Press.

Habermas, Jürgen. 1989. *Lifeworld and System: A Critique of Functionalist Reason.* Vol. 2 of *The Theory of Communicative Action.* Boston: Beacon.

Hann, Chris M. 1996. "Introduction: Political Society and Civil Anthropology." In *Civil Society: Challenging Western Models,* edited by Chris Hann and Elizabeth Dunn, 1–26. New York: Routledge.

———. 1998. Foreword to *Surviving Post-Socialism: Local Strategies and Regional Responses in Eastern Europe and the Former Soviet Union,* edited by Susan Bridger and Frances Pine, x–xiv. London: Routledge.

Hann, Chris, and Elizabeth Dunn. 1996. *Civil Society: Challenging Western Models.* New York: Routledge.

Hann, Chris, Caroline Humphrey, and Katherine Verdery. 2002. "Introduction: Postsocialism as a Topic of Anthropological Investigation." In *Postsocialism: Ideals, Ideologies and Practices in Eurasia,* edited by Chris Hann, 1–28. London: Routledge.

Hemment, Julie. 2004a. "Strategizing Gender and Development: Action Research and Ethnographic Responsibility in the Russian Provinces." In *Post-Soviet Women Encountering Transition: Nation Building, Economic Survival, and Civic Activism,* edited by Kathleen Kuehnast and Carol Nechemias, 313–33. Baltimore: Johns Hopkins University Press.

———. 2004b. "Global Civil Society and the Local Costs of Belonging: Defining Violence against Women in Russia." *Signs: Journal of Women in Culture and Society* 29 (3): 815–40.

Hinote, Brian P., and Gretchen R. Webber. 2012. "Drinking toward Manhood: Masculinity and Alcohol in the Former USSR." *Men and Masculinities* 15 (3): 292–310.

Hoffman, David E. 2003. *The Oligarchs: Wealth and Power in the New Russia.* New York: PublicAffairs.

Hoffmann, David L. 2003 *Stalinist Values: The Cultural Norms of Soviet Modernity, 1917–1941*. Ithaca, NY: Cornell University Press.

Höjdestrand, Tova. 2009. *Needed by Nobody: Homelessness and Humanness in Post-Socialist Russia*. Ithaca, NY: Cornell University Press.

Humphrey, Caroline. 2002a. "Does the Category 'Postsocialist' Still Make Sense?" In *Postsocialism: Ideals, Ideologies and Practices In Eurasia,* edited by Chris M. Hann, 12–15. New York: Routledge.

———. 2002b. *The Unmaking of Soviet Life: Everyday Economies after Socialism*. Ithaca, New York: Cornell University Press.

———. 2007. "Alternative Freedoms." *Proceedings of the American Philosophical Society* 151 (1): 1–10.

Hyyppä, Markku T., Juani Mäki, Olli Impivaara, and Arpo Aromaa. 2007. "Individual-Level Measures of Social Capital as Predictors of All-Cause and Cardiovascular Mortality: A Population-Based Prospective Study of Men and Women in Finland." *European Journal of Epidemiology* 22 (9): 589–97.

Idler Ellen L., and Yael Benyamini. 1997. "Self-Rated Health and Mortality: A Review of Twenty-Seven Community Studies." *Journal of Health and Social Behavior* 38 (1): 21–37.

Islam, M. Kamrul, Ulf-G. Gerdtham, Bo Gullberg, Martin Lindström, and Juan Merlo. 2008. "Social Capital Externalities and Mortality in Sweden." *Economics and Human Biology* 6 (1): 19–42.

Johnson-Hanks, Jennifer. 2005. *Uncertain Honor: Modern Motherhood in an African Crisis*. Chicago: University of Chicago Press.

Katzner, Kenneth. 1994. *English-Russian Russian-English Dictionary: Revised and Expanded Edition*. New York: John Wiley and Sons.

Kawachi Ichiro, Bruce P. Kennedy, Kimberly Lochner, and Deborah Prothrow-Stith. 1997. "Social Capital, Income Inequality, and Mortality." *American Journal of Public Health* 87 (9): 1491–98.

Kay, Rebecca. 2006. *Men in Contemporary Russia: The Fallen Heroes of Post-Soviet Change?* Surrey, UK: Ashgate.

———. 2007. Caring for Men in Contemporary Russia: Gendered Constructions of Need and Hybrid Forms of Social Security. *Focaal* 50: 51–65.

Kelleher C. Cecily, John Lynch, Sam Harper, Joseph B. Tay, and Geraldine Nolan. 2004. "Hurling Alone? How Social Capital Failed to Save the Irish from Cardiovascular Disease in the United States." *American Journal of Public Health* 94 (12): 2162–69.

Kennedy, Bruce P., Ichiro Kawachi, and Elizabeth Brainerd. 1998. "The Role of Social Capital in the Russian Mortality Crisis." *World Development* 26 (11): 2029–43.

Kennedy, Michael D. 2001. "Postcommunist Capitalism, Culture, and History." *American Journal of Sociology* 106 (4): 1138–51.

Kertzer, David I., and Tom Fricke, eds. 1997. *Anthropological Demography: Toward a New Synthesis*. Chicago: University of Chicago Press.

Khaltourina, Daria Andreevna, and Andrey Vitalevich Korotayev. 2006. *Russkyi krest: Faktori, mekanismi i puti preodoleniya demograficheskovo krisisa v Rossyi* [Russian

Cross: Factors, Mechanisms and Paths of Overcoming the Demographic Crisis in Russia]. Moscow: URSS.

———. 2008. "Potential for Alcohol Policy to Decrease the Mortality Crisis in Russia." *Evaluation and the Health Professionals* 31: 272–81.

Khrushchev, Nikita Sergeevich. 2006. *Memoirs of Nikita Khrushchev: Reformer, 1945–1964,* edited by Sergei Khrushchev. University Park: Pennsylvania State University Press.

Kiblitskaya, Marina. 2000. "'Once We Were Kings:' Male Experiences of Loss of Status at Work in Post-Communist Russia." In *Gender, State and Society in Soviet and Post-Soviet Russia,* edited by Sarah Ashwin, 90–104. London: Routledge.

Kideckel, David A. 1984. "Drinking Up: Alcohol, Class, and Social Change in Rural Romania." *East European Quarterly* 18 (4): 431–46.

———. 2008. *Getting By in Postsocialist Romania: Labor, the Body and Working Class Culture.* Bloomington: Indiana University Press.

Klein, Naomi. 2007. *The Shock Doctrine: The Rise of Disaster Capitalism.* New York: Metropolitan Books.

Koek, Huiberdina L. (Dineke), Michiel L. Bots, and Diederick E. Grobbee. 2003. "Are Russians Different than Other Europeans in Their Relation of Risk Factors to Cardiovascular Disease Risk." *European Journal of Epidemiology* 18 (9): 843–44.

Koester, David. 2003. "Drink, Drank, Drunk: A Social-Political Grammar of Russian Drinking Practices in a Colonial Context." *Anthropology of East Europe Review* 21 (2): 41–46.

Kornai, János. 1980. *Economics of Shortage.* Amsterdam: North-Holland Publishing.

Krantz, David S., and Melissa K. McCeney. 2002. "Effects of Psychological and Social Factors on Organic Disease: A Critical Assessment of Research on Coronary Heart Disease." *Annual Review of Psychology* 53: 341–69.

Kristenson, M., Z. Kucinskiene, B. Bergdahl, H. Calkauskas, V. Urmonas, and K. Orth Gomér. 1998. "Increased Psychosocial Strain in Lithuanian versus Swedish Men: The Livicordia Study." *Psychosomatic Medicine* 60 (3): 277–82.

Kristenson, M., Z. Kucinskiene, B. Bergdahl, and K. Orth Gomér. 2001. "Risk Factors for Coronary Heart Disease in Different Socioeconomic Groups of Lithuania and Sweden—the Livicordia Study." *Scandinavian Journal of Public Health* 29 (2): 140–50.

Kuehnast, Kathleen, and Carol Nechemias. 2004. "Introduction: Women Navigating Change in Post-Soviet Currents." In *Post-Soviet Women Encountering Transition: Nation Building, Economic Survival, and Civic Activism,* edited by Kathleen Kuehnast and Carol Nechemias, 1–20. Baltimore: Johns Hopkins University Press.

Kukhterin, Sergei. 2000. "Fathers and Patriarchs in Communist and Post-Communist Russia." In *Gender, State and Society in Soviet and Post-Soviet Russia,* edited by Sarah Ashwin, 71–89. New York: Routledge.

Kunitz, Stephen J. 1994. "The Value of Particularism in the Study of the Cultural, Social and Behavioral Determinants of Mortality." In *Health and Social Change in International Perspective,* edited by Lincoln C. Chen, 225–50. Boston: Harvard University Press.

Kürti L. 2000. "Uncertain Anthropology: Ethnography of Postsocialist Eastern Europe. A Review Article." *Ethnos* 65 (3): 405–20.

Lachenmeier, Dirk W., Jürgen Rehm, and Gerhard Gmel. 2007. "Surrogate Alcohol: What Do We Know and Where Do We Go?" *Alcoholism: Clinical and Experimental Research* 31 (10): 1613–24.

LaFont, Suzanne. 2001. "One Step Forward, Two Steps Back: Women in the Post-Communist States." *Communist and Post-Communist Studies* 34 (2): 203–20.

Lasker, Judith N., Brenda Egolf, and Stewart Wolf. 1994. "Community Social Change and Mortality." *Social Science and Medicine* 39 (1): 53–62.

Ledeneva, Alena V. 1998. *Russia's Economy of Favours: Blat, Networking and Informal Exchange.* Cambridge: Cambridge University Press.

Leon, David A., Laurent Chenet, Vladimir M. Shkolnikov, Sergei Zakharov, Judith Shapiro, Galina Rakhmanova, Sergei Vassin, and Martin McKee. 1997. "Huge Variation in Russian Mortality Rates 1984–94: Artefact, Alcohol, or What?" *Lancet* 350 (9075): 383–88.

Leon, David A., Lyudmila Saburova, Susannah Tomkins, Evgueny Andreev, Nikolay Kiryanov, Martin McKee, and Vladimir M. Shkolnikov. 2007. "Hazardous Alcohol Drinking and Premature Mortality in Russia: A Population Based Case-Control Study." *Lancet* 369 (9578): 2001–9.

Leon, David A., and Vladimir M. Shkolnikov. 1998. "Social Stress and the Russian Mortality Crisis." *Journal of the American Medical Association* 279 (10): 790–91.

Leon, David A., Vladimir Shkolnikov, and Martin McKee. 2009. "Alcohol and Russian Mortality: A Continuing Crisis." *Addiction* 104 (10): 1630–36.

Lett, Heather S., James A. Blumenthal, Michael A. Babyak, Timothy J. Strauman, Cliver Robins, and Andrew Sherwood. 2005. "Social Support and Coronary Heart Disease: Epidemiologic Evidence and Implications for Treatment." *Psychosomatic Medicine* 67: 869–78.

Levintova, Marya. 2007. "Russian Alcohol Policy in the Making." *Alcohol and Alcoholism* 42 (5): 500–505.

Leykin, Inna. 2011a. "Population Prescriptions: (Sanitary) Culture and Biomedical Authority in Contemporary Russia." *Anthropology of East Europe Review* 29 (1): 60–81.

———. 2011b. "'Population Prescriptions:' Pronatalism and the Fear of Underpopulation in Post-Soviet Russia." *Somatosphere,* December 26. *somatosphere.net/2011/12/ population-prescriptions-pronatalism-and-the-fear-of-underpopulation-in-post-soviet-russia.html.*

Liang, Jersey, Neal M. Krause, and Joan M. Bennett. 2001. "Social Exchange and Well-Being: Is Giving Better than Receiving?" *Psychology and Aging* 16 (3): 511–23.

Lincoln, Tim. 1997. "Death and the Demon Drink in Russia." *Nature* 388 (6644): 723.

Lindquist, Galina. 2001a. "Gurus, Wizards and Energoinformation Fields: Alternative Medicine in Post-Communist Russia." *Anthropology of East Europe Review* 19 (1): 16–28.

————. 2001b. "Transforming Signs: Typologies of Affliction in Contemporary Russian Magic and Healing." *Ethnos* 66 (2): 81–206.

————. 2001c. "Breaking the Waves: Voodoo Magic in the Russian Cultural Ecumene." *Kroeber Anthropological Society Papers* 86: 93–111.

————. 2006. *Conjuring Hope: Magic and Healing in Contemporary Russia.* New York: Berghahn.

Livschiz, Ann. 2006. "Children's Lives after Zoia's Death: Order, Emotions and Heroism in Children's Lives and Literature in the Post-War Soviet Union." In *Late Stalinist Russia: Society between Reconstruction and Reinvention,* edited by Juliane Fürst, 192–208. London: Routledge.

Lochner, Kimberly A., Ichiro Kawachi, Robert T. Brennan, and Stephen L. Buka. 2003. "Social Capital and Neighborhood Mortality Rates in Chicago." *Social Science and Medicine* 56 (8): 1797–1805.

Lynch, John W., George Davey Smith, George A. Kaplan, and James S. House. 2000. "Income Inequality and Mortality: Importance to Health of Individual Income, Psychosocial Environment, or Material Conditions." *British Medical Journal* 320: 1200–1204.

MacCallum, Gerald C., Jr. 1967. "Negative and Positive Freedom." *Philosophical Review* 76: 312–34.

Malyutina, Sofia, Martin Bobak, Svetlana Kurilovitch, Valery Gafarov, Galina Simonova, Yuri Nikitin, and Michael Marmot. 2002. "Relation between Heavy and Binge Drinking and All-Cause and Cardiovascular Mortality in Novosibirsk, Russia: A Prospective Cohort Study." *Lancet* 360 (9344): 1448–54.

Malyutina, Sofia, Martin Bobak, Galina Simonova, Valery Gafarov, Yuri Nikitin, and Michael Marmot. 2004. "Education, Marital Status, and Total and Cardiovascular Mortality in Novisibirsk, Russia: A Prospective Cohort Study." *Annals of Epidemiology* 14 (4): 244–49.

Manley, Rebecca. 2006. "Where Should We Resettle the Comrades Next? The Adjudication of Housing Claims and the Construction of the Post-War Order." In *Late Stalinist Russia: Society between Reconstruction and Reinvention,* edited by Juliane Fürst, 233–46. London: Routledge.

Marmot, Michael. 2004. *The Status Syndrome: How Social Standing Affects Our Health and Longevity.* New York: Owl Books.

McKee, Martin. 1999. "Invited Commentary: Alcohol in Russia." *Alcohol and Alcoholism* 34 (6): 824–29.

McKee, Martin, and Annie Britton. 1998. "The Positive Relationship between Alcohol and Heart Disease in Eastern Europe: Potential Physiological Mechanisms." *Journal of the Royal Society of Medicine* 91: 402–7.

McKee, Martin, Vladimir Shkolnikov, and David A. Leon. 2001. "Alcohol Is Implicated in the Fluctuations in Cardiovascular Disease in Russia since the 1980s." *Annals of Epidemiology* 11 (1): 1–6.

McKee, Martin, Sándor Szűcs, Attila Sárváry, Roza Ádany, Nikolay Kiryanov, Ludmila Saburova, Susannah Tomkins, Evgeny Andreev, and David A. Leon. 2005. "The Composition of Surrogate Alcohols Consumed in Russia." *Alcoholism: Clinical and Experimental Research* 29 (10): 1884–88.

————. 2000. "A Multilevel City Health Profile of Moscow." *Social Science and Medicine* 51 (9): 1295–1312.

Meshcherkina, Elena. 2000. "New Russian Men: Masculinity Regained?" In *Gender, State and Society in Soviet and Post-Soviet Russia,* edited by Sarah Ashwin, 105–17. London: Routledge.

Metzo, Katherine. 2009. "The Social and Gendered Lives of Vodka in Rural Siberia." In *Food and Everyday Life in the Post-Socialist World,* edited by Melissa Caldwell, 188–205. Bloomington: Indiana University Press.

Muntaner, Carles. 2004. "Commentary: Social Capital, Social Class, and the Slow Progress of Psychosocial Epidemiology." *International Journal of Epidemiology* 33: 674–80.

Muntaner, Carles, John Lynch, Marianne Hillemeier, Ju Hee Lee, Richard David, Joan Benach, and Carme Borrell. 2002. "Economic Inequality, Working-Class Power, Social Capital, and Cause-Specific Mortality in Wealthy Countries." *International Journal of Health Services* 32 (4): 629–56.

Muntaner, Carles, John Lynch, and George Davey Smith. 2001. "Social Capital, Disorganized Communities, and the Third Way: Understanding the Retreat from Structural Inequalities in Epidemiology and Public Health." *International Journal of Health Services* 31 (2): 213–37.

Navarro, Vicente. 2002. "A Critique of Social Capital." *International Journal of Health Services* 32: 423–32.

Nemtsov, Alexander. 2004. "Commentary: Is *Capital* the Solution or the Problem?" *International Journal of Epidemiology* 33 (4): 672.

————. 1996. "Problem: When People Drink, It's Society that Gets the Hangover." *Current Digest of the Russian Press* 49 (47): 12–14.

————. 1998. "Alcohol-Related Harm and Alcohol Consumption in Moscow before, during and after a Major Anti-Alcohol Campaign." *Addiction* 93 (10): 1501–10.

————. 2000. "Estimates of Total Alcohol Consumption in Russia, 1980–1994." *Drug and Alcohol Dependence* 58 (1–2): 133–42.

————. 2002. "Alcohol-Related Human Losses in Russia in the 1980s and 1990s." *Addiction* 97 (11): 1413–25.

————. 2003. "Alcohol Consumption Level in Russia: A Viewpoint on Monitoring Heath Conditions in the Russian Federation (RLMS)." *Addiction* 98: 369–70.

————. 2004. "Alcohol Consumption in Russia: Is Monitoring Health Conditions in the Russian Federation (RLMS) Trustworthy?" *Addiction* 99: 386–87.

Nemtsov, Alexander, and Vladimir M. Shkolnikov. 1994. "Jit' ili pit'" [To live or to drink]. *Izvestiya* 135, July 19.

Neufeld, Maria, and Jurgen Rehm. 2013. "Alcohol Consumption and Mortality in Russia since 2000: Are There Any Changes Following the Alcohol Policy Changes Starting in 2006?" *Alcohol and Alcoholism* 48 (2): 222–30.

Nicholson, Amanda, Martin Bobak, Michael Murphy, Richard Rose, and Michael Marmot. 2005. "Alcohol Consumption and Increased Mortality in Russian Men and Women: A Cohort Study Based on the Mortality of Relatives." *Bulletin of the World Health Organization* 83 (11): 812–19.

Nielsen, Finn Sivert. 2006. *The Eye of the Whirlwind: Russian Identity and Soviet Nation-Building; Quests for Meaning in a Soviet Metropolis.* Available at *www.anthrobase.com/Txt/N/Nielsen_F_S_03.htm.* Accessed October 31, 2010.

Notzon, Francis C., Yuri M. Komarov, Sergei P. Ermakov, Alexei I. Savinykh, Michelle B. Hanson, and Juan Albertorio. 2003. "Vital and Health Statistics: Russian Federation and United States, Selected Years 1985–2000 with an Overview of Russian Mortality in the 1990s." *Vital and Health Statistics* 5 (11): 1–55.

Notzon, Francis C., Yuri M. Komarov, Sergei P. Ermakov, Christopher T. Sempos, James S. Marks, and Elena V. Sempos. 1998. "Causes of Declining Life Expectancy in Russia." *Journal of the American Medical Association* 279 (10): 793–800.

Nuckolls, Charles. 1998. *Culture: A Problem that Cannot Be Solved.* Madison: University of Wisconsin Press.

Okólski, Marek. 1993. "East-West Mortality Differentials." In *European population,* Vol 2. *Demographic dynamics,* edited by Alain Blum and Jean-Louis Rallu, 165–89. Paris: John Libbey Eurotext.

Orth-Gomér, Kristina, Annika Rosengren, and Lars Wilhelmsen. 1993. "Lack of Social Support and Incidence of Coronary Heart Disease in Aged Swedish Men." *Psychosomatic Medicine* 55: 37–43.

Oushakine, Serguei Alex. 2009. *The Patriotism of Despair: Nation, War, and Loss in Russia.* Ithaca, NY: Cornell University Press.

Palahniuk, Chuck. 1999. *Fight Club.* New York: Henry Holt and Company.

Palosuo, Hannele. 2000. "Health-Related Lifestyles and Alienation in Moscow and Helsinki." *Social Science and Medicine* 51 (9): 1325–41.

Patico, Jennifer. 2002. "Chocolate and Cognac: Gifts and the Recognition of Social Worlds in Post-Soviet Russia." *Ethnos* 67 (3): 345–68.

Paxson, Margaret. 2005. *Solovyovo: The Story of Memory in a Russian Village.* Bloomington: Indiana University Press.

Peasey, Anne, Martin Bobak, Ruzena Kubinova, Sofia Malyutina, Andrzej Pajak, Abdonas Tamosiunas, Hynek Pikhart, Amanda Nicholson, and Michael Marmot. 2006. "Determinants of Cardiovascular Disease and Other Non-Communicable Diseases in Central and Eastern Europe: Rationale and Design of the HAPIEE Study." *BMC Public Health* 18 (6): 255.

Peck, M. D., V. Shankar, and S. I. Bangdiwala. 2007. "Trends in Injury-Related Deaths Before and After Dissolution of the Union of Soviet Socialist Republics." *International Journal of Injury Control and Safety Promotion* 14 (3): 139–51.

Perlman, Francesca, and Martin Bobak. 2008. "Socioeconomic and Behavioral Determinants of Mortality in Posttransition Russia: A Prospective Population Study." *Annals of Epidemiology* 18 (2): 92–100.

———. 2009. "Assessing the Contribution of Unstable Employment to Mortality in Post-transition Russia: Prospective Individual-Level Analyses from the Russian Longitudinal Monitoring Survey." *American Journal of Public Health* 99 (10): 1818–25.

Pesmen, Dale. 1995. "Standing Bottles, Washing Deals, and Drinking 'for the Soul' in a Siberian City." In "Culture and Society in the Former Soviet Union," ed. Nancy Ries. Special issue, *Anthropology of East Europe Review* 13 (2): 65–74.

———. 2000. *Russia and Soul: An Exploration.* Ithaca, NY: Cornell University Press.

Pine, Frances, and Susan Bridger. 1998. "Introduction: Transitions to Post-Socialism and Cultures of Survival." In *Surviving Post-Socialism: Local Strategies and Regional Responses in Eastern Europe and the Former Soviet Union,* edited by Susan Bridger and Frances Pine, 1–15. London: Routledge.

Plavinski, S. L., S. I. Plavinskaya, and A. N. Klimov. 2003. "Social Factors and Increase in Mortality in Russia in the 1990s: Prospective Cohort Study." *British Medical Journal* 326 (7401): 1240–42.

du Plessix Gray, Francine. 1989. *Soviet Women: Walking the Tightrope.* New York: Doubleday.

Popova, Svetlana, Jürgen Rehm, Jayadeep Patra, and Witold Zatonski. 2007. "Comparing Alcohol Consumption in Central and Eastern Europe to Other European Countries." *Alcohol and Alcoholism* 42 (5): 465–73.

Post, S. G. 2005. "Altruism, Happiness, and Health: It's Good to Be Good." *International Journal of Behavioral Medicine* 12 (2): 66–77.

Pridemore, William A., and Sang-Weon Kim. 2006. "Patterns of Alcohol-Related Mortality in Russia." *Journal of Drug Issues* 36 (1): 229–48.

Pushkin, Alexander. 1957. *The Captain's Daughter and Other Stories.* New York: Vintage.

Putnam, Robert. 1993. *Making Democracy Work.* Princeton: Princeton University Press.

———. 1995. "Bowling Alone: America's Declining Social Capital." *Journal of Democracy* 6: 65–78.

———. 1996. "The Strange Disappearance of Civic America." *American Prospect* 24 (Winter). *epn.org/prospect/24/24putn.html.* Accessed October 5, 2013.

———. 2000. *Bowling Alone: The Collapse and Revival of American Community.* New York: Simon and Schuster.

———. 2004. "Commentary: Health by Association; Some Comments." *International Journal of Epidemiology* 33 (4): 667–71.

Raikhel, Eugene. 2010. "Post-Soviet Placebos: Epistemology and Authority in Russian Treatments for Alcoholism." *Culture, Medicine and Psychiatry* 34 (1): 132–68.

———. 2012. "Radical Reductions: Neurophysiology, Politics and Personhood in Russian Addiction Medicine." In *Critical Neuroscience: A Handbook of the Social and Cultural Contexts of Neuroscience,* edited by Suparna Choudhury and Jan Slaby. New York: Wiley-Blackwell.

Raikhel, Eugene, and William Garriott, eds. 2013. *Addiction Trajectories.* Durham, NC: Duke University Press.

Ramstedt, Mats. 2009. "Fluctuations in Male Ischaemic Heart Disease Mortality in Russia 1959–1998: Assessing the Importance of Alcohol." *Drug and Alcohol Revue* 28 (4): 390–95.

Rehm, Jürgen, Urszula Sulkowska, Marta Mańczuk, Paolo Boffetta, John Powles, Svetlana Popova, and Witold Zatoński. 2007. "Alcohol Accounts for a High Proportion of Premature Mortality in Central and Eastern Europe." *International Journal of Epidemiology* 36 (2): 458–67.

Rethmann, Petra. 1999. "Deadly Dis-ease. Medical Knowledge and Healing in Northern Kamchatka, Russia." *Culture, Medicine and Psychiatry* 23: 197–217.

———. 2001. *Tundra Passages: History and Gender in the Russian Far East.* University Park: Pennsylvania State University Press.

Ries, Nancy. 1997. *Russian Talk: Culture and Conversation during Perestroika.* Ithaca, NY: Cornell University Press.

Rivkin-Fish, Michele. 1999. "Sexuality Education in Russia: Defining Pleasure and Danger for a Fledgling Democratic Society." *Social Science and Medicine* 49 (6): 801–14.

———. 2001. "Personal Transitions and Moral Change after Socialism: The Politics of Remedies in Russian Public Health." *Anthropology of East Europe Review* 19 (1): 29–41.

———. 2003. "Anthropology, Demography, and the Search for a Critical Analysis of Fertility: Insights from Russia." *American Anthropologist* 105 (2): 289–301.

———. 2004. "'Change Yourself and the Whole World Will Become Kinder': Russian Activists for Reproductive Health and the Limits of Claims Making for Women." *Medical Anthropology Quarterly* 18 (3): 281–304.

———. 2005a. *Women's Health in Post-Soviet Russia: The Politics of Intervention.* Bloomington: University of Indiana Press.

———. 2005b. "Bribes, Gifts, and Unofficial Payments: Towards an Anthropology of Corruption in Post-Soviet Russia." In *Corruption: Anthropological Perspectives,* edited by Dieter Haller and Cris Shore, 47–64. Ann Arbor, MI: Pluto.

———. 2006. "From 'Demographic Crisis' to a 'Dying Nation': The Politics of Language and Reproduction in Russia." In *Gender and National Identity in Twentieth-Century Russian Culture,* edited by Helena Goscilo and Andrea Lanoux, 151–73. DeKalb: University of Northern Illinois Press.

———. 2007. "The Politics of Reproduction and Nationalism in Russia." In *The Policies of Reproduction at the End of the 20th Century: The Cases of Finland, Portugal, Romania, Russia, Austria, and the US,* edited by Maria Mesner, Margit Niederhuber, Heidi Niederkofler, and Gudrun Wolfgruber, 157–79. Tampere, Finland: Tampere University Press.

———. 2010. "Pronatalism, Gender Politics, and the Renewal of Family Support in Russia: Towards a Feminist Anthropology of 'Maternity Capital.'" *Slavic Review* 69 (3): 701–24.

Rochat, Philippe. 2008. "Commentary: Mutual Recognition as a Foundation of Sociality and Social Comfort." In *Social Cognition: Development, Neuroscience and Autism,* edited by T. Striano and V. Reid, 303–17. Oxford: Blackwell.

———. 2009. *Others in Mind: Social Origins of Self-Consciousness.* New York: Cambridge University Press.

Rose, Richard. 1995. "Russia as an Hour-Glass Society: A Constitution without Citizens." *East European Constitutional Review* 4 (3): 34–42.

———. 1999. "Living in an Anti-Modern Society." *East European Constitutional Review* 8 (1–2): 68–75.

———. 2000. "How Much Does Social Capital Add to Individual Health? A Survey Study of Russians." *Social Science and Medicine* 51 (9): 1421–35.

———. 2002. "Social Shocks, Social Confidence and Health." *Studies in Public Policy* 362: 1–24.

Rozanski, Alan, James A. Blumenthal, and Jay Kaplan. 1999. "Impact of Psychological Factors on the Pathogenesis of Cardiovascular Disease and Implications for Therapy." *Circulation* 99: 2192–2217.

Rüthers, Monica. 2006. "The Moscow Gorky Street in Late Stalinism: Space, History and Lebenswelten." In *Late Stalinist Russia: Society between Reconstruction and Reinvention,* edited by Juliane Fürst, 81–102. London: Routledge.

Ryan, Michael. 1995. "Alcoholism and Rising Mortality in the Russian Federation." *British Medical Journal* 310 (6980): 646–48.

Saburova, Lyudmila, Katherine Keenan, Natalia Bobrova, David A. Leon, and Diana Elbourne. 2011. "Alcohol and Fatal Life Trajectories in Russia: Understanding Narrative Accounts of Premature Male Death in the Family." *BioMed Central Public Health* 11 (481): 1–10.

Sachs, Jeffrey D. 1995. "Why Russia Has Failed to Stabilize." In *Russian Economic Reform at Risk,* edited by Anders Åslund, 53–63. London: Pinter.

Sampson, Steven. 2002. "Beyond Transition: Rethinking Elite Configurations in the Balkans." In *Postsocialism: Ideals, Ideologies and Practices in Eurasia,* edited by Chris M. Hann, 297–316. New York: Routledge.

Sapolsky, Robert M. 2004. "Social Status and Health in Humans and Other Animals." *Annual Review of Anthropology* 33 (October): 393–418.

Schacter, Daniel. 1996. *Searching for Memory: The Brain, the Mind and the Past.* New York: Basic.

Scheffler, Richard M., Timothy T. Brown, Leonard Syme, Ichiro Kawachi, Irina Tolstykh, and Carlos Iribarren. 2008. "Community-Level Social Capital and Recurrence of Acute Coronary Syndrome." *Social Science and Medicine* 66 (7):1603–13.

Scheper-Hughes, Nancy. 1997. "Demography without Numbers." In *Anthropological Demography: Toward a New Synthesis,* edited by David I. Kertzer and Thomas Earl Fricke, 201–22. Chicago: University of Chicago Press.

Schwartz, Harry, 1965. *The Soviet Economy since Stalin.* Philadelphia: J. B. Lippincott.

Sen, Amartya. 1985. "Well-Being, Agency and Freedom." *Journal of Philosophy* 82: 169–221.

Shapiro, Judith. 1995. "The Russian Mortality Crisis and Its Causes." In *Russian Economic Reform at Risk,* edited by Anders Åslund, 149–75. London: Pinter.

Shevchenko, Olga. 2001. "Bread and Circuses: Shifting Frames and Changing References in Ordinary Muscovites' Political Talk." *Communist and Post-Communist Studies* 34: 77–90.

Shkolnikov, Vladimir M., Evgueni M. Andreev, David A. Leon, Martin McKee, France Meslé, and Jacques Vallin. 2004. "Mortality Reversal in Russia: The Story So Far." *Hygiea Internationalis* 4 (1): 29–80.

Shkolnikov, Vladimir M., Giovanni A. Cornia, David A. Leon, and France Meslé. 1998. "Causes of the Russian Mortality Crisis: Evidence and Interpretations." *World Development* 26 (11): 1995–2011.

Shkolnikov, Vladimir M., Mark G. Field, and Evgueniy M. Andreev. 2001. "Russia: Socioeconomic Dimensions of the Gender Gap in Mortality." In *Challenging Inequities in Health: From Ethics to Action,* edited by Timothy Evans, Margaret Whitehead, Finn Diderichsen, Abbbas Bhuiya, and Meg Wirth, 138–55. New York: Oxford University Press.

Shkolnikov, Vladimir M., David A. Leon, Sergey Adamets, Eugeniy Andreev, and Alexander Deev. 1998. "Educational Level and Adult Mortality in Russia: An Analysis of Routine Data 1979 to 1994." *Social Science and Medicine* 74 (3): 357–69.

Shkolnikov, Vladimir M., Martin McKee, Valeriy V. Chervyakov, and Nikolay A. Kyrianov. 2002. "Is the Link between Alcohol and Cardiovascular Death among Young Russian Men Attributable to Misclassification of Acute Alcohol Intoxication? Evidence from the City of Izhevsk." *Journal of Epidemiology and Community Health* 56 (3): 171–74.

Shkolnikov, Vladimir, France Meslé, and Jacques Vallin. 1995. "La crise sanitaire en Russie: I. Tendances récentes de l'espérance de vie et des causes de décès de 1970 à 1993." *Population* (French Edition), nos. 4–5: 907–43.

Shkolnikova, Maria, Svetlana Shalnova, Vladimir M. Shkolnikov, Viktoria Metelskaya, Alexander Deev, Evgueni Andreev, Dmitri Jdanov, and James W. Vaupel. 2009. "Biological Mechanisms of Disease and Death in Moscow: Rationale and Design of the Survey on Stress, Aging, and Health in Russia (SAHR)." *BMC Public Health* 9 (August 13): 293.

Sieff, Martin. 1991. "Russia's Needs Go beyond Freedom." *Washington Times,* final edition, September 3.

Siegrist, J. 2000. "Place, Social Exchange and Health: Proposed Sociological Framework." *Social Science and Medicine* 51 (9): 1283–93.

Silverstein, Merril, Xuan Chen, and Kenneth Heller. 1996. "Too Much of a Good Thing? Intergenerational Social Support and the Psychological Well-Being of Aging Parents." *Journal of Marriage and the Family* 58: 970–82.

Singer, Merrill, Freddie Valentin, Hans Baer, and Zhongke Jin. (1992) 2010. "Why Does Juan García Have a Drinking Problem? The Perspective of Critical Medical Anthropology." In *Understanding and Applying Medical Anthropology,* edited by Peter J. Brown and Ron Barrett, 307–23. New York: McGraw-Hill.

Sokolov, Mikhail. 2006. "Cruelty, Sex, and Pedagogical Authority: On Some Functions of Alcohol in Contemporary Russian Culture." *Kultura* (7–8): 17–19.

Solar, Orielle, and Alec Irwin. 2007. "A Conceptual Framework for Action on the Social Determinants of Health." Paper prepared for a meeting of the Commission on Social Determinants of Health, Vancouver, June 7–9.

Solzhenitsyn, Alexander Isaevich. 1981. *From under the Rubble.* Washington, DC: Regnery Gateway.

State Tretyakov Gallery. "Levitan, Isaak Illich: Over Eternal Quiet." *www.
tretyakovgallery.ru/en/collection/_show/image/_id/294*. Accessed November 1, 2010.

Stegmayr, Birgitta, Tatyana Vinogradova, Sofia Malyutina, Markku Peltonen, Yuri
Nikitin, and Kjell Asplund. 2000. "Widening Gap of Stroke between East and West.
Eight-Year Trends in Occurrence and Risk Factors in Russia and Sweden." *Stroke* 31
(1): 2–8.

Stillo, Jonathan. 2013. "'We Are the Losers of Socialism': Tuberculosis, Social Cases and
the Limits of Care in Romania." Unpublished manuscript.

Stoller, Eleanor Palo. 1985. "Exchange Patterns in the Informal Support Networks of the
Elderly: The Impact of Reciprocity on Morale." *Journal of Marriage and Family* 47
(2): 335–42.

Stone, Richard. 2000. "The Invisible Hand in Eastern Europe's Death Rates." *Science* 288
(5472): 1732–33.

Stuckler, David, and Sajay Basu. 2013. *The Body Economic: Why Austerity Kills;
Recessions, Budget Battles, and the Politics of Life and Death.* New York: Basic
Books.

Stuckler, David, Lawrence King, and Martin McKee. 2009. "Mass Privatization and the
Post-Communist Mortality Crisis: A Cross-National Analysis." *Lancet* 373 (9661):
399–407.

Sundquist, Jan, Sven-Erik Johansson, Min Yang, and Kristina Sundquist. 2006. "Low
Linking Social Capital as a Predictor of Coronary Heart Disease in Sweden: A Cohort
Study of 2.8 Million People." *Social Science and Medicine* 62 (4): 954–63.

Surtees, Paul G., Nicholas W. J. Wainwright, Robert Luben, Nicholas J. Wareham, Sheila
A. Bingham, and Kay-Tee Khaw. 2010. "Mastery Is Associated with Cardiovascular
Disease Mortality in Men and Women at Apparently Low Risk." *Health Psychology*
29 (4): 412–20.

Szreter, Simon, and Michael Woolcock. 2004. "Health by Association? Social Capital,
Social Theory, and the Political Economy of Public Health." *International Journal of
Epidemiology* 33 (4): 650–67.

Tennant, Christopher. 1999. "Life Stress, Social Support and Coronary Heart Disease."
Australian and New Zealand Journal of Psychiatry 33: 636–41.

Todorova, Maria, and Zsuzsa Gille, eds. 2010. *Post-Communist Nostalgia.* New York:
Berghahn.

Tomkins, Susannah, Tim Collier, Alexey Oralov, Lyudmila Saburova, Martin McKee,
Vladimir Shkolnikov, Nikolay Kiryanov, and David A. Leon. 2012. "Hazardous
Alcohol Consumption Is a Major Factor in Male Premature Mortality in a Typical
Russian City: Prospective Cohort Study 2003–2009." *PLOS ONE* 7 (2): e30274.

Tomkins, Susannah, Vladimir Shkolnikov, Evgueni Andreev, Nikolay Kiryanov, David A.
Leon, Martin McKee, and Lyudmila Saburova. 2007. "Identifying the Determinants
of Premature Mortality in Russia: Overcoming a Methodological Challenge." *BMC
Public Health* 7 (November 28): 343.

Transchel, K. 2006. *Under the Influence: Working-Class Drinking, Temperance, and
Cultural Revolution in Russia, 1895–1932.* Pittsburgh, PA: University of Pittsburgh
Press.

Treml, Vladimir G. 1997. "Soviet and Russian Statistics on Alcohol Consumption and Abuse." In *Premature Death in the New Independent States,* edited by José Luis Bobadilla, Christine A. Costello, and Faith Mitchell, 220–38. Washington, DC: National Academies Press.

Tumarkin, Nina. 1994. *The Living and the Dead: The Rise and Fall of the Cult of World War II in Russia.* New York: Basic.

Twigg, Judyth L. 2001. "Social Welfare: A Social Contract." In *Russia's Uncertain Economic Future: Compendium of Papers Submitted to the Joint Economic Committee.* U. S. Congress, 307-328. 107th Cong., 1st sess., S. Prt. 107-50.

———. 2003. "Social Capital in Russia's Regions." In *Social Capital and Social Cohesion in Post-Soviet Russia,* edited by Judyth L. Twigg, and Kate Schecter, 168–88. Armonk, NY: M. E. Sharpe.

Twigg, Judyth L., and Kate Schecter. 2003. Introduction to *Social Capital and Social Cohesion in Post-Soviet Russia,* edited by Judyth L. Twigg, and Kate Schecter, 3–16. Armonk, NY: M. E. Sharpe.

Uehling, Greta. 2004. *Beyond Memory: The Crimean Tatars' Deportation and Return.* New York: Palgrave Macmillan.

United Nations Population Division. 2009. *World Population Prospects: The 2008 Revision.* New York: United Nations, Department of Economic and Social Affairs.

Utrata, Jennifer. 2008. "Keeping the Bar Low: Why Russia's Nonresident Fathers Accept Narrow Fatherhood Ideals." *Journal of Marriage and Family* 70 (December): 1297–1310.

———. 2013. *Women without Men: Single Mothers and Gender Crisis in the New Russia.* Unpublished manuscript.

Utrata, Jennifer, Jean M. Ispa, and Simone Ispa-Landa. 2012. "Men on the Margins of Family Life: Fathers in Russia." In *Fathers in Cultural Context,* edited by David Shwalb, Barbara Shwalb, and Michael Lamb, 279–302. New York: Routledge.

Vàgerö, Denny, and Raymond Illsley. 1992. "Inequality, Health and Policy in East and West Europe." *International Journal of Health Science* 3 (225).

Verdery, Katherine. 1991. "Theorizing Socialism: A Prologue to the 'Transition.'" *American Ethnologist* 18 (3): 419–39.

———. 1996. *What Was Socialism and What Comes Next?* Princeton: Princeton University Press.

Walberg, Peder, Martin McKee, Vladimir Shkolnikov, Laurent Chenet, and David A. Leon. 1998. "Economic Change, Crime, and Mortality Crisis in Russia: Regional Analysis." *British Medical Journal* 317 (7154): 312–18.

Watson, Peggy. 1993. "The Rise of Masculinism in Eastern Europe." *New Left Review* 198: 71–82.

———. 1995. "Explaining Rising Mortality among Men in Eastern Europe." *Social Science and Medicine* 41 (7): 923–34.

Watts, Michael J. 1998. "Recombinant Capitalism: State, De-Collectivisation and the Agrarian Question in Vietnam." In *Theorizing Transition: The Political Economy of Post-Communist Transformations,* edited by John Pickles and Adrian Smith, 425–78. London: Routledge.

Weber, Gerard A. 2009. "Forsaken Generation: Stress, Social Suffering and Strategies among Working-Class Pensioners in Post-Socialist Moldova, Romania." PhD diss., City University of New York.

Weber, Max. 1995. *The Russian Revolutions.* Ithaca, NY: Cornell University Press.

Weidner, Gerdi. 1998. "Gender Gap in Health Decline in East Europe." *Nature* 395 (29 October): 835.

Wierzbicka, Anna. 2003. "Russian Cultural Scripts: The Theory of Cultural Scripts and Its Application." *Ethos* 30 (4): 401–32.

Wilkinson, Richard. 1994. "The Epidemiological Transition: From Material Scarcity to Social Disadvantage?" *Daedalus* 123: 61–67.

———. 1996. *Unhealthy Societies: The afflictions of Inequality.* London: Routledge.

———. 2005. *The Impact of Inequality: How to Make Sick Societies Healthier.* New York: New Press.

Wilkinson, Richard, and Kate Pickett. 2009. *The Spirit Level: Why Greater Equality Makes Societies Stronger.* New York: Bloomsbury.

World Bank, Development Research Group. 2013. *The World Bank: Data. data.worldbank.org.*

Yurchak, Alexei. 2006. *Everything Was Forever, until It Was No More: The Last Soviet Generation.* Princeton: Princeton University Press.

Zaridze, David, Paul Brennan, Jillian Boreham, Alex Boroda, Rostislav Karpov, Alexander Lazarev, Irina Konobeevskaya, Vladimir Igitov, Tatiana Terechova, Paolo Boffetta, and Richard Peto. 2009. "Alcohol and Cause-Specific Mortality in Russia: A Retrospective Case-Control Study of 48,557 Adult Deaths." *Lancet* 373 (9682): 2201–14.

Zaridze, David, Dimitri Maximovitch, Alexander Lazarev, Vladimir Igitov, Alex Boroda, Jillian Boreham, Peter Boyle, Richard Peto, and Paolo Boffetta. 2009. "Alcohol Poisoning Is a Main Determinant of Recent Mortality Trends in Russia: Evidence from a Detailed Analysis of Mortality Statistics and Autopsies." *International Journal of Epidemiology* 38 (1): 143–53.

Zdravomyslova, Elena, and Elena Chikadze. 2000. "Scripts of Men's Heavy Drinking." *Finish Review of East European Studies* 7 (2): 35–51.

Zdravomyslova, Elena, and Anna Temkina. 2012. "The Crisis of Masculinity in Late Soviet Discourse." *Russian Studies in History* 51 (2): 13–34.

Zemtsov, Ilya. 2001. *Encyclopedia of Soviet Life.* Piscataway, NJ: Transaction.

Zigon, Jarrett. 2010. *Making the New Post-Soviet Person: Narratives of Moral Experience in Contemporary Moscow.* Leiden: Brill.

———. 2011. *HIV Is God's Blessing: Rehabilitating Morality in Neoliberal Russia.* Berkeley: University of California Press.

Zubkova, Elena. 1998. *Russia after the War: Hopes, Illusions, and Disappointments, 1945–1957.* Translated by Hugh Ragsdale. Armonk, NY: M. E. Sharpe.

Zvolensky, Michael J., Roman Kotov, Anna V. Antipova, Ellen W. Leen-Feldner, and Norman B. Schmidt. 2005. "Evaluating Anxiety Sensitivity, Exposure to Aversive Life Conditions, and Problematic Drinking in Russia: A Test Using an Epidemiological Sample." *Addictive Behaviors* 30 (3): 567–70.

Index